T0320821

MODELS, MATHEMATICS, AND METHODOLOGY
IN ECONOMIC EXPLANATION

This book provides a practitioner's foundation for the process of explanatory model building, breaking down that process into five stages. Donald W. Katzner presents a concrete example with unquantified variable values to show how the five-stage procedure works. He describes what is involved in explanatory model building for those interested in this practice, while simultaneously providing a guide for those actually engaged in it. The combination of Katzner's focus on modeling and on mathematics, along with his focus on the explanatory performance of modeling, promises to become an important contribution to the field.

Donald W. Katzner is Professor of Economics and former Department Chair at the University of Massachusetts, Amherst. His published research spans several areas, including microeconomic and general equilibrium theory; the methodology of building models and of analyzing phenomena when measures of appropriate variables are neither available nor reasonably constructible; the analysis of uncertain economic phenomena when it is inappropriate to employ notions of probability; the impact of culture on economic behavior; and organizational issues within the economic firm.

Models, Mathematics, and Methodology in Economic Explanation

DONALD W. KATZNER

University of Massachusetts, Amherst

CAMBRIDGE
UNIVERSITY PRESS

CAMBRIDGE
UNIVERSITY PRESS

University Printing House, Cambridge CB2 8BS, United Kingdom

One Liberty Plaza, 20th Floor, New York, NY 10006, USA

477 Williamstown Road, Port Melbourne, VIC 3207, Australia

314-321, 3rd Floor, Plot 3, Splendor Forum, Jasola District Centre, New Delhi – 110025, India

79 Anson Road, #06-04/06, Singapore 079906

Cambridge University Press is part of the University of Cambridge.

It furthers the University's mission by disseminating knowledge in the pursuit of education, learning, and research at the highest international levels of excellence.

www.cambridge.org
Information on this title: www.cambridge.org/9781108418775
DOI: 10.1017/9781108291422

© Donald W. Katzner 2018

First published 2018

Printed in the United Kingdom by Clays, St Ives plc

A catalogue record for this publication is available from the British Library.

ISBN 978-1-108-41877-5 Hardback

For my grandchildren:
Sadie Alexandra
Ethan Benjamin
and
Chloe Emerson

Contents

Preface

My objective in this book is to bring into focus the interrelations between three elements or areas of investigation involved in economic explanation as well as the connections between those areas and economic explanation itself: first, the building of models as part of one possible approach to explaining economic phenomena; second, certain critical aspects of the mathematization that model construction frequently employs; and third, some features of the relevant methodological foundations upon which the model building explanatory program is based. I have commented on those aspects more expansively in the introduction and subsequent chapters that follow, and I have made some suggestions regarding the need to take a new view, not only of the status of economics as an explanatory discipline, but of the process of model building and in some respects the conceptual traps that arise in moving to real-world explanation.

In all that, of course, considerable and highly valuable contributions have been made by scholars whose efforts have preceded mine, and it is part of my intention to give full acknowledgment to the objectives that work has commanded. My present concern, however, is in the more practical and operational aspects of economic model building in a how-to-do-it sense, and while the more abstract issues of methodology that scholars have examined elsewhere inform my present argument, they do not engage my primary interest.

I should state that for the most part, I am an economic theorist who addresses methodological and philosophical issues that relate to my work through the lens of a practicing model builder. I believe that what I do and should be doing as an economist is to attempt to explain economic reality and thereby indirectly contribute to the making of economic policy and to matters that relate to the improvement of the human lot. The methodological and philosophical issues that I confront are those that bear upon the pursuit of this goal, namely, those that are concerned with the real-economic-world meaning and significance of the analytical approaches and techniques that I use. Over the years, many of my methodological and philosophical ruminations have found their way in bits and pieces, some considerably more extensive than others, into various parts of my published work. Parts of that previous work will be reflected in the present volume and I therefore record my thanks to the publishers and the holders of copyright for permission to reproduce from the following:

"In Defense of Formalization in Economics," *Methodus* 3, no. 1 (June, 1991), pp. 17–24. Published by the International Network for Economic Method.

"Our Mad Rush to Measure: How Did We Get into this Mess?" *Methodus* 3, no. 2 (December, 1991), pp. 18–26. Published by the International Network for Economic Method.

"The Misuse of Measurement in Economics," *Metroeconomica* 49 (1998), pp. 1–2. © John Wiley and Sons.

"The Significance, Success, and Failure of Microeconomic Theory," *Journal of Post Keynesian Economics* 24 (2001), pp. 41–58. © Taylor and Francis.

"Introduction: Science, Social Science, and Measurement," in my *Unmeasured Information and the Methodology of Social Scientific Inquiry* (Boston: Kluwer, 2001). © Springer.

"Why Mathematics in Economics?," *Journal of Post Keynesian Economics* 25 (2003), pp. 561–574. © Taylor and Francis.

An Introduction to the Economic Theory of Market Behavior: Microeconomics from a Walrasian Perspective (Cheltenham: Elgar, 2006).

"Introduction: Culture, Economics, and Economic Behavior," in *Culture and Economic Explanation* (London: Routledge, 2008). © Taylor and Francis.

Acknowledgments of more substantial reproductions of my earlier work appear in footnotes where appropriate.

Finally, I would like to thank Douglas Vickers for his extensive help and guidance in preparing this book.

Introduction

The methodology and analytics of model construction in the social sciences has lately attracted a good deal of interest, including valuable efforts by scholars in the economics discipline. The existing literature is extensive and important. But it tends to move in a somewhat different direction from that which is of concern in the present volume. That is, the focus of attention here exists in sharp contrast with the general scope, perspectives, and purposes of much of the literature which precedes it and which will be referred to elsewhere in this book.

The primary aim of subsequent chapters is to present a scheme of argument that throws necessary light on actual model building procedures that contribute to economic explanation. In particular, it develops and explores a five-stage model building format, including within it a number of elements having significant real-world relevance. That, in practitioner terms, permits the description of models that not only cohere in their separate elements but exhibit correspondences, or bridges, to empirical realities.

The sub-discipline of economic model building has for a long time, of course, occupied a place in analytical, as opposed to descriptive, economics. It has often existed on the level of unarticulated assumptions about the way the world works. But since the discipline of economics severed its attachment to moral philosophy and emerged to gain autonomous academic respectability, since Adam Smith enlightened economists about his pin factory and his functioning market concepts, since Ricardo and the classical economists understood the market system to function automatically at a level of high employment and economic welfare, since the neoclassicists embraced for analytical usage notions of full information, certainties of knowledge, and infinitely rapid market adjustment mechanisms — since those earlier developments, thinking about economic reality has increasingly employed well-specified models of the ways in which systems under investigation operate. It was not necessary in previous times to articulate a full model's construction to contemplate, for example, that if there should be an increase in market demand for a commodity without any change in supply conditions, there would, in the general scheme of things, be a rise in the price at which the market cleared or equilibrated. Indeed, such imaginations, based as they were inherently on not-fully-articulated models, soon found their way into the general public consciousness, quite apart from their developing significance for analytical economics.

But what will be seen as the increasing analytical sophistication of the subject, including, as will be noted, the expanded employment of mathematics for analytical purposes, has given rise also to specific, well-designated, and relevant models aimed at a more complete under-standing of market events and systems. That very development, it is of no small interest to observe, has proceeded at the same time as there has emerged some uncertainty among a number of economists as to the significance, and even the intellectual respectability, of their discipline. Such unease has been generated, in part, by criticisms that accuse the economics profession of, among other things, narrow-mindedness and a focus on irrelevance.[1] In light of those attacks, the growing literature on model construction in economics and the exploration of the methodologi-cal foundations that are relevant to it no doubt serve to blunt such criticism by allowing practitioners to communicate a broader and deeper sense of how their attempts at explanation relate to the real economic world and to the objectives of human betterment.

Some of the more recent contributions to this new perspective on economic modeling are contained within, or emanate from, the follow-ing: First, on the level of methodological foundations, Boumans and Davis define economic methodology as the "philosophy of science for economics." That is, economic methodology investigates "... the nature of the assumptions, types of reasoning, and forms of explanation used in economic science."[2] That includes the criteria or standards to be met when engaging in economic scientific activity and the basis and grounds whereby explanations produced by economic science may be said to explain

---

[1] See, for example, Bernstein [2], Hicks [6], Hutchison [7], Katouzian [8], Klamer and McCloskey [9], McCloskey [10], Ward [14], Woo [16], the collections of essays edited by Bell and Kristol [1], and Wiles and Routh [15], and the symposium, Has Formalization in Economics Gone too Far, in *Methodus* 3 (June 1991) pp. 6–31.

[2] Boumans and Davis [4, p. 1].

the economic phenomenon under investigation.[3] The Boumans and Davis book along with other recently published volumes such as, for example, those by Boland [3], Morgan [11], Reiss [12], and Ross [13], are, to a considerable extent, all concerned with economic methodology in that sense. Within that framework, contemporary economic methodology has moved in the direction of context-specific inquiries that relate to such topics as neuroeconomics, experimental economics, behavioral economics, and evolutionary economics.[4]

The present work, however, although it overlaps in certain respects with those interests, has, as has been indicated, a very different purpose and exists on a very different level. It is intended as a discussion of practical matters concerning principles of arrangement, organization, or procedure that relate to the process of the building of explanatory economic models. It identifies, in part, the steps that might be followed in actually constructing such a model and illustrates the manner in which those steps might, in practice, be carried out. Thus, by focusing on the nuts and bolts of model building, it attempts to point the way to the creation of improved explanatory models.

In the approach to the analysis of model construction that is here in view, questions arise with respect to the methodological relations that can or cannot properly be said to exist between the natural and the social sciences. For example, it is necessary to be sensitive to the meaning-content and the possible stability and explanatory significance of what might be adduced as economic laws as compared with the development and sustainability of laws in the physical sciences. Indeed, it is appropriate that, when faced with such juxtapositions, conclusions should be reached as to whether there exists an epistemological parity between the physical and the social sciences. For that reason a brief examination of relevant issues is included in Chapter 1. As indicated in the chapter, a number of salient considerations that do not warrant anticipation at this point suggest the absence of such parity and, in that regard, the resulting implications for economic theorizing are traced.

Two considerations, however, which will be seen to bear heavily on the results of the arguments to follow, warrant initial notice. The first has to do with the reality that economic activity and decisions occur in what will be referred to as real historical time. But what is involved in the phenomenon of historical time, which, in one way or another, economic reasoning must

---

[3] Ibid., pp. 1, 3.
[4] Hands [5, p. 72].

necessarily take into account, places a burden on analysis that does not bear on the physical sciences. That is because time, in many physical scientific formulations, is properly taken to be what will be denominated logical time. The details and the substantial significance of the difference between historical time and logical time will be elaborated in due course. It is sufficient to say for the present that in the reality-context of historical time, questions arise as to the stability over time of certain assumptions and identities generally contained in an economic analysis. In short, individual personal behavior patterns, and the analytical assumptions that are relevant to them, might be so unstable over time as to render it difficult to conclude that a true explanation of behavior and economic outcomes can be, or has been, determined. Several such considerations will be seen to bear on the inquiry into epistemological parity that was referred to earlier. And of course, the passage of historical time raises the issue of the extent to which knowledge of the past, or even of the present, can be confidently specified. As to the future, the recognition of historical time requires acknowledgment in one way or another for economic model building that the future is unknowable. A number of significant implications will be explored.

The second of the preliminary matters that warrant brief reference at this point has to do with what has been referred to as the increasing mathematization of economics as an analytical discipline. The background to that development, the reasons for it, and the nature of mathematical usage in economic argument (including model construction) will be considered at some length. In addition, it is also necessary to understand carefully on those levels the respects in which the differential calculus and other arithmetic-operations-requiring mathematical techniques that frequently find a place in economic model building may be employed in instances and cases where highly suspect results may follow. That often has to do prominently, as will be pointed out at length, with the possibly misleading deductions and conclusions that follow from the misuse of data or variable values that are measured in ordinal rather than cardinal or ratio terms. Further, an extended example of model building will be given in which the mathematics put to work appear in terms that render irrelevant the question of whether any kind of measurement is possible. Such ground has hitherto not been explored extensively in economic model building and will be seen to permit, in certain universes of discourse, models where pertinent variable values are unmeasurable or non-quantifiable. A logic of non-quantifiable mathematical relations has been developed in earlier writing and is briefly described in a simple, straightforward manner here.

In order to exhibit its potential explanatory significance it will also be adduced in the example mentioned above in which the building of a model of the structure of a firm or enterprise is set out in largely unquantified, set-theoretic terms.

In addition to what has already been said, it will be useful in concluding this introduction to provide a minimal indication of the issues that will be addressed in the first two chapters that follow. Chapter 1 provides a background view of the relations between the physical and the social sciences and the difficulty of asserting, as was previously mentioned, epistemological parity between them. Given the objective of economic model building that engages the present investigation, the principles of scientific testing and the disputes that have occurred in the development of them will be addressed. The conclusions will be seen to bear vitally on the entire enterprise of economic explanation.

Chapter 2 is concerned with a general discussion of the nature of models, their characteristics, and their relation to economic explanation. It concludes with a brief outline of the subsequent chapters, which, in part, identifies the location of the remaining topics alluded to above that do not appear in the first two chapters.

References

[1] Bell, D. and I. Kristol, eds., *The Crisis in Economic Theory* (New York: Basic Books, 1981).

[2] Bernstein, M. A., *A Perilous Progress: Economists and Public Purpose in Twentieth-Century America* (Princeton: Princeton University Press, 2001).

[3] Boland, L. A., *Model Building in Economics* (New York: Cambridge University Press, 2014).

[4] Boumans, M. and J. B. Davis, *Economic Methodology: Understanding Economics as a Science* (Basingstoke: Palgrave Macmillan, 2010).

[5] Hands, D. W., "Orthodox and Heterodox Economics in Recent Economic Methodology," *Erasmus Journal for Philosophy and Economics* 8 (2015), pp. 61–81.

[6] Hicks, J. R., "Some Questions of Time in Economics," *Evolution, Welfare, and Time in Economics*, A. M. Tang, F. M. Westfield, and J. S. Worley, eds. (Lexington: D.C. Heath, 1976), pp. 135–151.

[7] Hutchison, T. W., *Knowledge and Ignorance in Economics* (Chicago: University of Chicago Press, 1977).

[8] Katouzian, H., *Ideology and Method in Economics* (New York: New York University Press, 1980).

[9] Klamer, A. and D. N. McCloskey, "The Rhetoric of Disagreement," *Rethinking Marxism* 2, no. 3 (Fall 1989), pp. 140–161.

[10] McCloskey, D. N., "The Rhetoric of Economics," *Journal of Economic Literature* 21 (1983), pp. 481–517.

[11] Morgan, M. S. *The World in the Model: How Economists Work and Think* (New York: Cambridge University Press, 2012).

[12] Reiss, J., *The Philosophy of Economics: A Contemporary Introduction* (New York: Routledge, 2013).

[13] Ross, D., *Philosophy of Economics* (Basingstoke: Palgrave Macmillan, 2014).

[14] Ward, B., *What's Wrong with Economics?* (New York: Basic Books, 1972).

[15] Wiles, P. and G. Routh, eds, *Economics in Disarray* (Oxford: Basil Blackwell, 1984).

[16] Woo, H. K. H., *What's Wrong with Formalization in Economics? An Epistemological Critique* (Newark: Victoria, 1986).

1

Science and Economics

Science, as practiced by physicists, chemists, biologists, and other physical scientists, is no doubt one of our most successful and respected intellectual enterprises. Clearly, that success and respect have been intertwined with each other. On the one hand, science is looked up to because of its ability to explain and predict. Science explains the relations and causations that exist between facts and events and the phenomena of the world. That acquired explanation then enables prediction of future events and relations. In actual fact, science has resulted in an enormous extension of, and improvement in, the quality of life that many human beings lead. Medical and biological sciences have provided cures for numerous diseases and adequate food for expanding populations. Other segments of physical science (together with the technological developments they have spawned) have given us central heating, refrigeration, the automobile, plastics, television, the computer, the exploration of space, and much, much more. Thus success has bred respect. On the other hand, respect has brought increased funding into science along with the resources those funds provide, and it has encouraged many individuals to take up science as a career. Respect has therefore resulted in greater support for and the expansion of scientific activity, which, in turn, has brought forth more success. So pervasive and penetrating has been the combination of success and respect that it has led, in some quarters, to the glorification of science. Both those who practice it and scientific work itself are frequently held in the highest esteem. It is no wonder, then, that social science, and especially economics, has often attempted to cloak itself in the mantle of science.

But is social science really science? That, of course, depends on what is meant by the term "science." Unfortunately, several centuries of philosophical argument have failed to provide an exhaustive and universally accepted prescription that fully characterizes science. Indeed, with the

extensive appearance in the middle of the twentieth century of arguments
for the abandonment or modification of such comprehensive schemes as
positivism and falsificationism, the latter meaning that science is concerned
virtually exclusively with the disproof of hypotheses, some philosophers
seem to have become content to limit their discussions to describing the
properties of "good" science. In this vein, Kincaid [20], for example, while
retaining a place for the testing and potential falsification of hypotheses,
takes a broader view. Science, he claims [20, p. 21], is an activity that
generally "... promotes ... knowledge and truth." For him, good science
not only contains falsifiable statements, but it also fits data accurately, its
scope is wide, it coheres within itself and with established knowledge from
outside its purview, it is successful in obtaining useful information, and
it is objective in so far as human beings are capable of objectivity. Good
science also is subjected to tests. These tests must be capable of checking
specific, isolated hypotheses, of ruling out competing hypotheses, and of
making sure that it is the data that lead to the acceptance or rejection of the
hypotheses and not the background assumptions, or the conditions of the
environment in which the test is conducted. Finally, the explanations of
good science are either causal in nature or show how diverse phenomena fit
into common patterns.[1] Kincaid's purpose is to defend the social sciences,
and the thrust of his argument is that, pressed against these standards,
social science can be, and often is, good science.

Yet, even if one accepts the still-controversial proposition that social
science can be good science, it is nevertheless necessary to admit that there
are numerous differences between social science and the clearly more successful and more highly respected physical sciences. (A few of the successes
of the latter were mentioned at the outset.) The significance of some of
these differences is more contentious than that of others. But no matter how
contentious, such differences need to be recognized at the same time as the
objective of social science is taken to be identical to that of physical science,
namely that of explanation and then, in so far as the level of achieved
explanation permits, the prediction of possible future outcomes.

In the case of social science, the objects of study are human activities and
relations among human beings rather than actions of, and relations among,
non-sentient and unmotivated physical entities. And human activities
and relations depend on such elements as the knowledge, emotion, and
directedness of those who are acting and relating[2] – elements that have no

---

[1] Kincaid [20, pp. 50–55].
[2] e.g., Hayek [10].

counterpart in physical science. This means that acknowledgement of the ontological status of humanity necessarily pervades social science inquiry. Now, generally speaking, there are two different interpretations of human existence. On the one hand, individuals may be perceived as being totally constituted by the material pieces (e.g., neurons and other cells, molecules, atoms, etc.) of which they are made up. In particular, mental activities emerge in knowable ways from the physical component-pieces of the brain along with the relations between the appropriate collections of such pieces.[3] From this vantage point, which may be referred to as *philosophical materialism*, if enough were known about the properties of those material pieces (including the ways in which they interact with other material pieces both within and outside of the individual), then a person's behavior in any situation could be determined with a high degree of accuracy from a careful examination of his material characteristics and his environment. Allowing for interpersonal interactions, a parallel assertion could be made with respect to the behavior of an institution, which is, from the perspective of philosophical materialism, fully comprised of the people who form it.

On the other hand, it may be thought that human beings have cognitive capacities that go beyond, and are not solely determined by, their material parts. That is, knowledge of all the material facts about a person is not sufficient to explain his behavior. This implies that, in relation to the world in which human beings live and act, only the experiencing of things and events can directly interact with those extra-material cognitive capacities, since the material pieces cannot go that far. Of course, due to the individual's continually changing knowledge and circumstances, the interactions with respect to things and events can happen in any particular way only once, only when the individual makes intellectual contact with them, and only in the order in which those contacts actually occur. All mental processes, regardless of whether they relate to material or non-material elements, together with whatever knowledge has been accumulated, necessarily contribute to the making of an individual's decisions. It follows that experience and its orderly interaction with the extra-material capacities become of major significance in the generation of human behavior.

This latter view of the ontological status of mankind has many immediate consequences, five of which may be noted here: First, time cannot always be conceived in terms of the idea of "logical" time that physical science has

---

[3] See Bunge [4, pp. 8, 9].

generally assumed to be appropriate for investigating the physical world.[4]
That is, the relevant notion of time in social science is often "historical"
time, or that which is actually experienced by human beings, in which each
moment in history is unique, and in which time reversals (such as the re-use
through time of a fixed and fully specified optimization model thereby
permitting, say, an individual to take back a decision already made and
substitute a different one) are not possible.[5] Second, change in the world of
human beings has a different flavor, including far less foreseeable regularity,
than change in the physical world. Here the deliberative actions and
reactions of sentient individuals taking place amid the uncertainties created
by change are of paramount importance. And this becomes all the more
significant when it is recognized that, given existing knowledge, change may
not necessarily be even remotely predictable and may be produced instead
by unanticipated irregularities and shocks. That, of course, as will be seen
more fully in what follows, bears vitally on the compatibility of the twofold
objectives in the social sciences of explanation and prediction. Third,
because the objects of study in social science relate to human activities and
relations, the less-than-perfect knowledge possessed, that is, the considerable ignorance of the individuals in question,[6] along with the meanings
and interpretations they hold, have to be taken into account. Fourth, for
the same reason, motivations derived from, say, an assumed rationality, or
the drive to achieve the best result based on the contemplation of imagined
possible outcomes in the absence of full knowledge, become important
parts of explanation in social science. And fifth, to the extent that physically
identical persons have distinct experiences, interpretations of them, and
hence knowledge, their motivations and behavior in identical situations can
differ markedly. Thus, where one individual may be propelled by the desire
to be rational in the sense of, for example, maximization, another might

---

[4] Logical time orders events in an assumed sequence of occurrence without regard to the
manner in which these events are experienced in reality as past events, present events, and
future events. For a more complete discussion of the differences between this and the notion
of historical time introduced next, see Chapter 10 and Katzner [17, pp. 5–8]. Of course,
in some areas of physical science, for example in geology and in the dating of fossils, the
passing of historical time bears importantly on analysis and conclusions.

[5] To expand, in part, on the uniqueness idea, Vickers [31, p. 7] has characterized the human
condition in historical time as one with (a) a discontinuous epistemological status, in
that what the individual knows at each moment is unique (it depends on all that he
has experienced before), and (b) a continuous ontological status because there is no
modification, even across historical time, of his personhood.

[6] This ignorance includes not only large gaps in knowledge of the past and present, but also
a complete absence of knowledge of the future.

be directed by religious codes or cultural traditions. Of course, the middle three consequences on this list (the unpredictability of change, the absence of perfect knowledge, and the variety of motivations to action) also have relevance when the individual is regarded as the sum of his material parts alone. But clearly, the interpretation of human behavior in these respects depends on the commitment or otherwise to philosophical materialism. Regardless, in the physical as distinct from social sciences, neither knowledge, ignorance, meanings and interpretations, nor motivations driving actions exist as determinants of behavior by the objects of study.

At least three additional distinctions between the physical and social sciences arise less directly from, though not completely independently of, the humanness, or absence thereof, that is present in the objects of study. All three have significance regardless of whether the individual is taken to have a cognitive capacity that is independent of his material parts. One is that social scientists do not have nearly as much control as do physical scientists of the things that need to be held fixed in "laboratory experiments." All experimentation, indeed, more generally, attempts at corroboration with observed phenomena in all endeavors that strives to be scientific, rest on ceteris paribus or background requirements. And many of these are extremely difficult, if not impossible, to enforce in social science.[7] The second is that, it is often easier to quantify the elements of physical phenomena than those relating to social phenomena. More often than not, and quite apart from the problem in the social sciences of defining the salient and potentially decisive variables, appropriate scales on which to measure them do not even seem to exist. Issues and problems associated with these matters will be addressed in this and subsequent chapters.

Third, the nature of what is considered to be, say, economic science bears heavily on what is acceptable, valid, significant, or relevant explanation in the conduct of economic analysis. And in that determination, the economic science community plays a major role. The judgment of what an individual in the community sees as good economic science is based on that individual's own perceptions and observations as well as on those of others, including the perceptions and observations derived from institutions or established practices. Of course, the economics community itself is by no means homogeneous. Both across and within the two main

---

[7] This is not to say that the results of the relatively new field of experimental economics are useless. But many aspects of human experience cannot be controlled or duplicated in laboratory experiments. Thus individuals cannot be prevented from changing their minds and sometimes are threatened by loss of home or job that cannot be simulated in the laboratory with realistic force or power.

groups identified as orthodoxy and heterodoxy, there are often conflicting notions of what constitutes good economic science. Kitcher [21] argues that having such diversity maximizes scientific progress. Regardless, in all economic situations, where the objects of analysis are human actions and where accurate and meaningful measures of important variables, and laboratories with significant controls are absent, judging the quality or adequacy of an explanation requires different criteria than those appropriate for evaluating the behavior of non-sentient physical objects in the presence of accurate, meaningful measures, and significant laboratory controls. Additional details concerning the disparities between the physical sciences and economics are taken up in the remainder of this chapter and point further to the contrasts in judgmental criteria for good explanation between the two areas of investigation. The importance of this distinction arises in reference to the relevant evaluative criteria in economics in the fifth and last stage of model building described in Chapter 3.

Differences between the physical and social sciences like those described here have opened the door to specific philosophical debates. One perspective from which to enter such discussions, and one that will be seen to bear in various ways on the significance of the subject-matter of this volume, is to ask about the extent to which epistemological parity obtains between the physical and the social sciences. Now epistemology is concerned with such things as the origins of, the processes of creation of, the nature of, the limits of, and the validity and usefulness of knowledge. In particular, it has to do with the source, the meaning, and the competence of explanation. Explanation, in turn, has two parts: the thing being explained and the explanation of it. The former consists of the objects of inquiry; the latter is derived in terms of relations between those objects themselves and between those objects and others introduced for explanatory purposes. Questions relating to the presence or absence of epistemological parity between two discourses, then, would necessarily focus on comparisons of the properties taken to exist in their respective objects of inquiry, including the ability to identify and define clearly the variables relevant to that inquiry, and also on comparisons of the general character of the relations employed in their explanation.

Thus, to investigate whether social science attains epistemological parity with physical science, it is necessary to examine questions like (i) what is the origin and the method of formation of hypotheses about the objects of inquiry and explanatory relations involving them in the social sciences as opposed to the physical sciences? (ii) What, in each case, is the quality of, and the meaning of, the knowledge obtained upon subjecting those hypotheses to empirical tests? (iii) What is the possibility of establishing meaningful empirical tests in the respective sciences? (iv) What is the potential usefulness of that knowledge (in comparison with that of the physical sciences) in explaining and predicting the behavior of human beings and groups of human beings? And (v) to what extent, if at all, is investigation in social science more vulnerable to the intrusion of the values of the investigator than in physical science? In spite of the fact that the objects of inquiry in social science are the behavioral actions of, and relations among, sentient beings while those in physical science are not, epistemological parity between the two would still be established if it could be demonstrated, among other things, (a) that hypotheses in social science are provoked by universes of observation with the same characteristics as those in the physical sciences, (b) that the testing of those hypotheses permits the construction of meaningful explanations of past events, and (c) that the definitions of objects of inquiry in social science, and the analytical structures created to examine them, are sufficiently stable over time that conclusions formed on the basis of testing can be extrapolated into the future. In addition, it would need to be shown that human values do not interfere in the construction of explanation in social science to any greater extent than in physical science.

Now, a perception exists that, to date, social science has not been nearly as successful in contributing to human betterment as physical science, nor (probably as a consequence) has it been viewed with even remotely similar respect. This could be attributed to the relative infancy of the subject as a systematic intellectual discipline or, accepting the view that human beings are more than the sum of their material parts, it could be accounted for by citing the possibility that, for reasons cited above, social science is more limited in what it can do than physical science. In other words, it might not have been as successful in the tasks of explanation and prediction as the physical sciences. But it might also have something to do with an absence, in certain regards, of epistemological parity of social science with physical science, which may or may not be potentially correctable. Were that the case, once the reasons for the lack of parity are investigated and exposed, it might become possible, by removing some of the obstacles that are capable of elimination, to push social science epistemologically closer to physical science. To the extent that this could be accomplished, social science might then produce better explanation and more useful results. It would therefore become a more successful endeavor and, under those circumstances, the respect accorded to it might be considerably enhanced.

Not surprisingly, the question of epistemological parity between the
physical and social sciences, like the question of whether social science
is science, is unresolved and controversial. In covering themselves and
their work with the aura of science, many practitioners of social science
have sought, suggested, or implied complete epistemological parity. For
example, aspirations to epistemological parity may easily be inferred from
the assertion of Lundberg [24, pp. 24, 25], a sociologist, that sociology
has no choice but to "follow the rough road" that the physical sciences
have pursued. A similar inference for political science may be drawn
from Deutsch [8, pp. 7, 8]. And according to Hutchison [11, p. 38], some
economists have suggested the existence of an epistemological parity
between economics and physics that "... render[s] the methodological
analysis, prescriptions, strategy or tactics, derived from one ... entirely
appropriate, almost without qualification or reservation, to the other ... ."
But many other social scientists have dissented.[8] Moreover, both support
for, and opposition to, epistemological parity between the physical and
social sciences can be found among philosophers in their discussions
about, for example, the role of meanings, interpretations, and motivations
(rationality) in social science analysis.[9]

To give some idea of how the existence of epistemological parity
of social science with physical science can be considered further and
possibly refuted, three examples among many of the issues that could
be raised are considered here. These are, in turn, the status of laws and
the previously noted problems of the corroboration of statements and of
the measurement of variables.[10] It should be emphasized, however, that
numerous social scientists and philosophers do not accept the position
on the status of laws set out below, where emphasis is given to the role
of historical time and cultural differences in social science inquiry. The
historical-time perspective on laws, although it provides a reasonable basis
for much of what follows in this volume, is included here primarily for
illustrative purposes to clarify the notion of epistemological parity. Indeed,

---

[8] See, for example, Andreski [2, pp. 20–23], a representative of sociology, Ricci [26, pp. 286,
294–298] in political science, and Hutchison [12, p. 141] in economics. Campbell [6] and
Toulmin [30, pp. 504–508] suggest alternative approaches to epistemology itself that, if
accepted, would place the question of epistemological parity between physical and social
science in a different light.

[9] See, for example, the essays in Parts III and IV of the anthology put together by Martin
and McIntyre [25].

[10] Further discussion relating to laws may be found in Martin and McIntyre [25, Pt. II] and
Katzner [18], with respect to corroboration in Kincaid [20, Ch. 3] and with respect to the
measurement of variables in Katzner [14, 19].

subsequent chapters, though generally set in a logical time context, are largely independent of the attitude taken toward time, and their analytical significance does not turn exclusively on the conception of time that may be assumed to be relevant.

In physical science, a law is a universal statement that, while it establishes a cause and effect relation and provides a basis for explanation and prediction, is independent of any specific object to which it applies, and is also independent of time and place. It is generally accepted that, for example, the law of gravity in physics meets those requirements. But, with regard to social science, and from the perspective that the individual has a cognitive capacity that goes beyond the sum of his material parts, it has been argued by Shackle [27], [28, Ch. 7], Vickers [31], and others that the historical time environment in which human beings (both the objects of study as well as the investigator himself) live rules out the possibility of ever having knowledge of future human behavior. Only activities that have occurred in the past or are currently unfolding can (however imperfectly) be known. The actions of individuals, groups, and institutions that are yet to come cannot. And not only is the future unknown to humans; it is also unknowable. This absence of knowledge of the future, their argument goes on, precludes the specification of all probabilities, subjective or otherwise, of future events that relate to human behavior. On this view, an individual, for example, being a unique person and with unique knowledge at each moment of time, cannot say with certainty today what action he will take tomorrow because he does not know (even probabilistically) the conditions that will exist when tomorrow arrives, nor does he know how he himself will change in the interim. More generally, it is not possible to know in advance if any structure in place one day will still exist in the same form, or even exist at all, the next. For decisions and activities that are taken today create the structures, unknown today, that will stand tomorrow. Thus, for example, before the collapse of the Soviet Union in the 1990s, an astute observer might have been able to determine that that country was in serious trouble. He might even have been able to spin various scenarios depicting possible paths (including collapse) that the Soviet Union might have followed. But he would not have been able to predict, in the usual scientific sense of the term, its demise and the manner of its dissolution. In general, then, with such pervasive uncertainty about the future, prediction is neither tenable nor possible. Its untenability and impossibility arise from the general instability of structures over time and from the fact that actions in the present necessarily create an unknowable future. Indeed, structures that might form the basis of such predictions have been likened to the images in a kaleidoscope in their ability to dissolve "at a touch."[11] But, of course, it may still be possible for an individual under investigation to hold assumptions regarding the replication of past events as possible future outcomes, and to formulate decisions that rest upon those assumptions.

Accepting such an outlook in the conduct of inquiry, laws in the social sciences, unlike those in the physical sciences, cannot be projected into the future. Of course, one of the main reasons for establishing laws in the physical sciences is to achieve a degree of explanation that permits prediction. But in the social sciences, explanation to the same degree and prediction of the same kind cannot be achieved. Even explanation in social science that "precisely" explains a real phenomenon, although it might suggest predictive possibilities, has no formal predictive power because the real-world structures of the determining forces of observed phenomena are themselves subject to variation. Thus, although apparent regularities in the social sciences founded on past events may be observed, they still do not provide grounds for future projections in the same manner as do the well-established laws of the physical sciences. Laws in social science only apply to, and are relevant, for the past and present. They are not independent of time, and the quality of the knowledge they entail is insufficient for them to be used predictively as in physical science. It follows that, with respect to the time aspect of the status of laws, social science does not achieve epistemological parity with the physical sciences.

It can also be argued that because individuals from different cultures can be motivated to action differently, the laws of social science need also not be independent of place. This argument is made in three steps: First, behavior is derived from thought processes, more or less ordered and articulated, that result in the making of decisions. Thought processes, in turn, are mental acts that rely heavily on the symbols and their interpretations imported into the mind from the individual's cultural background. The motivations that guide those processes are also part of the cultural baggage included with the imports. Moreover, to make the decisions that generate behavior requires that the individual, in his decision-making thought processes, manipulates the imported symbols in culturally learned ways. It follows, then, that individual and institutional behavior (institutions are run by individuals) is significantly dependent on cultural backgrounds through the thought processes and motivations leading to the decisions that generate that behavior.

---

[11] Shackle [28, p. 42].

Second, significant cultural differences can arise across, and even within, societies. These differences often manifest themselves in ways that cause certain cultural traits to become dominant in some societies and not in others. For present purposes, a dominant trait is defined as one that appears to have more influence than most in generating individual behavior. Cultural traits become dominant when specific events occur that institutionalize those traits, making them a general motivating force for behavior in society at large. Of course, there may be many cultural traits that are common to two societies having different dominant traits. Moreover, cultural evolution has occurred in all societies over the ages in response to the events and histories that each experiences. And differences in histories are responsible, in part, for differences in dominant traits among them.

Third, and lastly, in constructing explanations of human behavior, social scientists abstract from reality to focus on the factors thought to be the most significant with respect to the issue at hand. Therefore, the elements on which attention centers must include the motivations at the time the action under investigation is taken arising from the dominant cultural traits of the society in which the action occurs. Since these motivations and traits can differ across societies, social science laws need not be independent of place. Acceptance of this argument would provide a further reason for a lack of epistemological parity between the social and physical sciences in relation to the status of laws.

Consider, next, one aspect of the issue of corroboration. This is the second example presented here of a domain in which epistemological parity between the social and physical sciences fails. Laboratory experimentation is usually the primary method of corroborating statements in the physical sciences. Such experiments, as pointed out above, are always conducted under appropriate ceteris paribus or background conditions. That is, standard experimental procedures invariably involve the holding of a specified number of variables fixed while the explanatory competence of other variables is investigated. Of course, the constancy of the ceteris paribus can never be complete even in physical science. And this means that any unexplained variance may be due to the omission of explanatory variables that have not been impounded in the ceteris paribus. Even so, without the ability to hold enough of the necessary variables and elements such as institutional structures fixed, laboratory corroboration would break down. But in the social sciences, it is often difficult to meet this standard and even to ensure that the constancy of the most significant of the requisite ceteris paribus conditions is actually enforced.[12] That is to say, there is

---

[12] Caldwell [5, pp. 156–157].

no reason to believe in the fixity over time of the conditions which to a greater or lesser extent may contribute to the determination of individual action. For example, suppose the behavior of an individual is thought to be rationally determined by his preferences. To corroborate this hypothesis, the characteristics of that person's behavior as revealed in repeated observations of it need to fit certain patterns. But since each observation is taken at a different moment in time, and since the individual's preferences exist only in his mind and are not, given the present state of social science, known to the investigator, any observation that contradicts the required pattern can always be explained away as a consequence of preferences that have changed through time. That is, the impossibility of knowing, as a practical matter, if the ceteris paribus restriction of fixed preferences is in play while observations are taken, precludes the drawing, with any degree of certainty, of inferences relating to the individual's motivations from observations of his behavior. This particular problem has to do with the possible lack of constancy of a certain element (in the present case, preferences) across time, and it arises from the sentientness of the individual whose behavior is under consideration. Whatever instability of individual preferences exists may be reflected in individual behavior regardless of whether it is thought that the behavior is determined by materialistic causation, on the one hand, or by reflected volitional response to a real situation, on the other. Alternatively, when dealing with data collected by government agencies, it is hard to determine exactly what remained constant, if anything at all, during the data-gathering process. It follows that the quality of knowledge provided by the testing of social science laws derived from past observations as described by those data is not the same as that furnished by tested physical science laws. And not only might the variables under investigation that are assumed to be unchanging actually vary over time, but the definitions of the variables themselves may have to be modified to meet new circumstances. For example, it is hard to imagine that the variable "automobile" remains constant through time. Thus there is more uncertainty attached to social science laws, and they are less reliable as elements of explanation. Corroboration, then, is a second area in which the social sciences seem to lack epistemological parity with the physical sciences.

Finally, there is the problem of measurement. Numerous yardsticks developed over many centuries such as rulers, balances, columns of mercury, etc., provide the means for at least cardinally (or intervally) measuring a broad variety of variables in the physical sciences.[13] These

---

[13] The notion of a cardinal measure is discussed in Chapter 5.

measures are, by and large, generally accepted and widely used. They are also meaningful both in terms of the logical structure upon which measurement generally rests and in terms of the use to which the numbers that represent measurements are normally put. There can be little doubt that the ability to measure precisely at cardinal or "higher" levels has played a major role in the successes enjoyed by the physical sciences.

But as has been remarked previously, measures like these are simply not available in many areas of social science. There are no generally accepted and appropriate yardsticks available for calibrating such abstract variables as freedom, honesty, culture, and enterprise. And, at present, in most cases there do not seem to be any good ideas of how to proceed in constructing scales on which they can be meaningfully and at least cardinally measured.[14] Indeed, and without ignoring the many empirical techniques that have been developed to handle unquantified variables (such as, for example, tests for association, the use of dummy variables in regression analysis, and the so-called logit model[15]), the lack of ability to measure is so endemic in the social sciences that numerous unquantified elements thought to be important are either represented by dubious but scalable "proxies,"[16] or excluded from analyses altogether. And numerous analyses themselves are not even undertaken because they involve the unmeasurable in decisive ways. These measurement difficulties point to a seemingly further departure from epistemological parity of social science with physical science in at least two respects: First, the use of proxy variables can only, at best, reduce to a minimal extent what might have been hoped for as the accuracy and relevance of the explanation produced by the analysis in question. At worst, it can render that analysis completely devoid of explanatory importance. For the use of a proxy implies the assumption

---

[14] In the earlier stages of the development of economics, it was thought that "utility" provided a cardinal measure of individual pleasure and pain. This derived from the well-known pleasure–pain calculus of Bentham's utilitarianism, and was endorsed by Jevons [13, Ch. 3] in 1871. In due course, however, economists came to the realization that utility actually measured pleasure and pain only ordinally.

To cite another illustration, while political scientists more or less agree on some of the structures or properties that cardinal measures of, say, political power should have (see, for example, Alker [1, pp. 197–206]), there is no general consensus on the particular measures that ought to be employed.

[15] These and a few others are described in Katzner [14, Chs. 12,13].

[16] Measures (or exact measures) are numbers that are generally accepted as calibrating exactly what they are intended to calibrate. Proxies are variables whose magnitudes everyone agrees do not capture exactly what is supposed to be gauged, but are used as "approximations" or representations anyway because exact measures are not available. Clearly, a proxy must be thought to have some relation to that which the proxy represents.

of a known, stable relation between the thing that is desired to be measured and the proxy.[17] And this assumption, which introduces knowledge where none formerly existed, is often not justified in reality. Second, rephrasing questions to avoid unquantified variables, or ignoring such questions and variables entirely, leads to the creation of a less significant, less distinguished, and less useful body of knowledge than would otherwise be the case. In either circumstance, the quality of knowledge produced by social science apparently cannot compare to the quality of knowledge fashioned by physical science and, as is the result in the other instances of failure to achieve epistemological parity with physical science described earlier, the efficacy and success of social science does not seem to be able to match that of physical science.

The apparent lack of epistemological parity, to the extent that it arises from the inability to measure in the social sciences, is an especially serious matter in the context of attempting to identify economics as a science. For since the end of the nineteenth century, humankind has become more fixated on numbers and measures than at any time in the past.[18] Society at large seems to have accepted the idea that for purposes of public discussion, knowledge requires measurement regardless of how meaningful the measures are. To repeat one popular refrain, "We simply have to be able to measure in order to know were we stand and if we are making progress." Academics, too, have fallen into line, measuring success by numbers of publications and subjective, numerical student evaluations of classroom performance.[19] Indeed, matters have progressed to the point at which, according to Eberstadt [9, p. 1], "... mankind lives under a tyranny of numbers" that is both injurious and enslaving, and likely to become worse.

The differences set out in earlier discussion between social and physical science apply with all their force to economics. But in spite of whatever difficulties these differences imply for the conduct of scientific inquiry in economics, economists as least as far back as Adam Smith used the word "science" to describe their discipline.[20] And the prototype for that science has always been the physical sciences. Because, as a consequence, economists have imported many of the analytical methods they employ from the physical sciences, and because those methods include the building of models the examination of which is the main focus of this book, it is

[17] See Katzner [16].
[18] Katzner [15].
[19] The fact that, in the latter case, the same number may mean different things to different student evaluators is ignored in the process of combining and analyzing their responses.
[20] Smith [29, p. 642].

worth taking a brief look as some of the physical-science methods, their epistemological foundations, and the importation of both into economics.

One way to set the stage is to go back to the Middle Ages that descended on Europe as the Roman empire declined and decomposed during the fourth and fifth centuries A.D. With political fragmentation dominating the ensuing millennium, the Catholic Church became the most powerful force uniting the European continent. Everyday life generally centered around religion and the study of God, and it was the Church that decided all questions relating to moral standards, religious practices, and religious dogma. Large segments of ancient Greek and Roman heritage, including much of the ancients' advancement in science, were deemed irrelevant, unimportant, or contrary to Church beliefs and were, to a considerable extent, ignored and forgotten. But in the fifteenth and sixteenth centuries, during the period known as the Renaissance, there was an awakening of interest in classical scientific inquiry. This led, in part, to a revolution in scientific thought that extended well into the seventeenth century. In particular, Copernicus, Kepler, and Galileo altered understandings of the heavens and earth and, in the case of Galileo, of how scientific analysis should and would proceed.

Before Galileo, one would consider, say, a stone falling to the ground and attempt to explain why it fell, and why it fell to the earth. The Aristotelians gave answers to these questions that survived through the Middle Ages: The stone fell because it had weight. Furthermore, since all objects in the universe, if left unrestrained, would move to their "natural places," and since the natural place of objects with weight was on the earth (i.e., assumedly at the center of the universe), the stone had to fall to the earth.[21] Galileo proposed to replace such superficial inquiry by measured analysis. But in so altering the focus and questions of scientific argument, his proposal implied nothing less than a change in the meaning of argument itself.[22] For instead of asking *why* the stone fell, Galileo would ask about the *characteristics of the stone* as it fell. Specifically, he would (i) express the most fundamental properties of the falling stone in terms of measures and use these measures to define quantitative variables, and (ii) analyze the falling stone by constructing relations among the variables that

---

[21] Kline [23, p. 172].

[22] From the perspective of the argument of this paragraph, the fact that the Aristotelian explanation happens to be qualitative and Galileo's is quantitative is of no consequence. The important point is the substantive change in the nature of explanation proposed by Galileo.

are built up deductively from axiomatic or observed principles.[23] Out of this procedure emerged, among other things, Galileo's measured law or "model" of uniform acceleration, namely, $d = kt^2$, where d is measured distance fallen after t units of measured time, and k is a numerical constant.

It was in this environment that Descartes articulated the first modern, unified approach to the creation of knowledge in the physical sciences. For Descartes [7], knowledge was gained by first thinking, theorizing, or reasoning about reality and then fitting what is observed or seen into the thoughts or theories already secured. From this perspective, known as *rationalism*, reality is made to correspond to thoughts. Several years later, an alternative approach, referred to as *empiricism*, was provided by Locke. He argued that one obtains knowledge by looking first, and then reasoning or building thoughts and theories to understand what has been seen, that is, thoughts are made to correspond to reality. Both approaches, then, dichotomize reasoning and seeing, and produce knowledge or truth by taking one to be prior to the other.

The perspectives that reason alone was the source of knowledge (rationalism), and that sensory experience was a precondition for reason (empiricism) were reconciled by Kant in the second half of the eighteenth century. Kant argued that while life experiences, including efforts to learn about history, natural laws, and human conditions, were the things on which reason operated, each person absorbed these experiences and reasoned with them in his own unique way, and with his own unique structure of categories. Thus, taking elements from both rationalism and empiricism, Kant, in a third perspective on the theory of knowledge, set the knowing individual off as an autonomous being, capable of his own personal construction of knowledge based on sensory perceptions. But by then, Comte had already introduced the notion of positivism, which was to become the basis for the development of a fourth approach to the construction of knowledge that was intended to replace the others as the "correct" approach to the formation of knowledge.

Positivism was the objective examination of observable phenomena for the purpose of discovering truths about them. *Logical positivism* (developed in the 1920s by the philosophically minded members of the Vienna Circle) was a system of logical thought in which knowledge of truth consisted only of meaningful statements that relate to observable phenomena.[24] Meaningful statements were either analytic (statements

[23] Kline [22, pp. 185–188].
[24] The remainder of this chapter is based on Caldwell [5].

whose validity depended solely on the definitions of the symbols they contained) or synthetic (statements whose validity was determined by the facts of experience).[25] Axioms or postulates, to the extent that they could not be empirically checked, fell into the former category. Logical analysis was made up of meaningful statements and used to clarify and draw synthetic conclusions about the truth content of propositions. Logical positivism emerged from positivism, the empiricist tradition, earlier work on symbolic logic or axiomatics, and work that showed anti-metaphysical or anti-speculative tendencies.

During the 1940s and 1950s, logical positivism matured into *logical empiricism*. This maturation involved the addition of three main elements. First, logical empiricism refined what it meant to confirm or successfully empirically check synthetic statements: A synthetic statement was confirmed if it repeatedly passed empirical tests of its validity without any negative instances of refutation. This was an early version of the notion of "confirmationism." Second, logical empiricism gave a specific identity, called the "hypothetico-deductive" model,[26] to theoretical structures or theories that, in part, expanded the concept of meaningfulness: A theory consisted of axioms, derivative propositions, and statements derived or deduced from a primary hypothesis based on the axioms, that purportedly described posited truth. These latter statements could refer to either observable or unobservable entities. Sentences involving only observables were considered to be meaningful (i.e., analytic or synthetic). Those containing unobservables could not be directly meaningful. The system as a whole became meaningful when some of its sentences involving unobservables, usually the derived ones, were translated into a form that permitted them to be indirectly observed and hence empirically tested. The unobservable elements of the theory thereby gained their meaningfulness indirectly. Third, the goal of inquiry (which formerly consisted only of description of truth) was redefined as explanation of truth that was based on a deductive or highly probable inductive argument (the two possibilities were called the "covering-law models") involving theories as described above. The deductive argument contained axioms or postulates from which the explanation of the thing observed was deduced. In the inductive argument, the thing to be explained could be inferred with a high degree of

---

[25] Ayer [3, p. 78].

[26] This notion of model, along with the idea of covering-law model introduced later, is distinct from the concept of model employed elsewhere in the present volume in that it lies on a different philosophical plane. The former refers to a model explaining the creation of knowledge in general; the latter to a model built to explain a real phenomenon.

probability from the postulates. Today, according to Caldwell [5, p. 199], "Philosophers seem agreed that explanation is an important goal (and some believe, the most important goal) of the scientific enterprise, and many accept the covering-law models as adequate depictions of legitimate scientific explanation."

Logical empiricism went into decline in the 1970s as criticisms of it gained widespread acceptance. Two of the more telling complaints were as follows: According to the first, identified with the name Karl Popper, statements and theories cannot be declared valid when they pass empirical tests. They can only be said to be consistent with the data employed. Testing based on other sets of data, not yet considered, available, or known, may yield inconsistencies with that data. Since tests can never be applied to all possible data sets, it is impossible to know if truth has been uncovered, and hence the primary objective of positivism to uncover truth cannot be attained. But when inconsistencies with data arise it may be concluded that the statements or theories have been falsified. The more tests a theory passes without falsification the more it has been confirmed. This is a later and more sophisticated version of the logical-empiricism notion of confirmationism noted above. Second, explanation can proceed by means other than building a theoretical structure that purports to accurately describe truth or what is actually going on. Two alternatives are to explain by the use of metaphors or analogies.[27]

In the years since the 1970s, no single, unified approach to inquiry has arisen in response to the decline of positivism. Instead, a variety of directions have been pursued, some of which "... emphasize the growth of knowledge over time, the dynamics of change within individual disciplines, and the actual practice of scientists. Universality is qualified by specificity; immutable verities are challenged by recognition of changing standards of investigation and patterns of thought; logical analysis is supplemented by and checked against the study of history."[28] Two examples are provided here.

Thomas Kuhn's approach begins with the notion of *paradigm* – a way of viewing and understanding the real world that provides a context for conducting analyses of it. Within a paradigm, legitimate areas of inquiry, both theoretical and empirical, and methods of investigation are clearly defined, and inquiry that articulates and extends the paradigmatic structure

---

[27] The terms "metaphor" and "analogy" are defined in Chapter 2. Although the definitions there are stated in reference to model building, they apply quite generally.
[28] Caldwell [5, p. 68].

(called normal science) is conducted. In the process of investigation, anomalies (inconsistencies with data or unexplainable phenomena) arise. These can lead to paradigmatic modification or replacement of the existing paradigm with a new one.

Imre Lakatos thought of inquiry as taking place within a dynamic system or *research program* that contained a collection of changing theories. Research programs consisted of a hard core of irrefutable, unchanging components of theories along with a belt of protection encompassing the refutable parts of them. It was within the protective belt that theoretical elements could be added, deleted, or altered as the results of investigations became clear. Research programs progressed or grew if they theoretically produced or empirically corroborated novel facts in their protective belts.

Over the years, many of the above ideas concerning the nature and source of knowledge have found their way into economics. Focusing attention on the period since the start of the twentieth century, it was Terence Hutchison who introduced positivism into economics in the late 1930s. Before that, economic methodology tended to stress subjectivism (introspection), methodological individualism, and the self-evident nature (through introspection) of the fundamental postulates of economic theory. Hutchison, the logical positivist, argued that this old methodology was not scientific because, in part, the propositions of pure theory, including economic models,[29] had no empirical content. Although it was not necessary that each statement in a theory be tested, at least a deductible implication of each had to be directly testable.[30] The use of introspection to establish the self-evidentness of the fundamental postulates was not legitimate because it did not demonstrate that those postulates had any connection to reality. In particular, one of the fundamental postulates, namely that of maximization by decision makers, was not appropriate because, in reality, decision makers face so much uncertainty and such a lack of information that they are actually unable to maximize in the sense that the theories employing that postulate require. The way out was through positivist empirical study of what decision makers actually

[29] The term "model" here refers to that which is built to explain a real phenomenon. Recall n. 26 on p. 23.

[30] This, at any rate, was Machlup's interpretation of Hutchison's position. In his response to Machlup, Hutchison denied that he was excluding indirect testability – that is, the testability of deductions from an untestable statement – when requiring that each statement of a theory be testable. But according to Caldwell [5, p. 143], much of Hutchison's work seems to contradict his denial.

do. Hutchison also imported falsification into economics as part of his positivist program.

Fritz Machlup thought that Hutchison's position was too extreme. Not all statements of a theory and, in particular, the postulate of maximization, could be and needed to be testable directly. In confluence with logical empiricism (the more sophisticated version of logical positivism), only derived "lower-level" statements had to be testable and subjected to empirical tests. Moreover, except for one glaring deviation, Milton Friedman, too, was primarily a logical empiricist. That exception was his belief that the goal of science was prediction (not explanation) and that the realism of assumptions or postulates did not matter. Caldwell [5, p. 173] refers to this approach as "methodological instrumentalism."

In the years following World War II, logical empiricism "... dominated the methodological rhetoric of economics."[31] It is not hard to understand why. In Caldwell's words [5, p. 220], "One of the most attractive features of logical empiricism was that it seemed to provide rigorous and objective formulas for identifying legitimate scientific procedure. The hypothetico-deductive model prescribed the structure and logical status of theories and theoretical terms; the covering-law models dictated which explanations were to qualify as scientific; and [the logical empiricist version of] confirmationism provided criteria for the appraisal [i.e., determining the truth or falsity] of theories. In a phrase, the logical empiricist program had prescriptive force." Today, logical positivism as a theory of knowledge seems to have lost some of its appeal among economists. Nevertheless, and continuing to quote Caldwell [5, p. 231], "In the construction and evaluation of their theories, most economists adhere to some variant of confirmationism or instrumentalism. Both of these approaches emphasize the testing of theories by their predictions. They differ in that instrumentalists consider the most highly confirmed theory the most useful instrument, whereas confirmationists consider the most highly confirmed theory the most probable: that is, confirmationists do and instrumentalists do not associate strength of confirmation with some notion of truth value."

Clearly, both confirmationism and instrumentalism still leave something to be desired as complete statements of a theory of knowledge. The former provides no persuasive way to choose between alternate and competing theories. For example, it furnishes no criterion for choosing between two theories that are confirmed to roughly the same degree. And just because one theory is confirmed to a higher degree than another, and hence might

---

[31] Caldwell [5, p. 4].

be thought to be more likely to be true, it does not follow that that theory is, in fact, true. Instrumentalism is relevant only when prediction is all that is of interest. And Popper's falsificationism, which is a part of both confirmationism and instrumentalism, "... runs into problems in application when interpreted strictly and loses prescriptive force when interpreted loosely."[32]

Caldwell's conclusion [5, p. 245] is that "... no universally applicable, logically compelling method of theory [or model] appraisal exists[,]" or if it does exist, "... we can never be sure that we have found it, even if we have." It follows that methodologies should be employed according to criteria other than those that relate to the seeking of truth. One possibility is to select a methodology that best fits the purposes of the investigation.

References

[1] Alker, H. R., *Rediscoveries and Reformulations* (Cambridge: Cambridge University Press, 1996).

[2] Andreski, S., *Social Sciences as Sorcery* (London: Deutsch, 1972).

[3] Ayer, A. I., *Language, Truth, and Logic* (New York: Dover, n.d.).

[4] Bunge, M., *Scientific Materialism* (Dordrecht: Reidel, 1981).

[5] Caldwell, B. J., *Beyond Positivism: Economic Methodology in the Twentieth Century*, rev. ed. (London: Allen & Unwin, 1991).

[6] Campbell, D. T., "Evolutionary Epistemology," in *Methodology and Epistemology for Social Science* (Chicago, IL: University of Chicago Press, 1988), pp. 393–434.

[7] Descartes, R., *Discours de la Méthode* (Leiden: Jan Maire, 1637).

[8] Deutsch, K. W., *The Nerves of Government* (New York: Free Press, 1996).

[9] Eberstadt, N., *The Tyranny of Numbers* (Washington: AEI Press, 1995).

[10] Hayek, F. A., "Economics and Knowledge," *Economica* n.s. 4 (1937), pp. 33–54.

[11] Hutchison, T. W., *Knowledge and Ignorance in Economics* (Oxford: Blackwell, 1977).

[12] Hutchinson, T. W., "On the Relations between Philosophy and Economics, Part II: To What Kinds of Philosophical Problems Should Economists Address Themselves?" *Journal of Economic Methodology* 4 (1997), pp. 127–151.

[13] Jevons, W. S., *The Theory of Political Economy*, 5th ed. (New York: Kelley, 1965).

[14] Katzner, D. W., *Analysis without Measurement* (Cambridge: Cambridge University Press, 1983).

[15] Katzner, D. W., "Our Mad rush to Measure: How Did We Get into this Mess?" *Methodus* 3, no. 2 (December, 1991), pp. 18–26. Reprinted in D. W. Katzner, *Unmeasured Information and the Methodology of Social Scientific Inquiry* (Boston, MA: Kluwer, 2001), Essay 2.

---

[32] Caldwell, [5, p. 244].

[16] Katzner, D. W., "The Misuse of Measurement in Economics," *Metroeconomica* 49 (1998), pp. 1–22. Reprinted in D. W. Katzner, *Unmeasured Information and the Methodology of Social Scientific Inquiry* (Boston, MA: Kluwer, 2001), Essay 8.

[17] Katzner, D. W., *Time, Ignorance, and Uncertainty in Economic Models* (Ann Arbor: University of Michigan Press, 1998).

[18] Katzner, D. W., "Economics and the Principle of Uniformity," *Economia Politica* 17 (2000), pp. 237–252. Reprinted in D. W. Katzner, *Culture and Economic Explanation* (London: Routledge, 2008), Essay 8.

[19] Katzner, D. W., *Unmeasured Information and the Methodology of Social Scientific Inquiry* (Boston, MA: Kluwer, 2001).

[20] Kincaid, H., *Philosophical Foundations of the Social Sciences* (Cambridge: Cambridge University Press, 1996).

[21] Kitcher, P., "The Division of Cognitive Labor," *The Journal of Philosophy* 87 (1990), pp. 5–22.

[22] Kline, M., *Mathematics in Western Culture* (New York: Oxford University Press, 1953).

[23] Kline, M., *Mathematics and the Physical World* (London: Murray, 1959).

[24] Lundberg, G. A., *Can Science Save Us?* (New York: Longmans-Green, 1947).

[25] Martin, M., and L. C. McIntyre, *Readings in the Philosophy of Social Science* (Cambridge, MA: MIT Press, 1994).

[26] Ricci, D. M., *The Tragedy of Political Science* (New Haven, CT: Yale University Press, 1984).

[27] Shackle, G. L. S., *Decision, Order and Time in Human Affairs*, 2nd ed. (Cambridge: Cambridge University Press, 1969).

[28] Shackle, G. L. S., *Epistemics and Economics* (Cambridge: Cambridge University Press, 1972).

[29] Smith, A., *An Inquiry into the Nature and Causes of the Wealth of Nations*, Modern Library ed. (New York: Random House, 1927).

[30] Toulmin, S., *Human Understanding*, v. 1 (London: Oxford University Press, 1972).

[31] Vickers, D., *Economics and the Antagonism of Time* (Ann Arbor, MI: University of Michigan Press, 1994).

2

Economic Models and Explanation

In confluence with the view of philosophers as indicated in the preceding chapter, an important aim of economic science, and that on which attention centers in this volume, is the explanation or clarification of worldly economic phenomena. The discerning of such phenomena could be completed with a single observation at a point in time or require repeated observations over a period of time. It should be noted, however, that in setting out to meet any explanatory aim, the complexity of human affairs is so detailed and extensive that it is beyond the capacity of human beings to explain any economic phenomenon by providing a fully exhaustive description of it. Clearly, then, explanation has to engage in abstraction from the minute particularities of the reality of the phenomenon whose explanation is sought. And this means that explanation of an economic phenomenon requires, at least in part, analysis of it. The explanation that is achieved may or may not carry with it an ability to predict.

Generally, analysis proceeds by organizing and exploring the thoughts one has about the phenomenon at issue. In economics there are a number of routes such organizations and explorations may take. To analyze by example requires the examination of highly detailed specific instances or case studies to illustrate the phenomena under consideration. Another form of analysis, storytelling, is the giving of a narrative account of the phenomena in which "... fact, theory, and values are all mixed together in the telling."[1] But the most common method of analysis in economics

---

[1] e.g., Ward [30, p. 180]. It is possible to think of storytelling as encompassing both description (including analysis by example) and model building in a static or dynamic context. For example, one might tell a story as description that incorporates "stylized" or hypothetical facts. Alternatively, a story might make use of elements of models, or employ both description and model building in its telling. But in all cases, the distinctive feature of storytelling is narrative. It is in this sense that storytelling is taken here to be distinct from and independent of analysis by example and model building.

involves the creation and study of models. And that is the main focus of attention here. It should be noted, however, that in the context of the epistemological considerations of the previous chapter, rationalism, empiricism, and falsificationism may or may not involve model building.

Models can be built for different reasons. They may be intended to suggest, according to Aydinonat [1, p. 119] "... what may be possible in the real world, ... show new ways ... [to] look at the world, ... or help ... evaluate the plausibility of ... conjectures about the world." They may be designed to identify the conditions under which certain outcomes might arise [1, p. 163], or the logical possibility of the occurrence of a sequence of observable values over time. The rationale for building models could also be to represent in a stylized way a possible structure or causal process in isolation, in which case the model built could be called *heuristic*, or to attempt to replicate past data and possibly predict future outcomes. Models built with the latter motive in mind may be referred to as *predictive*. And, of course, the reason on which present attention focuses is that models may be constructed to explain a particular phenomenon that has been observed.[2]

An explanatory model is an enlightening, artificial construction, the elements of which, by reason of their interrelation, produce with greater or lesser degrees of approximations a result that is the same as the actual observed event in the real world it purports to explain. Alternatively stated, a model of something – call the thing T – is a construct having enough in common with the observable facets of T that insight into T can be obtained by studying the construct. Einstein and Infeld [7, p. 33] gave the following physical-science illustration for physical models: Imagine a scientist is shown a watch with rotating hands and asked to explain how it works, but is not allowed to remove its cover. One way he might proceed is to obtain appropriate springs, gears, and whatever else might be required,[3] and build a model of the watch whose observable behavior duplicates the observed behavior of the original. It is then possible for him to give an explanation

---

What has been referred in the literature to as the "narrative method" or "narrative approach" is a special case of the notion of the general narrative in the above statement about storytelling. The narrative method requires the construction of a narrative made up of a unique sequence of events in time that involve human beings as actors. Narratives depicting what are considered to be static phenomena do not seem to be covered by the idea of narrative method. See Bruner [4, pp. 43–45] and Romer and Romer [26, p. 122].

[2] An alternative role for explanation described by Sugden [29] and not considered here is to create a model first and then look for something in the real world that it explains.

[3] Why he might choose specific gears, for example, or even why he might choose gears at all does not matter for present purposes.

of how the model behaves by claiming that the original watch works like, or as if it were, the model. Obviously, the objective in constructing this model is that of creating a structure that explains the operation of the watch. Evidently, there are many different models, and hence explanations, that could be built. But all explanations (not only those whose sole objective is to describe a structure) operate by identifying something in the model (here, the movement of the model's hands) with what is observed (the movement of the hands on the original watch). In economics, of course, models are usually not physical things. Rather they are mental constructs based on assumptions, abstract concepts, and relations among variables. But in many cases, they function in much the same way as in the Einstein–Infeld example. Thus, economic model building is different from description and from analysis by example in that it purports to provide a general explanation of the thing being scrutinized; it is different from storytelling in that it focuses on relations among variables rather than on narrative.

In economics, moreover, what is observable are data consisting of prices, quantities, incomes, and so on. The unobservables frequently consist of the determinant elements of economic decisions and actions, and it is hypotheses about them and their interrelatednesses that often constitute the inner workings of the economist's model built to explain the observed data. Such a model is intended to reproduce the same observed behavior (data) as that generated by the unseeable inner works of the real economy. In addition to hypotheses on unobservables, sometimes assumptions are introduced with respect to observables. The latter may limit the observable domain over which the model may be said to apply. Economic models, then, do not have the physical qualities of models of watches. Instead they are usually mental configurations, created by the economist to explain certain observations and, in their formal-logical form, are made up of things such as variables, parameters, relations, and assumptions and propositions derived from them. They also abstract from a multitude of possible forces to concentrate on the minimum number necessary for explanation, and their properties are understood as properties of the model and not properties of that which is the object of explanation. Nevertheless, economic models generally operate in the same way as suggested in the watch example.

Clearly, economic models, being mental forms, do not themselves exist in the real observable economic world. Nor do the properties they imply of the observable phenomena under investigation. Models and their properties are fictions, useful for understanding and explanation, that exist only in the minds of investigators. The assumptions and relations of a model may be, to a greater or lesser degree, "appropriate" or "relevant," and may or may not identify or be associated with directions of causality thought to be inherent in the phenomena under investigation.

Models are often parts of theories. A theory is a system of ideas containing its own forms of concepts, assumptions, arguments, propositions, and frequently models. But it is much more than a generalized version of a model. For each of these elements is interconnected in such a way that the propositions, arguments, models (if present), and conclusions of the theory derive their purpose and force in relation to each other. The manner in which the elements of a theory are tied together provides its distinctive character. Because, it is the notion of model independently of any theory that is relevant here, all aspects of the concept of theory that do not relate to models are ignored.

Six observations concerning this conceptualization of the idea of an explanatory economic model should be noted. First, the definition of model does not require that the variables under consideration be capable of measurement. Nor does the fabrication of any particular model impose a similar condition. In the absence of measurement, a variable's values can be specified as distinct and discrete verbal descriptions. The variable itself is the thing that can take on as values any description in the appropriate collection of verbal descriptions. Relations among such unmeasured variables can be defined in standard set-theoretic terms and used in model building in much the same way (except, of course, that numbers are not available) as relations among measured variables. Thus, without measurement, a procedure analogous to maximization or minimization can be envisaged. Systems of simultaneous functional relations can be formulated and, under certain conditions, their solutions expressed as functions of parameter values. And in the same context, systems of dynamic, periodic, functional relations can be analyzed for their stationary paths and stability properties.[4] General illustrations of these structures and a more detailed discussion of them are provided in Chapter 5. A lack of ability to measure, then, is no barrier to the pursuit of model building in economics.

Second, it is implicit in the definition of model given above, and consistent with the discussion of empirical positivism, falsificationism, and confirmationism in Chapter 1, that there should exist, in models that are meaningfully relevant to the economic reality under examination, acceptable accordances between the model and the observed facets of the

---

[4] Katzner [11], [14] presents a full discussion and proof of these claims.

phenomena being explained.[5] There should exist, that is, bridges linking the model and the relevant observed facts of quantified or nonquantified empirical reality. By that is meant that specifically observable or knowable occurrences of real-world characteristics, outcomes, or events, which, as has been said, may or may not be describable by quantifiable data, must be seen to stand in a one-to-one relation with elements or components of the model.[6] Although no attempt will be made here to describe what constitutes "acceptable accordances" between a model and reality, most assuredly each economist has some idea of the nature of the accordances that are acceptable to him, if not the adequacy standards of the economics profession at large. Furthermore, these accordances are crucial to the overall acceptability of the model proposed. Without such accordances, any analysis based on the model would be regarded as having little significance and relevance for explaining the phenomena under investigation.

Third, as previously indicated, all models that make a meaningful attempt to throw explanatory light on economic actuality are constructed through a process of abstraction. Reality is sufficiently complex that it cannot all be included in the specification of a model. Things have to be left out. This is so in defining variables, quantitative or not, as well as in characterizing relations.[7] Indeed, the very attempt to construct explanatory models is undertaken in the absence of an ability to describe exhaustively actual states of affairs in a satisfactory way. Thus the contents of, or the purported explanation derived from models are, at best, only supposed approximations of real or observed phenomena that are relevant only under certain conditions and possibly at certain times, and cannot have universal applicability.[8] It follows that, in contemplating what were referred to as accordances between the model and the real phenomenon that is being explained, and between the final explanation offered by the model and that phenomenon, larger or smaller imprecisions, divergences, and exception may arise. To handle each significant imprecision, divergence, or exception requires either a separate model addressed specifically to the issues involved, or a generalization of the original model that gave birth to the imprecision, divergence, or exception. The former leads to "localism" in analysis; the latter to models that assert less and less about the real-world phenomena in question.[9]

---

[5] See, for example, Keynes [16, p. 296].
[6] The idea of a bridge will be discussed more fully in the next chapter.
[7] A discussion of the kinds of things that are omitted appears in Chapter 6.
[8] Katouzian [10, pp. 157, 158].
[9] See Woo [31, pp. 29–31, 69, 70].

Fourth, models, as described here, are to be regarded as analogies or metaphors.[10] The distinction between analogy and metaphor is subtle; the following statement of their divergence will serve for present purposes. When modeling the observed behavior of a consumer, for example, to say that the model is an analogy is to think of the consumer as behaving "something like" that set out in the model. But to take the position that the model is a metaphor means that, with respect to the limited environment to which it applies, the consumer's behavior is thought of as being captured or explained with a high degree of literalness by the model's statement or, in other words, that the consumer is interpreted as behaving exactly and in all particulars as does the model. Klamer and Leonard provide formal definitions of metaphor and analogy that are consistent with the distinction provided here: A metaphor transfers the attributes of one object to another [19, p. 46]; an analogy is "a sustained and systematically elaborated metaphor, where one system of relationships is joined to another" [19, p. 45]. In economics, metaphors are sometimes established implicitly through the use of the phrase "as if," as employed above in discussing the Einstein–Infeld watch example. Thus, for example, under appropriate conditions a particular consumer's observed behavior may be explained as if he were a constrained utility maximizer. The difference between analogies and metaphors is that in the first case the model itself (apart from its variables and relations) is an approximate similarity or likeness; in the second it is an "as if" representation.[11] But in either case, the model likens observed reality to mental constructions in which reality is conceived of in terms of the constructions. In this way models serve as both an instrument of thought or explanation and as devices for communicating in an intelligible manner.[12] Their force lies in that they focus thoughts in precise ways, in that they provide standards for judging real-world behaviors, and in that they transfer the sense of one person's vision to another.

Fifth, because of the something-like or as-if nature of economic models, and because of the level of abstraction they employ, it does not follow that

---

[10] Although the idea of metaphor dates at least to Aristotle (see, for example, Klamer and Leonard [19, p. 22]), it was not recognized until 1983 that "economics is heavily metaphorical" (McCloskey [21, p. 502]). Indeed, Mirowski [22] has argued that many of the models of neoclassical economics are metaphors that were incompletely copied from pre-Einsteinian physics.

[11] This is not to exclude the approximateness that comes about in the variables and the relations from the abstraction process described above.

[12] McCloskey [21].

such models are necessarily capable of immediate concrete application, in the sense of precise and accurate description to specific real-world situations. Economic models, as noted above, do not exist in reality though they themselves are, of course, "real" in the sense that their formal-logical description is stated and communicable. They are mental constructions that are quite distinct from, albeit hypothetical approximations to, the reality to which they relate. To confuse a model of a person, a firm, or an economy with, respectively, an actual person, an actual firm, or an actual economy, is to commit what Machlup called the "fallacy of misplaced concreteness." According to Machlup [20, p. 9], the fallacy occurs when theoretical symbols are used "as though they had a direct, observable, concrete meaning." What a model normally does do, of course, is to establish principles and modes of causation that can be applied only in very broad and general ways.

Sixth, all models, in their construction, are subject to what may be called the "angle of vision" that the scholar who builds them brings to his work. Angles of vision emerge from pre-analytical persuasions arising out of backgrounds and experiences, and they influence, in turn, the nature of the questions asked and the assumption content of the analyses put forward to answer them. In this way, and in a very broad sense, all scholarly enterprise, in particular model building, is inescapably contaminated by ideology, politics, culture, and values.[13]

The economic phenomena that explanatory economic models purport to address largely consist of economic behavior or the consequences of that behavior. The models themselves can be constructed with one or more explanatory objectives in mind. One possible objective could be merely to center attention on describing the manner in which an actual economic entity may be structured. Such a construction could be thought to clarify the characteristics of the phenomenon in question and explain how its various possible parts might cohere. For example, a model, similar to that set out in Chapter 7, may be designed to identify the possible elements of a real firm and show how those elements could fit together in explaining what the total phenomenon of a firm might look like. An alternative objective of explanatory model-building in economics is to focus directly, as in the case of the model of the watch noted earlier, on the explanation of observable outcomes. Explanation in this case will, no doubt, necessitate the building of a structure. But the entire thrust of argument is pointed toward developing outputs of the structure for explaining the observable

---

[13] See Myrdal [23, pp. vii,viii].

outcomes. The outcomes to be explained could come from a single entity such as the inputs and outputs of a firm, or from an entity made up of multiple units like the prices and quantities across a microeconomy. In the latter case, of course, the model would be concerned with clarifying how possible relations between consumer and firm may achieve the outputs that represent the observed simultaneous appearance of all market price and quantity outcomes.

Evidently, an explanatory economic model built to depict the possible structure of an entity may also, although not of primary importance, produce outputs that might be of use in explaining observable outcomes. Although these outputs are only a by-product of structural creation, they are still outputs in the same sense as those obtained from a model whose main purpose is to explain observable outcomes. And since, as previously indicated, the latter models rely on structure, it follows that, in many cases, an economic model may be interpreted in terms of either of the two objectives described here, namely, to explain a structure or to explain behavior. For example, a model of the firm might have as its objective an explanation of how the various elements of the firm might fit together or interact with each other to produce output and hire inputs. Alternatively, its purpose might be to explain the hiring-of-input and supply-of-output behavior of the firm.

Consider now the outputs produced by a model regardless of whether the objective of the model is to explain the structure of an observed economic entity or observed economic behavior. These outputs fall into at least two categories or styles: When the consequences of economic behavior, that is the outcomes of the behavior that is observed, are at issue either as a by-product of a structure or as the primary focus of a model, the model outputs are typically collections of variable values as in the price and quantity outputs of demand–supply models of isolated markets. On the other hand, if the underlying reasons or motivations for economic behavior, say the decision mechanism that generates the observed behavior, are under investigation, the model outputs are often behavioral functions whose function values in the decision mechanism case are usually regarded as the result of economic choice. Behavioral-function outputs could also identify patterns of macroeconomic evolution over time as generated, for example, by Kaldorian or Kaleckian growth models.

It is worth examining these two styles of model outputs in greater detail. The difference between them may be thought of in terms of a distinction between aspects of initial conceptualizations of the observed phenomena (i.e., the entity or event) that the model is intended to explain.

Taking up the behavioral-function style first, the relevant aspect of the initial conceptualization centers around the following kinds of questions: Can some kind of structure or the component parts that make it what it is and give rise to a representation of the entity's or event's observed behavior, be specified; who are the decision-makers within the economic structure in view, or what is the mechanism recognized in the structure that produces its representation of the observed behavioral outcome; how do decision-makers, if present, make the decisions that lead to the structure's representation of the observed outcome, or how, respectively, does the mechanism operate to cause the structure to function in a way that enables it as a whole to realize its representation of that outcome? To answer such questions, the phenomenon, apart from whatever elements might be structurally appropriate in constructing a model, can be visualized in terms of potentially repeatable observations in which certain observed variables may be thought of as dependent on certain other observed variables (e.g., consumer purchases as prices and incomes vary, firm input purchases and output sales arising from various input and output prices, and the time path of real output as time passes). Then an economic frame or structure is built that constitutes an explanatory model within which depictions of repeated action can take place, and analysis can then proceed to focus on the model's representation of the observed behavior in question. The output produced by the model is expressed as a behavioral function or functions where both independent and dependent variables are observable (e.g., respectively, consumer demand functions, firm input demand and output supply functions, and an equation relating real output to time) and the model as a generator of those functions can be employed as an explanation of the observed behavior. Moreover, the functions produced by the model can possibly be estimated from actual repeated observations, and the properties of those functions (as derived from the model) can possibly be tested against the properties of the observations. Estimation and testing would be two ways of corroborating the presence of what has been referred to earlier as bridges from the model to the observed phenomenon. And, of course, such a model can be used as the basis for predictions of future action. A model that generates this style of output may be called a *multi-output* or a *function-output* model.

Turning to the other style of model output where the consequences of economic behavior rather than the motivations or reasons for it are at issue, the relevant aspect of the initial conceptualization of the observed entity or event is conceived of as being produced or represented by only a single observation, that is, one observation of each of the values of a specific collection of variables (e.g., the price and quantity transacted in an isolated market, and those appearing simultaneously in all markets of the economy). Here a different set of questions arises: What is the entity or event in real economic life that has been observed; how can that entity or event best be captured and conceived for what it is; why did it, respectively, arise or happen in the way it did; and can it arise or happen again? In this case, too, a structure (e.g., respectively, intersecting market demand and supply curves, and utility and production functions which, upon appropriate maximization, lead to the economy-wide excess-demand functions that equate to zero as in the [Walrasian] general equilibrium model,[14] or alternatively, a system of linear equations with the fixed production coefficients of the so-called classical model as set out by Pasinetti [24, Ch. 5]) is built that constitutes an explanatory model. But now the structure plays a different role in the explanation of an economic organization in focusing on the representation of a possible single, stand alone outcome rather than on representing possible repeated actions that might occur within it, and analysis proceeds to work out the manner in which the variable values representing that outcome arise in the model structure's framework. The output of the model is a single collection of variable values that are observable (e.g., respectively, the price and quantity variables of the supply–demand model of an isolated market or the vectors of price and quantity variables across the microeconomy in the general equilibrium or classical microeconomic model). Here the variable values that are actually observed and taken as produced by or representative of the entity or event to be explained are identified with the output produced by the model and, in light of that identification, the model can be used to explain these observations. The full model itself does not admit empirical tests, although some of its component functions might still be representative of repeated observed behaviors and hence capable of being estimated or tested as indicated earlier in relation to the multi-output model. Were the latter to be so, bridges to the observed phenomenon could be confirmed through empirical estimation or testing beyond the forced linkage arising from identifying the observed variable values produced by or representing the entity or event with the model's output. Alternatively, it might be possible to extend the model in such a manner as to derive

---

[14] Of course, the objective of constructing these model structures might only be, as with the model of the watch mentioned earlier, to explain how a market or, respectively, a microeconomy operates. In that situation, the specific outcome of the model might not be of interest.

within its framework a behavioral function that might be representative of observable behavior. Examples of such extensions appear in Chapter 7. Of course, the model as initially formulated is generally not in a state that would permit prediction of future variable values. A model that leads to this style of output will be called a *single-output* or *variable-value-output* model.

The dichotomy that gives rise to multi- versus single-output models evidently applies to phenomena that are viewed as static and not considered to evolve over time,[15] although, in that case, repeated observations across time can possibly be taken. (A phenomenon may be said to evolve over time if at least one manifestation of an aspect of it at one moment or in one period of time may be thought to depend, at least in part, on manifestations that arose at past moments or in past periods.) But clearly, the dichotomy also applies to phenomena that are considered to evolve over time. A dynamic model with a stable stationary state or equilibrium and in which observations of the phenomenon under consideration are explained by identifying them with that equilibrium is a single-output model (e.g., the tâtonnement general equilibrium model with price adjustments reacting to non-zero excess demands over time[16]). A dynamic model representing a phenomenon, the observations over time of which are explained as evolving along a non-equilibrium time path in the model, is a multi-output model (e.g., models whose time-path outputs converge, diverge, or oscillate around an equilibrium path such as a cobweb model or a model of hyperinflation). The function output in this latter case typically consists of periodic or, when quantification is present, difference equations whose variables depend continuously on time.

The previous discussion of model objectives and outputs in economic analysis may be succinctly summarized as follows: Some multi- or single-output models are constructed to explain the structure of an existing economic entity. Others are fabricated to explain the outcomes resulting from the operation of an entity or an event.

Consider now, in greater detail, the relation between model building and explanation. Explanation and models that explain have been characterized in terms of such differing notions as causality, idealization, unification, credible worlds, etc.[17] However, it is not necessary at this point to delve into the details that these categories present. Several of them will be

---

[15] The notions of static and dynamic models are considered more extensively in Section 10.2.

[16] In a tâtonnement model, trading is not permitted until the equilibrium outcome is reached.

[17] For example, Reiss [25]. Heuristic and predictive models as described above may also, in the appropriate context, be explanatory.

briefly noted in the next chapter. For now, the following definition is sufficient: By the term "explanation" (which includes the idea of "models that explain") is meant first, a statement of the economic significance of the main features and empirical characteristics of the phenomenon in view; second, revelation and clarification of the reasons why the observed phenomenon is what it is; and third, the degree to which the presence of the phenomenon in the economic system is likely to be continued, and the economic implications that follow from such continuation. That is, to explain something is to render it intelligible, to show how it fits into the world of which it is a part, and to furnish the genesis, source, and potential significance of it. Explanations of economic phenomena, then, require the elucidation of the forces and their implications that cause those phenomena to appear and possibly continue to appear. In particular, explanations of economic behaviors and outcomes consist of providing reasons why the given behaviors and outcomes occurred.

Explanation is correct if it gives what is thought to be an accurate picture of that which is actually going on; it is erroneous if it does not. To the extent that the viability of the model involved in explanation is supported by empirical testing against data culled from an appropriately relevant time period, correct explanation may provide the basis for prediction. (Prediction is not sufficient for correct explanation because it may be derived from irrelevant causes.) However, due to the inachieveability of full verification and the inadequacies of the economist's laboratory with respect to the inability to hold the necessary control variables fixed (recall the discussion of Chapter 1), it is not possible in many circumstances to test statistically or otherwise determine whether an explanation is correct – even when considerable data are available. Thus the viability of economic argument, that is its ability to provide a "true" explanation of a state of affairs, often rests on the judgment of the investigator as to its "reasonableness." But in the end, such reasonableness has, in turn, to be based on the relevance (also suggested in Chapter 1) of the explanation to the cultural environment in the context of which the observed state of affairs is generated. When the latter cultural environment is the same as that of the investigating economist, the judgment of an explanation's validity becomes personal – introspective in character and derived from private life experience. That is, the judgment is then dependent to a considerable degree on the cultural background of the investigator. In that case, for him to be ready to accept an explanation, the investigating economist has to feel that its assumption content accurately reflects his own perception of, and his own understanding of the relevant relations within, the reality being explained.

Clearly, the competence of a model to produce an explanation depends, in substantial part, on the method of the model's construction, on the suitability of its assumption content, and on the accordance of its component parts with real economic elements, thereby avoiding spurious correlations with actual facts. Moreover, when observing an economic phenomenon at any given moment of time, only a single observation is possible.[18] To explain this observation as the output of a model constructed for that purpose, then, the model has to determine a unique output. For example, a consumer buying a basket of commodities in a supermarket, buys only one basket. Attempting to explain that purchase using the traditional model of consumer behavior in which demand functions may be multi-valued does not yield a complete explanation of this consumer's behavior. It only provides limits on what the consumer might have bought. And although the model might be set so that the actual basket purchased falls within those limits, it does not fully explain the acquisition of the specific basket in question.

Another activity sometimes related to explanation in which economists engage, and which often involves model building, is problem solving. Whereas explanation usually requires the articulation of a vision with the previously elucidated characteristics, to solve problems is to answer specific questions. The questions could be of the same kind as those arising with respect to explanation (e.g., how is the price of a good determined in the market in which the good is bought and sold). But they need not (e.g., what is the extent to which quantities demanded vary with changes in price or income). In the former case, problem solving compels explanation in the setting out of a vision leading to the construction of a model; in the latter, explanation, vision, and model construction are not necessary. For, with respect to the latter, techniques could be used which could be shown to have been logically derived from a vision-based model, but are presented without any reference at the time of their employment to the structure or content of the vision or model itself. In that circumstance, problem solving focuses solely on a narrowly defined, isolated matter. The broader issues such as (i) the relationship between similar problems, (ii) the interaction of their solutions and, if present, their association with explanations, visions, and models, and (iii) the conditions under which solutions, explanations, visions, and models could be extended and applied elsewhere may be ignored in problem solving but remain an integral part

---

[18] Of course, this does not preclude the possibility of taking repeated observations at different subsequent times.

of explanation. Thus explanation is often a more general activity having significantly far-reaching implications than immediate problem solving. Since problem solving, even when not explicitly linked to explanation, may often be implicitly related to it as previously described, problem solving will not be considered further.

According to Bird [2, p. 89], good explanation has at least three additional characteristics beyond the provision of satisfactory reasons for an event as described earlier: Good explanation should have power to explain in detail distinct facts. The more it can explain and the greater the detail, the greater its power. It should be as simple as possible. The use of Occam's razor to reduce assumption content would certainly contribute to that simplicity. And, lastly, it should have the "... ability to integrate and combine with other explanations." [19]

To illustrate an economic model that provides good explanation in this sense, consider the general equilibrium model of a perfectly competitive economy whose purpose is to explain and clarify the simultaneous, interacting behavior of real agents as observed in price and quantity data throughout the real microeconomy. That single-output model focuses on the notion of equilibrium (i.e., a position of rest with no tendency to change) and, in the tradition of methodological individualism,[20] is built up by making assumptions about the preferences, technologies, and behaviors of fictitious, individual agents. Having accepted the questions this model addresses, and having accepted the equilibrium approach and the assumptions upon which the answers provided by the model are to be based, the economist has no choice but to pursue the relevant analyses and inquire into the existence, uniqueness, and stability of equilibrium in the model. An easy way to see why this must be so is to focus attention on a solitary, real-world market in isolation. Imagine one were to observe that market during a particular period of time. In that case, one could see that a specific quantity of the commodity was traded at a specific price or, in other words, one would observe a single point in commodity-price space. Subsequent observation in the following period would yield a second point with, say, a higher price and a larger quantity. In building a single-output model to explain how these points came to be seen, the economist could assume (a) that there exist two downward-sloping distinct market demand curves each passing through one, but not the same, observed point, and

---

[19] Further discussion of (good) explanation may be found in Elster [8] and Kincaid [17], [18].
[20] A definition and discussion of methodological individualism appears in Chapter 10.

(b) that there exists only one upward-sloping market supply curve passing through them both.[21] Then, since each observed point is identified as a market equilibrium point in the model,[22] each could be explained either as analogous to, or as if it were, the output of the interaction of supply and demand. The economist could also assert that the movement from the first point to the second occurred because of an increase in demand. Clearly, equilibrium must exist in the model for this explanation to work. If, moreover, the equilibrium in the model were not unique, then the explanation would be incomplete; it would allow the observed point to be identified with more than one equilibrium, each with its own properties, and no way to tell which theoretical properties should be identified with the seen point. Finally, when the observed point changes from the old to the new, the old equilibrium in the model is replaced by a new one. But if the latter equilibrium were not stable, then whatever dynamics there were in the model could prevent navigation within it from the old to the new equilibrium and, in that circumstance, the explanation given for the observed movement from the one point to the other would break down. An alternative interpretation of reality would be to locate observed points along time paths that converge to equilibria in the model rather than to identify them specifically as equilibria. But in either case the questions of existence, uniqueness, and stability have to be explored because that is the only way to be sure that the model can be linked to the real world.

A similar argument applies to the full general equilibrium model with many goods and many agents. And in spite of the fact that considerable resources and energy have already been devoted to the investigation of the existence, uniqueness, and stability questions in this context, satisfactory answers are available only in the case of existence. The problem is that, although sufficient conditions for uniqueness and stability are known, these conditions are not very general and, contrary to the tenets of methodological individualism, are typically expressed as restrictions on aggregated, that is market, excess demand functions. Furthermore, it is not clear if it will ever be possible to give satisfactory general uniqueness and stability conditions that are stated with respect to the preferences,

---

[21] The assumption of a single supply curve is sufficient but not necessary for the construction of this model.

[22] Note that, as suggesteded earlier, demand curves, supply curves, and equilibrium points cannot exist in reality. They can only be present in models. Similarly, to prove that equilibrium exists and is unique and stable in a model can never imply that unique and stable equilibria exist in the real world.

technologies, and behaviors of the individual agents.[23] Therefore, if generality and methodological individualism are to be maintained, even more resources and energy will have to be diverted to the analyses of general equilibrium models. And if this quest fails, then without even questioning the realism of their assumptions or the relevance of the conclusions derived from them, the general equilibrium model will have to be discarded because it is unable to provide a viable explanation of that which can be observed.

Subject to this last stipulation, the qualities of good explanation can be observed in the earlier mentioned example of the general-equilibrium model. Indeed, the general-equilibrium model interpreted as an analogy or as a metaphor provides a deterministic representation of, and reasons for, observed market behavior. It is powerful, relatively simple, and can integrate with other explanations (e.g., certain models of international trade and of economic growth). It is also elegant, and appealing, and has led to what are considered by many to be significant results. Of course, to the extent that a more realistic model of the full microeconomy could be developed that also satisfies the criteria for good explanation, that model would presumably be considered a better explanation of microeconomic reality.[24]

Similar considerations apply to the remaining examples of models used as illustrations earlier – the cobweb model of an isolated market, the classical model of the microeconomy, and Kaldorian and Kaleckian macroeconomic models of economic growth. In all of these cases, the existence, uniqueness, and stability of equilibrium solution values or growth rates determined by the simultaneous equations of the model are often essential characteristics for meeting the criteria of good explanation and to be thought by economists to be both significant and appealing. The same can be said of many other explanatory models in economics.

The six observations made earlier regarding the various features of economic models influence the modus operandi of model building. In particular, the question of economic realism, or the potential robustness of the explanation that the model achieves, will depend critically on the extent to which, at one or more stages of the exercise, the accordances referred to earlier between the model and real economic data and outcomes can be established. Those accordances will rest, in part, on the severity of the degree of abstraction that inheres in the model and that, in turn, will hang

---

[23] See Katzner [15].

[24] One such candidate has been proposed by Katzner [13, Chs. 9–11] in the context of the environment of historical time, ignorance, and nonprobabilistic uncertainty championed by Shackle [27, 28].

on the precise universe of inquiry in which the model is provoked. The severity of abstraction, moreover, will necessarily vary as real conditions warrant and may assume acute proportions when the variables employed are nonquantifiable.

With these issues in view, model building in economics may be thought of as a constructive process that develops by passing through a number of levels or stages. Five stages may be identified, starting with (i) the formulation of an initial vision, then proceeding through three additional stages in which (ii) an inaugural formulation of a model with primary assumptions, (iii) secondary assumptions and manipulations, and (iv) empirical testing where appropriate are sequentially tacked on, and ending with (v) the making of a judgment as to the cogency, relevance, and significantness of the model produced. The details of this process and matters related to it are considered in Chapter 3. In the course of that discussion, the explanatory significance of different types of models with respect to their objectives and outputs will be explored.

Model building in economics is often associated with mathematics and numerically measured variables. In relation to the former, one may wonder why this is so and how did it happen. With respect to the latter, measurement or quantification, as pointed out earlier, is actually not necessary to have perfectly rigorous and meaningful mathematical models that explain economic activity. The issues are taken up respectively in Chapters 4 and 5.

There are, to be sure, other matters that relate to model building in economics. These include more extensive and deeper explorations into the relation between theory and model, into how and why models impart knowledge,[25] into the interactions between causality and model building,[26] and into the testing of economic models.[27] However, with a few exceptions interspersed throughout general argument, further inquiry along these lines is beyond the scope of the present volume. Instead, attention is focused on more mundane matters having to do with the practicalities of model building as indicated in the following.

Chapter 6, "Issues Relating to the Construction of Models from Scratch," explores in some detail the exercise, scope, and usefulness of model building in economics. The particular questions it addresses include: what does model building do, how does it do it, and what are its prerequisites,

---

[25] A survey of some of the literature on these matters is provided by Dohnen [6, pp. 193–196].
[26] See, for example, Cartwright [5].
[27] See, for example, Boland [3].

limitations, power (expanding on that notion introduced earlier), and potential. The answers to these questions are developed in terms of the stages of model building set out in Chapter 3, and are illustrated in Chapter 7 by the actual building, from the very beginning, of a model with two objectives. The main purpose is, by focusing only on the structure created, to clarify the possible characteristics of, and the efficiency properties of certain organizational forms that a firm might assume. A second objective is to extend the model to explain as a by-product particular outcome behaviors in and of those organizational forms. Since the variables in this analysis are, for the most part, non-numerical, the chapter also serves to provide an example of a complete application of analysis without measurement to a static, theoretical topic. That is, it depicts the process of proceeding from "dialectically appearing" reality, through abstraction, to the construction of an "arithmomorphic" model employing unmeasured variables[28] and, finally, to some theoretical results. Of course, the same process applies when appropriate measures of the variables in question are available.

It will become apparent in due course that the discussions in Chapters 3–6 are designed to lead cumulatively to the exposition of the concrete example of model building contained in Chapter 7. Those intervening chapters, therefore, should be read with that motivation in mind. Chapters 8–10, summarized in the following paragraphs, consider different methodological issues that are not a part of this cumulating argument.

Many investigations in economics do not seem to construct models in accordance with the five stages set out in Chapter 3. Often construction begins with stage (iii) and ends there or with stage (iv). Of course, stages (i) and (ii) could be passed over if use is being made of a model developed by another investigator who has, in published venues, already worked out the particulars of the model at those stages. But if the early-stage tasks have never been undertaken, and there are many instances in which they have not, then the vision at stage (i) and the assumption content at stage (ii) are necessarily imposed implicitly by the assumptions invoked at stage (iii). Unfortunately, as described and informally illustrated in Chapter 3, this latter procedure has the potential of introducing early-stage elements into the analysis that can turn out to be inappropriate for the purposes at hand. In Chapter 8, "The Implicit Assumption Requirements of Later-Stage

---

[28] As will be indicated in Chapter 6, reality necessarily arises dialectically in that the concepts and variables of any reasonably complete description of it do not have clear boundaries and overlap their opposites. An arithmomorphic model is one that is built up from variables whose values are all distinct and discrete. These ideas are due to Georgescu-Roegen [9, pp. 43–47].

Model Building," the details of some examples of the assumptions and implied visionary elements implicitly imposed by starting at stage (iii) are spelled out.

Economists sometimes build models in which one or more of the variables involved, such as effort in efficiency wage models, can, at best, be only ordinally and not cardinally measured.[29] Because numbers on ordinal scales can be modified by arbitrary increasing transformations without changing their information content, this raises possible issues regarding the logical viability of structures built with them. For example, transforming an ordinally measured variable with respect to which a function has a unique maximum value can modify that function to such an extent that a maximum no longer exists.[30] Hence the meaning and significance of a model based on the maximization of a function with respect to an ordinally measured variable is called into question. Chapter 9, "Ordinality and the Adequacy of Analytic Specification," examines the implicit links between a model containing ordinal variables and its underlying unquantified counterpart that are needed to render the former a viable theoretical construction. The chapter demonstrates that when the underlying unquantified structure is unknown, it is necessary, in order to make any sense of the model, that the permissible transformations of scale applicable to the ordinal variables have to be arbitrarily restricted beyond that which is permitted by dint of the ordinality itself. This adds an additional layer of arbitrariness beyond that which naturally and necessarily enters the model-building process as described above. In the case of the efficiency wage model, sustainability requires that the only usable transformations of the ordinal effort scale employed in that model are those which are multiples of each other. The possibility of an underlying structure being known but unspecified is also considered.

The volume continues with a discussion in Chapter 10 of several of the different kinds or categories of models heretofore not considered that economists use for explanatory purposes. These categories will serve as the basis for pairwise comparisons of models exhibiting the following characteristics: statics vs dynamics, partial equilibrium vs general equilibrium, individualist vs structuralist, certainty vs uncertainty, and within the latter category, probabilistic uncertainty vs nonprobabilistic uncertainty. Finally, Chapter 11 provides some general concluding methodological comments.

---

[29] The notion of ordinal measurement is characterized in Chapter 5.
[30] Mathematical illustrations appear in Chapters 5 and 9. For a more complete discussion of the issues involved, see Katzner [12].

References

[1] Aydinonat, N. E., *The Invisible Hand in Economics: How Economists Explain Unintended Social Consequences* (London: Routledge, 2008).

[2] Bird, A., *Philosophy of Science* (Montreal and Kingston: McGill-Queen's University Press, 1998).

[3] Boland, L. A., *The Methodology of Economic Model Building: Methodology after Samuelson* (London: Routledge, 1989).

[4] Bruner, J., *Acts of Meaning* (Cambridge, MA: Harvard University Press, 1990).

[5] Cartwright, N., *Hunting Causes and Using Them* (Cambridge: Cambridge University Press, 2007).

[6] Dohnen, T. J., "Building and Using Economic Models: A Case Study Analysis of the IS-LM Model," *Journal of Economic Methodology* 9 (2002), pp. 191–212.

[7] Einstein, A. and L. Infeld, *The Evolution of Physics* (New York: Simon & Schuster, 1938).

[8] Elster, J., *Explaining Social Behavior: More Nuts and Bolts for the Social Sciences* (New York: Cambridge University Press, 2007).

[9] Georgescu-Roegen, N., *The Entropy Law and the Economic Process* (Cambridge, MA: Harvard University Press, 1971).

[10] Katouzian, H., *Ideology and Method in Economics* (New York: New York University Press, 1980).

[11] Katzner, D. W., *Analysis without Measurement* (Cambridge: Cambridge University Press, 1983).

[12] Katzner, D. W., "The Misuse of Measurement in Economics", *Metroeconomica* 49 (1998), pp. 1–22. Reprinted in D. W. Katzner, *Unmeasured Information and the Methodology of Social Scientific Inquiry* (Boston, MA: Kluwer, 2001), Essay 8.

[13] Katzner, D. W., *Time, Ignorance, and Uncertainty in Economic Models* (Ann Arbor, MI: University of Michigan Press, 1998).

[14] Katzner, D. W., *Unmeasured Information and the Methodology of Social Scientific Inquiry* (Boston, MA: Kluwer, 2001).

[15] Katzner, D. W., "The Current Non-Status of General Equilibrium Theory," *Review of Economic Design* 14 (2010), pp. 203–219.

[16] Keynes, J. M., Letter to R. F. Harrod, July 4, 1938, in *Collected Writings* v. 14, D. Moggridge, ed. (London: Macmillan, 1973), p. 296.

[17] Kincaid, H., *Philosophical Foundations of the Social Sciences* (New York: Cambridge University Press, 1996).

[18] Kincaid, H., *Individualism and the Unity of Science* (Lanham: Rowman & Littlefield, 1997).

[19] Klamer, A., and T. C. Leonard, "So What's an Economic Metaphor?" in *Natural Images in Economic Thought: Markets Read in Tooth and Claw*, P. Mirowski, ed. (Cambridge: Cambridge University Press, 1984), pp. 20–51.

[20] Machlup, F., "Equilibrium and Disequilibrium: Misplaced Concreteness and Disguised Politics," *Economic Journal* 68 (1958), pp. 1–24.

[21] McCloskey, D. N., "The Rhetoric of Economics," *Journal of Economic Literature* 21 (1983), pp. 481–517.

[22] Mirowski, P., *More Heat than Light* (Cambridge: Cambridge University Press, 1989).

[23] Myrdal, G., *The Political Element in the Development of Economic Theory*, P. Streeten, trans. (London: Routledge & Kegan Paul, 1953).

[24] Pasinetti, L., *Lectures on the Theory of Production* (New York: Columbia University Press, 1977).

[25] Reiss, J., "The Explanation Paradox," *The Journal of Economic Methodology* 19 (2012), pp. 43–62.

[26] Romer, C. D. and D. H. Romer, "Does Monetary Policy Matter? A New Test in the Spirit of Friedman and Schwartz," *NBER Macroeconomics Annual* 4 (1989), pp. 121–170.

[27] Shackle, G. L. S., *Decision, Order and Time in Human Affairs*, 2nd ed. (Cambridge: Cambridge University Press, 1969).

[28] Shackle, G. L. S., *Epistemics and Economics* (Cambridge: Cambridge University Press, 1972).

[29] Sugden, R., "Credible Worlds: The Status of Theoretical Models in Economics," *The Journal of Economic Methodology* 7 (2000), pp. 1–31.

[30] Ward, B., *What's Wrong with Economics?* (New York: Basic Books, 1972).

[31] Woo, H. K. H., *What's Wrong with Formalization in Economics? An Epistemological Critique* (Newark: Victoria, 1986).

3

The Stages of Model Building in Economics[1]

As described in Chapter 2, economic behavior or the consequences of that behavior are frequently the subject matter of explanatory economic models. Models of this sort can be built for the purpose of explaining, respectively, certain aspects of a phenomenon that are observed or how an economic phenomenon generates outcomes. In the first instance the emphasis is on the model's structure; in the second it is on the model's output. When there is interest in the model's output either as the main focus of the model or as a by-product, one of at least two styles of outputs may emerge. These styles give rise to what has been called the multi- or function-output model and the single- or variable-value-output model.

It should also be recalled that the function-output model is often built on the foundation of economic choice. From Hausman's perspective [11, p. 73], the structure of the standard model of choice consists of preferences (in the general sense of judging one alternative to be better than or equally as good as another), beliefs, and constraints as determinants of choices. With respect to the traditional multi-output model of consumer demand, individual preferences and beliefs are combined into a preference ordering among baskets of commodities, and preference orderings and price-income constraints combine to determine choices and hence behavior [11, p. 19]. In the case of the firm, the typical model sets out to show how the firm's operating decisions are determined: First, its preference ordering among input mixes and output levels is developed as dependent on constraining prices and resource endowments, beliefs about technological possibilities, and the firm's desire for larger net returns. These preferences then generate

---

[1] This chapter is taken with minor modifications and additions from my paper of the same title in *Studies in Microeconomics* 4 (2016), pp.79–99. © Sage Publications India. Reproduced with permission.

the firm's choices and behaviors [11, p. 42]. The models that produce the behavioral functions described here can be combined and enlarged to obtain the general equilibrium model whose structure fabricates an output that is a collection of variable values consisting of prices and quantities across the microeconomy. In this sense, the general equilibrium model is a variable-value-output model. However, building the general equilibrium model could also be interpreted as having as its only objective the description of a possible structure that explains how the general microeconomy operates. This chapter is concerned with the procedure whereby the function-output and the variable-value-output models are constructed.

Remember, too, that a model of T has been described as a construct having enough in common with T so that insight into T can be gained by studying the model. In economics, models are mental formulations intended to relate to economic phenomena. Boumans [3, pp. 2–4] thinks of models as instruments of investigation that aid in achieving an understanding. They are built by "...fitting together elements from disparate sources." The latter include "...policy views, mathematical concepts and techniques, metaphors and analogies, stylized facts and empirical data." These pieces are homogenized and harmonized into a single form and merged into a single structure. It is a trial-and-error activity. The main thrust of what follows is to describe and explore some of the characteristics of the manner in which this homogenization and harmonization process in the construction of models can be carried out.

Weisberg [26, p. 209] identifies a three-stage procedure for the construction of models in general and which applies to explanatory economic models in particular: "In the first stage, a theorist constructs a model. In the second, she analyzes, refines, and further articulates the properties and dynamics of the model. Finally, in the third stage, she assesses the relationship between the model and the world if such an assessment is appropriate." The present chapter considers a five-stage approach that builds on Weisberg's structure and in which his first and third stages are each split into two parts. It will be seen that this enlargement of Weisberg's structure leads to a deeper and more detailed conceptualization of the process of building a model. The possible problems that can arise by ignoring the initial steps when constructing models are then described. In this context, the relation of models to the reality they purport to explain, along with their empirical testing, is also considered. The chapter concludes with a brief discussion of the place of explanatory model building in the overall methodological scheme.

It should also be pointed out that the main focus here is to marshal those considerations and logical relations which, taken together, point to what might be considered an optimal way of coming to grips with the problem of economic explanation. In that sense, the ensuing presentation may be interpreted as being connected to two distinct and alternative contexts. First, attention may be paid primarily to the ways in which economic model building is designed to elevate the more significant aspects in the explanation of actual phenomena. Since economic model builders attempting to explain economic phenomena have appeared, historically, not to have been seriously concerned with a detailed specification of the procedures involved in such an exercise, the ensuing discussion may be viewed as more normative than descriptive in that it provides a proposal for directing model building toward possibly more fruitful explanation. Second, from a purely methodological perspective, the following can be viewed as suggesting conceptual steps or stages that may be employed as an aid in describing and understanding explanatory economic model building activities. These stages are heuristically relevant in clarifying the process of model construction and furnish a conceptual framework that rationalizes certain aspects of the model building program.

3.1 Model Construction

As previously indicated, the concept of model building in explanation as contemplated here is described in terms of five procedural steps. The advantages and limitations of approaching model construction in this way will be considered later on. For now, it should be noted that the approach is quite distant from instrumentalism in that the relation of assumption content to the real-world activity under investigation is highly significant, and that as suggested earlier, prediction is only a secondary by-product of explanation. The five steps or stages may be identified as follows:

(i) *Formulate an initial image of the phenomenon in question and its characteristics.* According to Schumpeter [21, pp. 561–562], "... the thing that comes first [in every scientific venture] is Vision. That is to say, before embarking upon analytic work of any kind we must first single out the set of phenomena we wish to investigate and acquire 'intuitively' a preliminary notion of how they hang together or, in other words, of what appear from our standpoint to be their fundamental properties." This will involve an accounting of various aspects of the phenomenon under review, recognizing that it may be described with respect to single or multiple outcomes and in terms of (a) measurable, (b) non-quantified or non-quantifiable, or (c) proxy variables. If the phenomenon is seen as a single-outcome happening, the initial image of it will focus on an interpretation of the structure that produces a representation of the observed outcome. If it is viewed as a multi-outcome event, attention will center on a depiction of behavioral characteristics and interaction. From the latter vision, a process of abstraction will bring into focus a conceptual structure containing potential relations among those elements that appear to be most important for explanatory purposes. The abstraction procedure requires the isolation of certain elements thought to be most important for the purpose at hand from the influence of other elements deemed to be less important.[2]

(ii) With the objective of explaining a single- or multiple-outcome in view, *formalize these initial thoughts in a model that employs relations among appropriate variables.* In this inaugural conceptualization of possible explanatory relations, it is not necessary to consider in full detail the extent to which the model is operational or the usefulness of the model for explaining aspects and possible iterations of the phenomenon. That is, specific answers to questions of measurement, if appropriate, of the empirical testability of the model, and of the availability of analytical techniques to manipulate and, assuming testability, to test the model, are ignored. Nevertheless, the potential correspondence between real-world occurrences and the model builder's analytical conceptions will, of course, still be influential.[3]

In the process of formalization, a number of assumptions, referred to below as primary assumptions, will have been made. It will subsequently emerge that an important relation exists between the assumption content of the model (including both primary and what will shortly be called secondary assumptions) in its full specification and its overall explanatory competence, coherence, and empirical relevance. For that reason, it is useful at this point to clarify the distinction between what has been designated as primary assumptions and secondary assumptions.

Primary assumptions form part of the initial stage of formalization of the model and have to do with such things as the characteristics of human behavior, possible institutional structures influential in economic outcomes, and human motivations for economic decisions and choices. Thus, consistent with frequently adduced assumptions relevant to the explanation of commodity market activity, the assumption may be made, for example, that decision makers behave in accordance with some appropriately specified objective of benefit or preference satisfaction. Such an assumption may derive from an underlying tenet of generalized economic rationality present in the cultural background of the individuals under consideration. Similarly, assumptions regarding institutional structures may reflect perceptions of the nature of competition and regulatory

---

[2] This is Mäki's notion of "essential isolation." See Grüne-Yanoff [7, p. 98].

[3] With respect to predictive models, these first two stages are necessary in order to avoid the spurious correlation between predictors and that which is predicted.

constraints, resource availabilities and their freedom of movement, and the availability of finance.

The model as constructed thus far, with the initial vision of stage (i) taken into account and with its primary assumption content of stage (ii), provides an abstract description that makes sense as an incomplete representation of how the real world might actually operate or be described. (These two stages correspond to Weisberg's first stage.) That depiction, for example, may bring into focus individuals with particular preference orderings and motivations, pursuing their own self-interest, and facing institutional and resource limitations. But incompleteness arises because the representation may not yet have sufficient substance to rigorously and logically assert that the behavior to be explained could follow from the primary assumptions alone. The missing material is furnished by the secondary assumptions.

The purpose of secondary assumptions, to be introduced at the next stage (stage (iii)), is to complete the model so as to render it capable of explaining the phenomenon under consideration. This will include, in part, making the model amenable to analytical exploration and empirical investigation. Illustrations of these kinds of assumptions might involve specifying, say, mathematical forms or properties of preference orderings and associated utility functions if preference satisfaction is contemplated in stage (ii) as a primary assumption and represented in stage (iii) as utility maximization; ignoring or modifying, in specific situations, some of the primary assumptions introduced at stage (ii); and introducing quantified proxy variables in place of unmeasured or ordinally measured variables present at stage (ii). In the latter case, it will be relevant to consider certain difficulties and possibilities of misinterpretation that may arise in the use of the calibrated proxies.

(iii) *Operationalize the model.* (This relates to Weisberg's second stage.) By this is meant both the possible introduction of new elements and the manipulation of the relations among the variables of the model to extend and complete the analysis, to examine the implications of the assumptions, and to derive, if possible and not already present in the relations that structure the model, empirically testable hypotheses.

Notwithstanding the care with which primary assumptions may be brought in at stage (ii), the process of operationalizing will usually involve the introduction of secondary assumptions of the sort indicated earlier.[4] As

---

[4] As noted earlier, it is certainly possible for a model builder who is using or extending a model constructed by someone else to employ the same primary (stage (ii)) and secondary

will be argued in what follows, secondary assumptions often have implicit assumption counterparts that may be implied at the level of the primary assumptions of stage (ii). That is, these counterpart assumptions that are now seen to be relevant because of the operationalization at stage (iii) may significantly alter the initial structure of assumptions introduced at the earlier stage. And such counterparts may not have been acknowledged or taken into account at stage (ii). Of course, had such implicit primary-level assumptions been explicitly introduced as primary assumptions at stage (ii), they would frequently (though not necessarily) imply, respectively, the corresponding secondary assumptions. In any case, the presence at the level of stage (ii) of implicit assumption counterparts to the secondary assumptions of stage (iii) raises the issue of how well these counterparts fit with the earlier initial image and its initial formalization in stages (i) and (ii). This matter plays an important role in judging the cogency, relevance, and usefulness of the model in stage (v) described below.

(iv) *When appropriate, subject the model to empirical tests.*[5] Where quantified variables are employed, this will be accomplished by using standard statistical and econometric techniques. For instances when the explanatory model is structured by nonquantifiable variables, a variety of alternative methods is also available.[6] It should be noted, however, that all empirical tests compare model properties with observed data – quantified or unquantified. And construction of that data involves considerable abstraction that removes it a significant distance from reality, often farther than the vision of stage (i) or the preliminary formulation of stage (ii). To identify in the general automobile market, say, the number of automobiles sold at a particular price requires the condensation, respectively, of quantities of many different products and their varying prices into a single pair of numbers.

In order to proceed to the empirical testing of an explanatory model, it is first necessary to be clear on a preliminary, preparatory step that must be taken. Let observation provide a set of data that is to be explained. To illustrate, that set may contain the price and quantity of a commodity seen in a single market during a period of time, a consumer's purchases of baskets of commodities at various prices and incomes at various moments of time, or a sequence of aggregate real output quantities produced by

---

(stage (iii)) assumptions of the original model. But this does not absolve the copier of the need to discuss these assumptions and give reasons why they are relevant to explaining the phenomenon on which the copier's attention is focused. Moreover, if the copier is making changes in the original primary or secondary assumptions, those changes require justification too.

[5] With heuristic models, such empirical corroboration may not be necessary.

[6] See Chapter 5 for several possibilities. More extensive discussion may be found in Katzner [13, Chs. 12, 13].

the macroeconomy across time. In each case, a model is constructed from certain assumptions regarding economic behavior that are thought to have given rise to the observed data. As is implicit in the discussion on pp. 35–36, some model outputs, here to be called model outcomes, describe the way in which real-world elements would appear if the model were an accurate representation of reality. The preparatory step to empirically testing the model is to assume a correspondence between the relevant model outcomes and the data in question. That correspondence, which is, of course, subject to subsequent test, is what permits it to be said that the model explains the observed data. In the examples provided above, the observation of the price and quantity in the single market may be explained as described on pp. 42–43 as occurring at the intersection of market demand and supply curves; the consumer's purchases at various prices and incomes may be explained as points on a demand function derived from constrained utility maximization, and the sequence of aggregate real outputs of the macro economy may be explained as outcomes in a Kaldor, Goodwin, or Kalecki economic growth model. At this juncture, no actual empirical test of any of these models has been undertaken.

Given the assumptions of an explanatory model, sometimes those assumptions, especially the secondary ones, will imply that certain outcomes of the model including, possibly, the variable values or relations acted on directly by the model's assumptions, necessarily exhibit certain properties. With respect to the constrained utility maximization model, the assumed linearity of the budget constraint and the absence of prices and income as independent variables in the utility function force the demand functions to be homogeneous of degree zero; in some Kalecki models, the assumptions imposed such as, for example, that the price level is set by a mark-up from unit costs, results in a growth rate of aggregate real output that is inversely related to the share of profit in aggregate income (the price level times aggregate real output). When properties such as these are present, empirical testing can go forward. To perform an empirical test, then, the properties that apply to those model outcomes identified with the observed set of data at issue can be compared to the properties of that observed data. That is, regarding the test of homogeneity of a demand function derived from constrained utility maximization, the observed data can be checked to see if the consumer's purchases remain constant when all prices and income have been multiplied by the same positive number. In the case of the particular Kalecki growth model under consideration, the observed sequence of aggregate real outputs and further observations of corresponding profit share data could be examined to determine if a decline or increase in the profit share (and hence a rise or fall in labor's share) is associated with a respective expansion or contraction of the rate of growth of aggregate real output. Employing statistical techniques when available, to the extent that, in the judgment of the investigator, the properties of the model outcomes and those seen in the observed data are consistent with each other, the explanatory model has passed the empirical test. The question of what it means to pass an empirical test in terms of determining what might be called the validity of a model will be discussed further below. For now, however, note that passing an empirical test in relation to one set of observed data does not guarantee that the model will pass the same empirical test when exposed to enlarged or alternative data sets such as data observed at different times or over different periods of time. Furthermore, in the case of the demand–supply model, there are usually no assumptions that impose properties on the price–quantity pairs occurring at intersection points. For that reason, the demand–supply model, although capable of explaining price–quantity data in an isolated market, is unable to be empirically tested in the sense described here.

More generally, models built for the purpose of explaining the possible structure of a phenomenon and how it might function frequently do not generate properties of their outcomes and do not admit of direct empirical tests of their explanatory competence. The same is typically true of single-output models (whose purpose is often structural explanation) as they are usually formulated. For example, in addition to the demand–supply model of price determination in an isolated market, the two single-output models of the microeconomy discussed earlier, viz., the general equilibrium and classical models, both of which could also be viewed as models with the sole purpose of describing a structure, have this nontestable characteristic.[7] Apart from other possible connections, these models are linked to reality in that observed prices and quantities are interpreted as equilibrium prices and quantities in the relevant model. Even without empirical testing, the usefulness of these models in explanation is clear: Their explanatory competence exists at a high level of intuitive satisfaction even in the absence of empirical tests, and the models

---

[7] Of course, the component relations of the supply–demand model and certain component relations of the general equilibrium model are testable in isolation. And there are, moreover, special formulations of the general equilibrium model extended by letting endowments vary that can also be tested for explanatory competence. With respect to the latter, see Brown and Matzkin [4]. Recall that, as pointed out in Chapter 2, in general the component parts of single-output models may be testable and the models themselves may sometimes be extended to provide testable implications.

themselves are robust by reason of their apparent continued empirical relevance. Indeed, the model explaining observed prices and quantities in an isolated market has passed into the public domain and stands as the basis for often-seen-and-heard assertions of the form, "Reductions in supply have led to price increases." And the general equilibrium model is typically regarded as a way of thinking about the microeconomy as a whole, and as a part of the theoretical basis for capitalism – the economic system that is thought to largely structure economic behavior in the Western world today.

(v) In light of any empirical tests that have been undertaken, *make a judgment of the explanatory significance or competence of the model including its cogency (that is, the manner in which its parts fit together to provide explanatory significance) and its relevance to the real phenomenon under investigation, and its possible usefulness for purposes of explanation and prediction.*

Of course, judgments of cogency and relevance are highly personal in nature and reflect the values and interests of the person undertaking the investigation. Nevertheless, as pointed out in Chapter 1, these judgments are still formed in relation to, and constrained by, the standards of what is considered to be economic science. That science in contrast to physical science, recall, deals with thinking and motivated beings, and is severely limited by the unavailability of laboratory controls and the difficulties that may arise in the measurement of significant variables. Returning to Caldwell's conclusion cited at the end of that chapter (p. 27) that even in this framework (or perhaps because of it?) no universally compelling way to evaluate models exists, it follows that there is still considerable leeway for subjectivity on the part of the investigator to play an important role in arriving at the judgments required in stage (v). With these ideas in mind, a model may be judged cogent if it provides, in the view of the investigator, a satisfactory explanation of the phenomenon it was constructed to explain. Cogency may also require that the elements of the model be internally consistent in the sense that there are no contradictions among them. The judgment of relevance necessitates a determination by the investigator as to the extent to which the various constituent parts of the model do, in fact, directly or indirectly reflect what are thought to be observable real-world relationships and economic structures. In particular, it has to take into account what has been referred to as the bridges to reality that may or may not be present in the model. A bridge, recall, establishes a direct connection between an element of a model and the observable real world. Examples will be provided shortly. The notion of bridge encompasses not only those connections to reality that relate to the primary- and secondary-assumption content present in the model, including whatever implicit assumption counterparts present at the level of stage (ii) that are implied by the secondary assumptions added at stage (iii). It also includes those connections that are corroborated upon subjecting, when possible, parts of the model to empirical estimations and tests.

It should be emphasized that the existence of a bridge can be confirmed either as a result of an empirical estimation or test, or when an element of the model appears in the judgment of the investigator as a sensible representation of a real-world object. Bridges can be present at each of stages (i)–(iv) of the model building process. They can exist as links between established cultural tenets of societies and assumptions of motivation directing behavior in economic models (e.g., the cultural value of self interest arises in the assumption that individuals buy what they most prefer or maximize utility) as well as between model conclusions and observed facts (e.g., the macroeconomic conclusion that under certain conditions income tax cuts will stimulate the growth of GDP can be associated with the increase in GDP observed after the US income tax cuts of 1964). Relevance would likely require, in at least one of the first four stages mentioned, at least one link to reality that is sufficiently adequate for an investigator to accept the model as a possible explanation of the phenomenon in question. The more links, and the more stages at which such links are present, the greater the confidence the investigator might have in the model's explanatory competence. (Stages (iv) and (v) as described here correspond to Weisberg's third stage.)

In all of this, the knowledge, skill, and imaginative insight of the investigator is critical. Such elements, to the extent that they are present, could enhance the meaningfulness and persuasiveness to the investigator of the explanation secured and might lead to acceptance of the model by others as an adequate statement of what is going on.

Four aspects of the foregoing scheme of model building call for comment. First, what have been referred to as secondary assumptions (stage (iii)) often have to do with assumed forms of, or assumed properties of, the logical relations that inhere in the model's configuration. Those secondary assumptions, such as the secondary assumptions identified in the utility-maximization example to be discussed later or the Cobb–Douglas production function employed in various models of the firm, may, as suggested earlier, be present in order to facilitate the manipulation of the model in moving to its deductive conclusions and implications. This is a crucial aspect of model construction in that it develops and extends the model to the point at which, at least in principle, it is possibly linkable, in ways not available in earlier stages, to potential observations that are identifiable with, and thought to be representative of, the phenomenon being explained. These observations could be expressed in terms of either numbers or words. In the latter case, they would consist, as has been previously indicated, of verbal descriptions of realizations of various forms of such things as, for example, security or freedom. Thus operationality or passage from the second to the third stage does not necessarily imply transition from an unquantified to a quantified state.[8]

Second, and expanding on the last point, it should be emphasized that none of the five stages of explanatory model building as described here depend in any way on an ability to measure the variables on which attention is focused. As will be suggested in Chapters 5 and 6, and seen to a considerable extent by example in Chapter 7, vision in its entirety can be imagined, all primary and secondary assumptions can be stated, all parts of all structures can be formulated, and all manipulations of variables and relations and all empirical tests can be accomplished in an unquantified context. Model building as an intellectual enterprise can proceed in the complete absence of measurement.

Third, in relation to the possible testability of the multi-output model (explicitly noted only in stage (iv) above) and in addition to the possible testability of particular behavioral components and extensions of the single-output model, an important point of scientific procedure should be kept in mind. The pertinent part of the content of any stage of the model building process may be regarded as part of the model outcome and subjected to tests for empirical relevance. The particular statement or posited relation that is subject to test may be an assumption or, as previously suggested, one of several deductive implications that are considered to be potentially significant. That is, with respect to the latter, scientific explanation may legitimately proceed by submitting to empirical test not only or exclusively what may be considered as a final hypothesis designed to explain empirical states of affairs, but also what might be a logical deduction from such a hypothesis or from the earlier assumption content of the model.

A simple example will illustrate what might be envisaged in that connection. Consider the preceding case of the single-output model of a market for a particular commodity. In reference to the assumed demand curve component in that example, it could be anticipated that at lower market prices a larger quantity of the good will be demanded. That

---

[8] See Section 5.1.

would conceivably arise because one might imagine that each individual in the market may demand a larger quantity at the lower price, and/or because at the lower price new purchasers may enter the market. Now it might be thought useful to make a preliminary empirical test of such a possibility, that is, to empirically establish or falsify, at least tentatively, and in general terms, the assumption of a negative inclination of the posited demand curve. Additionally, the test might contribute to further assumptions or hypotheses regarding things like the elasticity of demand and the elasticity of buyer substitution between the commodity at issue and other commodities. To accomplish this test, observations might be made of the number of buyers in the market at successive points in time and their purchases at different commodity prices. And statistical procedures might be employed to control for various buyer characteristics such as demographic classes and income categories. Tests of this sort may be referred to as subsidiary tests because they direct attention to side issues rather than to the main thrust of argument. Nevertheless, conclusions may be drawn from these tests that point to higher degrees of confidence in the final empirical relevance of the model, its overall explanatory competence, and its possible usefulness for purposes of prediction.

Fourth, the limitations of empirical testing in models that admit to such testing also deserve comment in relation to what has been referred to earlier as model validity. On the one hand, a model that survives empirical tests may be thought of as provisionally confirmed as one possible explanation of the phenomenon under investigation. But that by itself does not signify that a different model, and hence an alternative explanation, might not also pass similar tests. Nor does it provide a final guarantee that the explanation generated by the model is correct and relevant to the matter at hand. Of course, and as will be seen in the utility maximization model illustration that follows, the absence of such a guarantee does not mean that the model is not useful. But in light of this particular limitation, cogency and relevance as judged by the investigator need not rely on full correctness. They could also be based, in addition to the results of tests, on further considerations involving judgments as to the meaningfulness and appropriateness of both primary and secondary assumptions and the theoretical results that ensue from them. To illustrate, a model concluding that sunspot activity causes economic activity, even if consistent with observed data, may be rejected on the grounds that the correlation between sunspot and economic activity is spurious. Generally, of course, correlation does not imply causality. In the sunspot case, the judgment may be made that the correlation does not provide an accurate causal explanation of what is actually going on. On the other hand, conditions may exist in which a model that is apparently refuted by a test could nevertheless be adjusted in certain ways to enable it to be viewed as a cogent and relevant explanation. Such a situation may arise because of acknowledged deficiencies in the test or inadequacies in the manner in which the stage (ii) specification of the model was operationalized. In the latter instance, the model's explanatory competence could be improved by adjustment of the third-stage specifications, i.e., the secondary assumptions, that led to its operationality.

An example with a more technical frame of reference than those presented earlier will serve to illustrate the method of proceeding that is here in view. Consider the standard multi-output utility-maximization model of consumer purchasing behavior in which elements such as uncertainty, savings, and altruism are ignored. Imagine that this model is to be constructed from scratch. The modeling process begins (stage (i)) by envisaging the consumer as an individual who buys different commodities at various prices, whose choices are constrained by the prices of goods and the amount of money he has to spend, and whose behavior is a reflection of his own self-interest. At the level of stage (ii) an initial model is developed that contains two primary assumptions: The consumer has a preference relation among baskets of commodities that is consistent, i.e., reflexive and transitive,[9] and, in each purchasing situation, he buys that basket that is the most preferred among the options available to him. Since baskets of commodities are already quantified, there is no measurement issue. In stage (iii) the model is often operationalized by first introducing secondary assumptions to permit the expression of preferences in terms of a utility function that is to be maximized, and also to guarantee the existence of unique utility-maximizing baskets. One collection of such assumptions is that the preference relation is also total[10] and representable by a continuous (utility) function defined over a Euclidean commodity space, and that the utility function is increasing, and strictly quasi-concave. Then the model is manipulated to derive, from the constrained maximization of utility, demand functions and their empirically testable properties. Observe that the assumptions of totality and continuous representability are already expressed at the same level (i.e., the level of preferences) as the primary assumptions, while those of increasingness and strict quasi-concavity can easily be reduced to, or expressed at that level. To follow through on stage

---

[9] A relation such as $\geq$ defined on D is *reflexive* when $x \geq x$ for all x in D. It is *transitive* if $x' \geq x''$ and $x'' \geq x'''$ imply $x' \geq x'''$, for all x', x'', and x''' in D.

[10] The relation $\geq$ on D is *total* provided that, for all x' and x'' in D, either $x' \geq x''$ or $x'' \geq x'$.

(iv), appropriate empirical tests are undertaken and an analysis is made of the extent to which the model fits the available data.

In the last stage (stage (v)), a judgment has to be made as to the cogency and relevance of the model as it may be applied in an attempt to explain empirical outcomes at different moments or periods of time. It turns out that in the present example a number of qualifying considerations imply that the results of empirical tests or analyses may not help with such a judgment. On the one hand, to empirically test or analyze the model, repeated observations of a consumer's purchases at varying prices and incomes have to be made. But since, as pointed out in Chapter 1, such observations are necessarily taken across a specific period of time, any instance emerging in the observed data that might be thought to contradict or refute the model through inconsistencies with the derived properties of demand functions can always be explained away in terms of changing preferences over time from one observation to another.[11] Of course, it must be borne in mind that problems may arise regarding the quality of the empirical data-set against which the model is being tested or estimated. As a case in point, the very definition of a particular commodity represented in the data, the commodity's availability, and its desirability in relation to competing or complementary goods may vary as time passes due to technological innovation. Such modifications provide additional reasons why observed data may contradict the properties of demand functions derived from constrained utility maximization.

On the other hand, confirming instances, as previously noted, do not necessarily guarantee that the model is an accurate explanation of what is really going on. And alternative models may also achieve believable degrees of confirmation. Confirming instances, moreover, may appear reliably to establish adequate explanation without disclosing the real underlying causation of the observed outcomes. Thus they do not necessarily provide a true and accurate explanation of actual behavior. But the vision of stage (i) and the primary assumptions based on it of stage (ii) may, on several grounds, still seem appropriate in many cases: first, because of the bridge to reality linking the buying circumstances in the model (i.e., the limits imposed by prices and money available) to circumstances similar to what a real consumer actually faces when making purchases; second, because of the bridge between preferences in the model and the seemingly plausible

---

[11] Caldwell [5, pp. 156–157]. Of course, there may be reasons why, in particular situations, inconsistencies revealed by empirical tests might be taken as evidence that the theory should be rejected.

fact that real individuals actually have preferences among buying options; and third, because of the bridge, present at least for Western economies, generally linking the effort in the model to buy the most preferred option with self-interest in the real Western world. (Self-interest is a fundamental tenet of the cultural milieu in which actual purchasing behavior takes place in the West and hence, as a rule, may be understood as a driving force behind behavior in Western economies.[12]) Account should also be taken of the fact that the secondary assumptions and their implicit assumption counterparts at the level of stage (ii) are logically necessary to ensure that preference or utility maximization can take place. As such, the secondary assumptions do not seem to interfere significantly with the main thrust of the explanation produced by the model. Therefore, in the context of this example (with uncertainty, saving, and the possibility of such elements as altruism ignored), the utility maximization model may be judged as both a cogent and relevant explanation of numerous instances of consumer purchasing behavior. According to the criteria set out in Chapter 2, it is also good explanation.

Leaving the specific example behind, as a general proposition, it does not matter that, in many instances, there may not actually be enough information available to real decision makers to calculate maximum values from the equations of a model. Indeed, one could make such an assertion – Simon [22, pp. 79–84] has already done so – with respect to the determination of constrained utility maximizing baskets in the consumer model described above. But as previously indicated, economic models are abstractions and, apart from what have been recognized as empirical bridges, are not intended to link all of their structural elements in a one-to-one manner with real-world data or conditions. All that matters is that at one stage at least there is an accordance between the model and the reality under investigation that imparts a recognizable degree of explanatory competence to the former. Given this link, it is perfectly reasonable to explore, in an abstract context, the general structures of that model, possible directions of causality that relate to it, and the implications of the model itself. Moreover, it may be possible to extend and further develop the model at the level of stage (iii) so as to obtain additional specific results that might potentially be identifiable with observable data. And in spite of any lack of information available to real decision makers (the results

---

[12] Katzner [14]. This is not to say that motivations other than self-interest might not drive behavior in particular circumstances.

of whose actions are being investigated), the usefulness of the model in providing an explanation of the real phenomenon at issue is preserved.[13]

To show how a specific investigation might fit into the five-stage methodological structure proposed here, consider the model of herd behavior developed by Banerjee [2]. The purpose of Banerjee's model is to provide an explanation of why it might be rational for an individual making a decision to be influenced by the decisions that others have made. The discussion of his stage (i) vision suggests that the reason why such a procedure could be rational is that the decisions of others may mirror information that the decision maker in question does not have. Reflecting back on the stage (i) vision, the model, upon analysis, shows that a consequence of everyone relying on the information contained in the observed decision of others in making their own decisions is herd behavior – everyone does what everyone else does even though their own information might suggest doing something different.

In stage (ii), Banerjee sets out a game-theoretic model in which individuals make decisions sequentially in a fixed order. Each person knows the choices of those who made decisions before him, but not the information upon which those decision were based. In stage (iii) the model is analyzed to determine the unique decision rule adopted by all participants. Welfare properties are also considered, and the model is extended to consider such things as alternative payoff structures and requiring the order in which decisions are made to be endogenous. There is no attempt at stage (iv) empirical testing and no stage (v) overall judgment of the model is provided although some of the model's weaknesses are described.

3.2 The Difficulty with Ignoring Stages (i), (ii), and (v)

While the general methodological statement of the stages of explanatory model building set out earlier may seem rather straightforward and even obvious, many investigations in economics do not appear to follow the pattern it sets out. In particular, stages (i), (ii), and (v) are often ignored or considered only in a superficial manner. Economists may recognize and acknowledge one or more of these stages, and perhaps even give lip service to them. But without taking full cognizance of the entire scheme of stages and their implications, they may fail to address the questions of how

---

[13] None of this is intended to denigrate in any way Simon's substitute of satisficing for maximizing behavior (as will be described in the next chapter). Simon's approach yields a different model that has different strengths and weaknesses, and that may or may not be judged to provide a better explanation at the level of stage (v).

and to what extent their constructions relate to and explain real economic phenomena. Clearly, the answers to these latter questions relate to the stage (v) judgment of explanatory competence of the built model. Without a statement of that judgment (taking it to be positive – for otherwise the model would be discarded) the model would be left defenseless, rendering the explanation it provides more vulnerable to its critics.

Whatever the difficulties in dealing with stages (i) and (ii) of the methodology set out above, those difficulties can be compounded by the fact that in economics it often happens that many, if not all of the variables of the model at those stages are not capable of appropriate quantification. Some are not even ordinally quantifiable. Since techniques for handling the unquantified in a formal way, though available,[14] are not well known, a lack of ability to quantify may make coming to terms with stage (ii) and possibly even stage (i) seem intractable. This may be one reason why scholars have often tended to neglect those stages and proceeded directly with the operational models of stage (iii).

But regardless of the reason, when stages (i), (ii), and (v) are ignored, attention necessarily focuses only on stage (iii) and possibly on stage (iv). That is, a model in operational form is assumed, manipulated and, perhaps, tested. (For instance, the inquiry might begin by assuming the presence of a functional relation with certain properties or, more particularly, of a functional relation of a specific form.) And little attention is paid to many of the assumptions at the primary level or stage (ii), both those that are implied from the introduction of secondary assumptions and those that, being primary, are not, and both of which are now mostly implicit in the operational statement of the model. But without explicit expression of all stage (ii) level assumptions, it is not possible to know the full extent of the assumption content of the model. Moreover, since the primary-level assumptions are located at stage (ii) and are in that sense "nearer" to reality than the secondary assumptions and the operational model of stage (iii), and since the primary-level assumptions are therefore more closely related to the initial contemplations of stage (i), they are critical in judging the cogency and relevance of the model. It follows that without knowing all primary-level assumptions of the model, the ability to carry out the judgment of stage (v) can be significantly impaired.

Because, as indicated at the beginning of Chapter 2, models generally can be built for different purposes, none of this is intended to imply that

---

[14] Chapter 5 below describes them in a highly simplified context. For more general discussion, see Katzner [13, 15].

successful model building must, of necessity, always take stage (i) and (ii) considerations into account.[15] But it does suggest the dangers of not doing so.

To illustrate the problem and see what is at stake, suppose, in the standard utility-maximization model described previously, the further secondary assumption of an additive utility function

$$u(x) = f^1(x_1) + \cdots + f^I(x_I),$$

(where u and the f^i are functions, the x_i represent scalar quantities of good i with $i = 1, \ldots, I$, and x is the vector $(x_1, \ldots, x_I)$) with positive first-order and negative second-order derivatives of each function f^i everywhere, is included as part of the operationalizing process of stage (iii). It is well known that with such a utility function, as the individual's income rises his demand for each good increases, that is, there are no inferior goods.[16] Although, as indicated earlier, characteristics such as the absence of inferior goods cannot be conclusively refuted (or affirmed) by observing demand behavior, this still seems rather strange. But it is demonstrated in Section 8.2 that the implicit assumption counterpart at the level of stage (ii) of the secondary assumption of additivity is that the individual's preference ordering is such that preferences among quantities of each commodity alone are independent of the quantities of the other commodities that could be held by that individual.[17] And as part of the initial stage (i) and stage (ii) formulation, this might not seem to be appropriate in many cases. By looking at the stage (ii) implication of this secondary assumption, then, possible grounds are obtained for arriving at the judgment in stage (v) that the model is inadequate.

This is not to say that additive utility functions are never to be employed under any circumstances.[18] For example, the assumption of additivity could be invoked to demonstrate that even under such a severe restriction,

---

[15] As an example of constructing a model first and looking for something for it to explain (recall n. 2 on p. 30), "...Volterra began his investigation of Adriatic fish by not looking directly at those fish or even at the statistics gathered from the fish markets, but by constructing a model [in which] he imagined a population of predators and prey, each with only two properties. [He then discovered] some very general properties of predator-prey models, ones that apply far more widely than the particular case he had in mind" (Weisberg [26, pp. 222–223]).

[16] For example, Katzner [12, p. 91].

[17] The argument is similar to that establishing the relationship between "additive preferences" and the existence of an additive utility function representing them.

[18] Nor is it to accuse the classical economists such as Jevons, Walras, and Marshall of bad modeling because they assumed additive utility functions. Their models, after all, were based on the knowledge complex of the time. It was the subsequent advancement of

certain confounding issues (such as, say, the presence of asymmetric information) could arise, thus suggesting that without that restriction, matters could be even more complex and difficult to deal with (e.g., Sugden [24, p. 9]). But when confining interest to the explanation of an individual's demand behavior, such an assumption might not, in the judgment of the investigator, seem to be suitably representative of his preferences.

The issue raised by this example, namely that ignoring the implications of secondary assumptions at the primary level can exclude vital information necessary to arrive at a judgment of the cogency and relevance of a model, may arise in many different ways in model building directed toward explanation. As a second illustration, turn attention to the standard long-run model of the perfectly competitive firm. The stage (i) vision consists of such elements as technology playing a role in the production of outputs, and the firm reacting to market dictates in its own self-interest. In stage (ii), a production function is introduced, input and output market prices are taken to be fixed and, given these parameters, and the firm is assumed to hire inputs and produce outputs so as to maximize profit (total revenue minus total cost). At the operational level of stage (iii), at least two significant secondary assumptions arise. First, a distinction is drawn between durable physical capital and nondurable inputs so that normal profit (the minimum return on the investment in durables necessary to keep the owners of the firm from removing their investment in it) can be characterized as the economic reward of the physical capital inputs. Second, sufficient properties on the production function are imposed to enable the maximization to take place. Implicit in the distinction between physical capital and nondurable inputs is the further secondary assumption that the two kinds of inputs can be treated identically in determining the firm's profit-maximizing position in the sense of equating the first-order partial derivatives of the profit function to zero.[19] It follows that the firm's optimal input mix and optimal output level depend only on input and output prices and the firm's production function. It is also concluded that even though the free entry of perfect competition drives profit to its designated normal level and above-normal profit to zero, the firm is content to continue to hire inputs and produce outputs.

However, the secondary assumption of treating physical capital inputs in the same way as nondurables implies, at the level of stage (ii), that

knowledge that made it possible at a later date to see that additive utility comes with some potentially unfortunate baggage.

[19] Other problems associated with this approach to physical capital are not considered here.

significant consequences of the manner in which physical capital has been incorporated in the model are not usually consistent with observable fact. In particular, the practice requires that the firm's revenue at any instant in the model be sufficient to cover the full cost of the physical capital inputs – a characteristic that is often incompatible with reality. For in real-world situations, the cost of physical capital will generally be amortized over its useful life and, were this accounted for in the model, the optimal input mix and optimal output level would be influenced, in addition to prices and the production function, by the cost, at the margin, of carrying the physical capital inputs over those inputs' lives.[20] Once again, by looking at the implications of the secondary assumptions significant properties of the model are revealed that may lead to the judgment that the original model should be rejected or at least modified.

Robinson's criticism [20] of the aggregate capital variable in the neoclassical production function may be interpreted in similar terms. That is, neoclassical analyses of economic distribution and growth at the time might be said to have started at the operational level (stage (iii)) by postulating such a production function without considering the meaning of the capital variable at the lower stage (i) and (ii) levels.[21]

[T]he production function has been a powerful instrument in miseducation. The student of economic theory is taught to write O = f (L,C) where L is a quantity of labour, C a quantity of capital and O a rate of output of commodities. He is instructed to assume all workers alike, and to measure L in man-hours of labour; he is told something about the index-number problem involved in choosing a unit of output; and then he is hurried on to the next question, in the hope that he will forget to ask in what units C is measured. Before ever he does ask, he has become a professor, and so sloppy habits of thought are handed on from one generation to the next.

[20, p. 81]

Robinson's paper draws out the unfortunate consequences of ignoring this stage (i) and stage (ii) issue.

To provide an example in the more recent literature, consider the market for used automobiles as analyzed by Akerlof [1, pp. 489–492]. Akerlof presents his model as "..., a finger exercise to illustrate and deepen ... [certain] thoughts ... rather than for importance or realism." From that perspective, Akerlof begins with a stage (i) description of his vision of the market. He notes the price difference between new and used automobiles

---

[20] Katzner [16, pp. 551–553].
[21] For example, Stigler [23, especially Ch. 12]. Harcourt [9, p. 11] considers this volume to be a case-book example of neoclassical economics during the period.

and the presence of what he later refers to as asymmetric information, viz., that the seller of the used car typically knows more about it than the buyer. Akerlof's analysis then specifies a stage (ii) demand–supply model for the used car market in which the "average quality" of used automobiles traded and the market price are determined. His stage (iii) extension of the model adds two types of utility functions: cars with uniformly distributed quality and the derivation of the market demand and supply functions from the maximization of utility.

If, now, notwithstanding Akerlof's important contribution on the level on which his analysis was presented, it was desired to move his model further toward realism, a number of obstacles arise. To begin with, creating a model with market demand and supply functions requires additional abstraction from that already present in the vision of stage (i). And the presence of an unmeasured quality variable requires employment of different abstract conditions (which Akerlof ignores) to ensure the existence of solutions than are normally required.[22] However, this movement away from the real phenomenon being explained by these stage (ii) constructions is normal in many analyses and cannot usually be overcome. But in stage (iii), Akerlof assumes an additive utility function and, implicitly, that average quality can be measured on a ratio scale. The potential difficulty with the first of these stage (iii) assumptions has already been discussed; that with the second arises from the considerable arbitrariness introduced by taking a variable to be ratio measured when, at best, it is only ordinally measured.[23] Both assumptions tend to push the model considerably farther from reality than the distance already present in stages (i) and (ii) and might, even if some empirical corroboration were available, lead to a stage (v) rejection of the model as an explanation of the used automobile market.

3.3 Models and Their Relation to the Real World

Consider, now, in the context of the stages of model building described here, how models generally relate to and explain the real world. These considerations, of course, will delineate part of the background within which the judgments of stage (v) are reached.

Clearly, in moving across stages (i)–(iii), more and more abstraction takes place. Models become increasingly idealized and "false" as accurate representations of reality in the sense that they are less and less closely

---

[22] For example, pp. 109–114. See also Katzner [13, pp. 90–94].
[23] See Chapter 9.

related to what is actually present in the real world.[24,25] The most significant and extensive deviations from reality are likely to occur in the transition from stage (ii) to stage (iii) with the introduction of secondary assumptions and possible measures of particular variables.[26] According to Wimsatt [27, pp. 28–29], this distancing from actual existence due to the process of abstraction can be attributed to a variety of sources, including the constructing of the model as an approximation that cannot be fully applicable to any situation, and ignoring certain relevant variables so that the model lacks coverage of significant aspects of the real phenomenon under investigation. In spite of their falsity, however, false models, as is implicit in earlier discussion, are often judged by investigators to be cogent and relevant, and therefore accepted as explanations of that which is to be explained. Indeed, Wimsatt [27, pp. 30–32] suggests that the construction of false models can help in the search for alternative models (still false) that provide better explanations of the reality under consideration. In terms of the present proposal, Wimsatt's suggestion might mean contemplation of the extent to which the construction of a false model conforms to the five-stage procedure described here and the implications that that holds for possible testing of the model and its coherence. In light of these considerations, changes might be made that turn the false model into one that provides a more satisfying explanation.

There are also a number of other ways to approach models and model falsity that can make a false model acceptable as an explanation of an observed phenomenon. These alternatives are entirely independent of the five-stage procedure, although many are still consistent with it. Four of the later approaches are now considered as illustrations.

Hausman [10, p. 41] is content as long as the false model provides knowledge of the real world despite its distant-from-reality perspective. That very problem, of course, has been addressed in the successive stage

---

[24] This gives rise to what has been called the "explanation paradox" in that economic models at the same time are both explanatory and false. See Hands [8].

[25] The meaning of the phrase "false model," which is employed only in the present chapter, should not be confused with the idea of the "falsification of a model." The former refers to a model that, as will be seen, is acceptable even though it does not fully represent the reality it purports to explain; the latter to the rejection of a model because it is not consistent with the data against which it has been tested.

[26] Adding assumptions to those of stage (ii) to arrive at stage (iii) may make it easier to fit the model to a given set of quantified or unquantified data. But, as pointed out earlier, such data already involve substantial abstraction from the real phenomenon at issue. Hence any movement of this kind from stage (ii) to stage (iii) is properly regarded as increasing the distance of the model from reality to at least that already present in the data.

model building procedure previously explored in which the possibility of bridges from model assumptions to the empirical world speaks to questions regarding the degree of closeness to reality of the model's conclusions.

To consider the ability of a model to provide knowledge in a particular case, focus on the static geometric supply–demand model set out in Chapter 2 explaining how the observed price of a single commodity is determined and how it rises and falls during a period when rapid inflation is not present. (Here, the identification of assumptions with the various stages of model building is left to the reader.) The commodity at issue is assumed to be homogeneous and bought and sold in a single isolated market. This, as previously noted in a different context, is already an abstraction which, necessarily, is not present in reality. Thus, gasoline, even within a single country, is not homogeneous and is sold in many places and under varying circumstances. The same is true of the "observed price" which, at the empirical level, is often taken to be an average of observed prices over a collection of locations and similar products. Regardless, demand and supply curves are postulated that relate single quantity values to single price values and that are assumed to be stable for the period or moment of time in question. Of course, such curves are further abstractions that do not exist in actuality. Moreover, all other forces that may be operating in the market are ignored. When an observed price-quantity point is to be explained, both demand and supply curves are assumed to pass through that same observed point. The observed price is then viewed as the equilibrium output of the interaction of these geometric representations of demand and supply. Furthermore, an observed rise in price, say, is said to be a consequence of either an increase in demand or a reduction in supply.

In spite of its abstract nature and its distance from actuality, most economists would probably agree that this false model still yields knowledge of real economic activity. And, as pointed out earlier, the explanation it provides is so useful and resonates so strongly as an understanding of what is going on that it has passed from the realm of academic economics into the public domain. Of course, when the media write or speak of demand and supply, they do not explicitly refer to curves. But the model is certainly lurking in the background and imparts substance and meaning to their assertions.

False models are admissible as explanation to Mäki [18, p. 78] because, to him, they are idealizations that exclude, in the judgment of the investigator, the presumably less significant real phenomena from involvement and influence in their analytical structures, thereby permitting a sharper focus on the key factors or what is thought to be most important. That is, it is the isolation arising in stage (i) of model building that gives models their significance. Even with false assumptions, models still represent real phenomena by resembling them "...in relevant respects and sufficient degrees.... Thanks to this resemblance, the examination of ...[the model] will convey information about ...[the reality under investigation]" (Mäki [17, p. 11]).

Sugden [24] accepts false models as explanation since, from his perspective, they create credible worlds, that is, "... descriptions of how the world could be" [24, p. 18]. Gaps between the credible worlds and reality are filled by what Sugden refers to as inductive inference. The more credible the model, the more confidence in the inferences. What counts in determining credibility is a "...harmonious relationship between the assumptions of the model, and between the model and what we know about the causal structure of the [real] world."[27]

Evidently, for Hausman, Mäki, and Sugden, the degree of acceptability of a model notwithstanding its falsity would depend on how well, from their individual vantage points, the model relates to and explains reality. That determination, again, is precisely what is presented as the objective of the five-stage model building methodology elucidated above. To a considerable extent the ability to relate and explain rests on the nature of the stage (iii) secondary assumptions and what they imply at the nearer-to-reality stage (ii) level. And thus model building that neglects stages (i) and (ii), and begins at stage (iii) leaves important questions concerning its viability and acceptability somewhat in doubt.

According to Morgan [19, p. 178], false models are acceptable as explanation because, for her, they aid in understanding the real world by telling stories about that world. "Modeling involves a style of scientific thinking in which the argument is structured by the model, but in which the application is achieved via a narrative prompted by an external fact, an imagined event or question to be answered. Economists use their economic models to explain or understand the facts of the world by telling stories about how those facts might have arisen." To illustrate in the demand–supply model described earlier, the structure of the argument or model is the intersecting demand and supply curves, and the stories consist of such narratives as how an observed outcome is a consequence of the interaction of the forces of demand and supply, or how an increase in price has come about through an enlargement in demand or a decline

---

[27] This is Mäki's [17, p. 12] interpretation of Sugden's position.

in supply. The stories form a bridge as described earlier that spans the gaps between model structures and the realities the models purport to explain. Both the structures and stories emerge from the vision described in stage (i) of model building set out earlier.

It is, of course, always possible to develop a story to enhance a model's argument after the model has been built. This was certainly the case with the auctioneer story associated with Walras' general equilibrium model of price determination, which was created long after Walras set out his model.[28] But, from what seems to have emerged from stage (i) considerations, Walras [25, p. 84] had his own story of price determination based on brokers or criers who negotiate market transactions. In any case, the dangers of adding a story after a model is built in which stage (i) considerations are not taken into account are similar to those of starting model construction at stage (iii): Irrelevancies can be introduced that tend to push the model farther from the realities of the phenomenon the model purports to explain and may impair the ability to reach a positive judgment of the model in stage (v). Although the auctioneer story that currently accompanies the general equilibrium model allows easy visualization of the mathematical workings of that model, it still adds further unrealism to it.

3.4 Recapitulation and Further Commentary

Previous discussion has focused on the relations between the various elements or content of models as they occur at different stages of their construction. In addition to the observations made in that connection, a number of further comments will serve to clarify and summarize earlier results. It is convenient to begin by returning to the method of explanatory model building in economics described in Section 3.1. As suggested in that section, models are often built to explain observable phenomena. Apart from such items as prices and quantities, there are circumstances in which the phenomena being observed consist of unquantified elements with respect to which the attribution of numerical measures is not evident. Thus, the necessity is frequently imposed on an investigator to model real-world phenomena in such a way as to somehow achieve explanation in the face of measurement difficulties.

What has been referred to earlier as the stage (i) level of model construction is the vision leading to an initial collection of elements

---

[28] Fisher [6, p. 26] suggests that the auctioneer story was invented by Schumpeter in his lectures to students and introduced into the economics literature by Samuelson.

abstracted from real situations to focus attention on what is deemed to be important and significant. It is among these elements that, in passing to stage (ii), inaugural variables are defined and relations among them first postulated. Properties of the relations may also be introduced as additions to these primary assumptions. At the operational level of stage (iii), numerical measures may (or may not) be brought in to quantify what is not quantified, and analytical techniques that require numbers like the calculus (or those that do not) can be applied to manipulate the relations. But, in the sense described earlier, the taking of each of these subsequent actions removes the model or analysis one step farther from the reality it purports to explain. Clearly, the stage (i) and stage (ii) levels are those parts of the analysis that usually come closest to the actual real-world phenomena under scrutiny. For this reason, then, the content of the primary assumptions introduced at stage (ii) would typically have to be a part of what is kept in mind in order to make a conclusive judgment of the relevance of an analysis to the real-world question being addressed.

It should also be recalled that what constitutes empirical corroboration of a model or its testing against reality often occurs at a higher level of abstraction from reality than that of stages (i) and (ii). That is because secondary assumptions of convenience are frequently introduced to manipulate the model so as to obtain empirically testable propositions. In addition, numerical measures of economic variables, when present, are often proxies that, at best, only approximate what is supposed to be measured. And, notwithstanding the fact that some proxies reflect what is intended to be measured more effectively than others, the exact relationship between what the proxies are supposed to measure and what they actually measure is not known. Even when measures are not available or when "exact" (non-proxy) measures are, the non-numerical or numerical data against which the model is tested are still, as described earlier, some distance from reality. It follows that what passes for a test is actually not a test at all, but rather, only a way of obtaining an empirical conjecture of what might be. The relevance of the model still depends on a stage (v) judgment by the investigator based on the content of the model at the levels of stage (i) and stage (ii).

Unfortunately, as suggested earlier, many practitioners of explanatory economic model building do not pay much attention to these first two stages in building their models. Analyses frequently start by specifying operational or partly operational models with only quantified variables. Functional relations among them with specific properties are postulated and analytical manipulation proceeds from there. Questions about the meaningfulness of the measures employed and the relation of the structure to the levels of stages (i) and (ii), and hence to the real phenomenon under investigation, are not considered. But until those questions are given serious attention, no judgment can be made about the relevance of the analytical endeavor to the real phenomena at issue. In many cases, the arbitrariness of such an approach is clear and its usefulness may be questionable.[29]

Alternatively, greater relevance and less arbitrariness may be easier to achieve by actually starting model construction at the level of stage (i) itself. (The process was illustrated in reference to the standard constrained utility-maximization model in Section 3.1.) Assumptions might then be introduced at stage (ii) that, at the outset of the analysis, seem to fit the reality at issue, and argument at later stages would then proceed from those assumptions. This approach, however, might necessitate, in the later-stage arguments, the keeping of the analytical structure in unquantified form and the using of the rules of analysis without measurement (Chapter 5) to pursue the manipulation of functions and derive conclusions. In that case, manipulative tools requiring quantification, such as the calculus, could not be employed. But at least from this perspective, the relevance of the model or the analysis based on it would be determined up front and would not become an issue that might cause the entire endeavor to be discarded later on.

Discussion in this chapter has been substantially confined to questions relating directly to model building addressed to economic explanation, and, following from that, the respects in which the explanatory competence of a model can be adjudicated by the investigator in the light of relevant observable or empirical phenomena. It will be useful, in concluding the chapter to comment briefly on the broader question of the location of present argument in the larger complex of issues having to do with appropriate methodologies for economic analysis in general. The relation of the five-stage procedure of model building developed here to instrumentalism has already been noted at the outset.

Leaving aside mere description and focusing only on attempts at analytical economic explanation, two alternative methodological approaches to economic explanation can, in rather broad strokes, be referred to as "rationalist" on the one hand or "positivist" on the other. Recalling Chapter 1, rationalism comes to expression in the view that economic explanation properly proceeds by deductive implications from a given set

---

[29] Forms of arbitrariness, different from those suggested here, that arise from using inappropriate forms of measurement (e.g., cardinal measures where only ordinal measures are warranted) will be taken up in Chapter 9.

of initial assumptions about human behavior and the environment in which that behavior takes place. The positivist perspective, which in the present usage of the phrase includes both logical positivism and logical empiricism, elevates the necessity for the derivation of testable hypotheses to enhance the competence of economic explanation in explaining real phenomena. Without delving into these methodological approaches in further detail, it is clear that at the initial stages of model building, i.e., stages (i) and (ii), elements of rationalism are apparent. That is so to the extent that the primary assumptions of stage (ii) refer in general to basic postulates underlying human behavior, as well as to specific assumptions about real-world environmental or contextual structures. The deductive procedures that are generally associated with a rationalist approach are reflected in stage (iii) of model building, where the progress to the derivation of a testable hypothesis is carried out, preparatory to empirical testing at stage (iv). But it should be equally clear that the procedure of model building proposed here is in no sense simply or solely deductivist in its starkest rationalist sense. To the contrary, that procedure makes every necessary nod to positivist persuasions in significant twofold respects.

First, what should be seen as a highly significant aspect is the bridges to the real world, which are intended to fasten the analysis to genuine observable or empirical phenomena at appropriate points. As such, they often illuminate the way to the construction and content of appropriate empirical tests of stage (iv). Second, the insistence on testing the model at stage (iv) when possible is in itself designed to incorporate in the model construction process the possibility of a genuine correspondence to real-world occurrences in the sense that the relevance as well as the explanatory cogency of the model is thereby ascertainable.

The deliberate introduction to the model building argument of elements of both a priori rationalism and positivism rescues the argument from the aridity of severe rationalism that might not necessarily have any relevance to real-world situations and conditions at all, and from the mere descriptive handling of so-called facts of economic reality which, in itself, will generally be without explanatory content. Moreover, what is to be seen as a highly significant aspect of the model building process is the need for reactive relations between the secondary assumptions that appear at stage (iii) and the primary assumptions at stage (ii). The examples of that interrelation that have been given confirm the way in which the robustness of the model is preserved, as necessary adjustments in the contours of the model are made, and the ways in which, as a result, the explanatory competence of the model is, hopefully, maximized.

References

[1] Akerlof, G. A., "The Market for 'Lemons': Quality Uncertainty and the Market Mechanism," *Quarterly Journal of Economics* 84 (1970), pp. 488–500.

[2] Banerjee, A. V., "A Simple Model of Herd Behavior," *Quarterly Journal of Economics* 107 (1992), pp. 797–817.

[3] Boumans, M., *How Economists Model the World into Numbers* (London: Routledge, 2005).

[4] Brown, D. J. and R. L. Matzkin, "Testable Restrictions on the Equilibrium Manifold," *Econometrica* 64 (1996), pp. 1249–1262.

[5] Caldwell, B. J., *Beyond Positivism: Economic Methodology in the Twentieth Century* (London: Allen & Unwin, 1982).

[6] Fisher, F. M., "Adjustment Processes and Stability," in *The New Palgrave*, v. 1, J. Eatwell, M. Milgate, and P. Newman, eds. (London: Macmillan, 1987), pp. 26–28.

[7] Grüne-Yanoff, T., "Mäki's Three Notions of Isolation," in A. Lehtinen, J. Kuorikoski, and P. Ylikoski, eds., *Economic for Real: Uskali Mäki and the Place of Truth in Economics* (London: Routledge, 2012), pp. 96–111.

[8] Hands, D. W., ed., "Symposium on the Explanation Paradox," *Journal of Economic Methodology* 20 (2013), pp. 235–292.

[9] Harcourt, G. C., *Some Cambridge Controversies in the Theory of Capital* (Cambridge: Cambridge University Press, 1972).

[10] Hausman, D. M., "Laws, Causation, and Economic Methodology," in H. Kincaid and D. Ross, eds. *The Oxford Handbook of Philosophy of Economics* (New York: Oxford University Press, 2009), pp. 35–54.

[11] Hausman, D. M., *Preference, Value, Choice, and Welfare* (New York: Cambridge University Press, 2012).

[12] Katzner, D. W., *Static Demand Theory* (New York: Macmillan, 1970).

[13] Katzner, D. W., *Analysis without Measurement* (Cambridge: Cambridge University Press, 1983).

[14] Katzner, D. W., "Western Economics and the Economy of Japan," *Journal of Post Keynesian Economics* 21 (1999), pp. 503–521.

[15] Katzner, D. W., *Unmeasured Information and the Methodology of Social Scientific Inquiry* (Boston, MA: Kluwer, 2001).

[16] Katzner, D. W., *An Introduction to the Economic Theory of Market Behavior: Microeconomics from a Walrasian Perspective* (Cheltenham: Elgar, 2006).

[17] Mäki, U., "The dismal Queen of the social Sciences." In U. Mäki, ed, *Fact and Fiction in Economics: Models, Realism, and Social Construction* (Cambridge: Cambridge University Press, 2002), pp. 3–32.

[18] Mäki, U., "Realistic Realism about Unrealistic Models," in *The Oxford Handbook of Philosophy of Economics*, H. Kincaid and D. Ross, eds. (New York: Oxford University Press, 2009), pp. 68–98.

[19] Morgan, M. S., "Models, Stories, and the Economic World," in *Fact and Fiction in Economics: Models, Realism, and Social Construction* U. Mäki, ed. (Cambridge: Cambridge University Press, 2002), pp. 178–201.

[20] Robinson, J., "The Production Function and the Theory of Capital," *Review of Economic Studies* 21, no. 2 (1953), pp. 81–106.

[21] Schumpeter, J. A., *History of Economic Analysis* (New York: Oxford University Press, 1954).

[22] Simon, H. A., *Administrative Behavior*, 2nd ed. (New York: Macmillan, 1957).

[23] Stigler, G. J., *Production and Distribution Theories: The Formative Period* (New York: Agathon, 1968).

[24] Sugden, R., "Credible Worlds: The Status of Theoretical Models in Economics," *The Journal of Economic Methodology* 7 (2000), pp. 1–31.

[25] Walras, L., *Elements of Pure Economics*, W. Jaffé, trans (Homewood: Irwin, 1954).

[26] Weisberg, M., "Who Is a Modeler?" *British Journal for the Philosophy of Science* 58 (2007), pp. 207–233.

[27] Wimsatt, W. C., "False Models as Means to Truer Theories," in *Neutral Models in Biology*, M.H. Nitecki and A. Hoffman, eds. (New York: Oxford University Press, 1987), pp. 23–55.

4

Models and Mathematics

Model building in economics is often, though not always, mathematical,[1] and frequently a part of what is referred to as formalization. Indeed, the latter may be defined as the development and analysis of relations among variables that constitute part (or all) of an economic model. Justifications for the use of mathematics and formalization, and hence the mathematical type of model building, by economists (and others) go back quite some time. Cournot [2, pp. 2–5] and Jevons [10, pp. xxi–xxv, 3–5] believed that certain forms of reasoning in economics are mathematical in character. Walras [33, pp. 47,48] thought that to be scientific is, in part, to be mathematical. More recently, Suppes [30] provides seven reasons why formalization is desirable: It aids in the clarification of conceptual problems and the building of logical foundations, in the bringing out of explicit meanings of concepts, in standardizing terminology and methods, in permitting the development of a general vision without obstruction by inessential details, in allowing the attainment of a greater degree of objectivity, in setting out the precise conditions required for the analysis to be considered, and in obtaining the minimal assumptions necessary for statement of the analysis. Debreu [3, p. 275] cites linguistic convenience and the ability to obtain deeper understanding and analytical extensions that might not otherwise be possible. Mathematical reasoning, according to Gorman [5, p. 273], is important in economics because it helps in determining "... what implies what. It is from the solid basis of such knowledge that one can make imaginative leaps into the unknown." For Solow [29,

---

[1] For examples of non-mathematical models in economics see Marshall's [21] model of the consumer in Book III, his model of the firm in Book IV, and his model of the market in Book V. Of course, parts of these models are translated into mathematical language in several of Marshall's appendices. They were fully translated into that language by others later on.

p. 33], mathematical reasoning is preferred because, ceteris paribus, it is more exposed: "… what you see is what you get." And Weintraub [35, pp. 178,179] argues that, since we comprehend our economic world by creating mental structure, and since doing mathematics is creating mental structure in its "purest form," mathematics is naturally important and relevant in economic analysis.

It should be noted that criticisms of the use of mathematics in economics are more often criticisms of the uses to which mathematics is put rather than the use of mathematics itself.[2] Mathematical models that do not meet the requirements of the constructive five-stage method set out in the previous chapter, whose assumption content is regarded as inappropriate in relation to the problem at hand, or which are used to address inappropriate questions are certainly subject to criticism – but not necessarily for the use of mathematics as such.[3] In any case, subsequent discussion in this volume deals almost exclusively with models in mathematical form.

However, it should also be kept in mind that the discussion in Chapters 2 and 3 of the abstractness and approximateness of models in general applies with all its force to the case of mathematical models. Indeed, the separation of mathematics from reality was observed long ago by Einstein [3, p. 233]:

As far as the propositions of mathematics refer to reality, they are not certain; and as far as they are certain, they do not refer to reality.

---

[2] There are, of course, exceptions. The following two are well-known: First, Lawson [20] has argued that mathematical deductivist reasoning is the source of substantial unreality in much of economic analysis because it necessarily restricts that analysis to consideration of stable, isolated, and invariant closed systems. Actuality, on the other hand, is more realistically understood in terms of unstable, interlinked, and changing open systems. Lawson's position [19] also points to the use of mathematical functions as a particular source of unreality since they unrealistically imply a stable and isolatable relationship between the variable in the functions range and those in its domain. These arguments have been criticized by, respectively, Setterfield [25] and Katzner [17]. Second, as partly suggested earlier (n. 10 on p. 34), Mirowski [22] claims that the mathematics of neoclassical economics was developed by copying certain metaphors of nineteenth-century physics and that, since the neoclassical copiers failed to carry over a crucial part of those metaphors, neoclassical economics is wanting in terms of the structural standards to which its physical counterpart adheres. Without meeting those standards, neoclassical economics flounders, awash in arbitrariness. Mirowski [22, pp. 397–398] seems to believe that to avoid that arbitrariness, all economic science must, of necessity, be firmly grounded in fully intact metaphors taken from, or in analogies to, physical science. But, as pointed out in Chapter 1, social science is different from physical science in that, in part, it focuses on sentient human beings rather than on non-sentient physical objects. This implies that fundamentally different forms of (often irregular) behavior have to be explained in social science investigations, and hence that analogies to, and metaphors taken from, physical science are not necessarily relevant in that endeavor.

[3] See Katzner [11].

And this separateness is one expression of the abstractness and approximateness of models in mathematical form.

Although there were earlier forays into economics, as a general observation it may still be said that mathematics invaded and spread throughout economics during the same period in which positivism entered and gave way to falsification as the means for determining truth. And clearly, mathematics has been enlisted in the service of both positivism and falsification in economics. Apart from the advantages listed above, then, it is still reasonable to ask why model building in economics became mathematical. Why, that is, in moving from the vision of stage (i) to the initial and incomplete model of stage (ii), and then to the full operational model of stage (iii), were the formulations of model structures expressed in the language of mathematics? What kinds of forces or motivations might have propelled economists in the mathematical direction? Is there something in the subject-matter of economics that lends itself, or pushes the analyst, to take up mathematics in his model building? If so, why is it there? It is not only that economic models became mathematical; but economics itself or, more precisely, economic theory, became overwhelmingly mathematical. Although other social sciences have employed mathematics in parts of their analytical structures, none has incorporated mathematics as extensively or as completely as economics. Why has that been so?

Tentative answers to these questions might begin by considering three motivations that could have inspired economists to introduce mathematics into their work in a serious way. The first is to make use of existing human capital. Most of the early contributions to mathematical model building in economics were made by mathematically trained individuals like Cournot and Walras who had left their original fields of interest to enter the realm of economic discourse. They saw there an opportunity to apply their accumulated capital of mathematical knowledge in a new and different way. As more and more economists learned mathematics as a means to further their professional ends in whatever form mathematics may have been available at the time, they, too, developed vested interests in the use of mathematics. And given the time and energy put into mastering it, those investments would be hard to discard. Hence they, too, had incentives to look for new ways to apply their acquired knowledge of mathematics in the building of economic models.

A second motivation could have come from the desire for scientific respectability. As pointed out in Chapter 1, science as practiced by physical scientists has been widely venerated. On the one hand, such science has been highly regarded for its ability to explain and predict physical phenomena. And on the other, the fact that that science has been understood to have been the foundation upon which considerable improvements in the quality of human life have been built has only increased the respect accorded it. Indeed, physical science and those that practice it have frequently been held in the highest esteem. It comes as no surprise, then, that economists would want their efforts to be thought of as scientific.

Now it has also been argued in Chapter 1 that economics cannot be a science in the same sense as the physical sciences. But that does not mean that in the quest for scientific respectability economists might not have attempted to import into their subject what they could of the methods of the physical sciences. And one element of scientific expression that was clearly importable into economics was mathematics. The use of mathematics could then be thought to add an aura of the scientific to economics in its enforcement of precision in the articulation of concepts and results, in its enhancement of clarification in the logical structure of argument, and in its creation of sharp delineation of the boundaries of the analysis as a whole. The addition of such elements into economic discourse could not but help to increase its scientific respectability. From this vantage point, one is not taken aback by Walras' belief that, as previously indicated, mathematics is one of the prerequisites for science.

The third motivating force that may have led economists to resort to mathematics in their work is the quest for what might be called epistemological security or feelings of security with respect to claims of truth. On one level, the resort to mathematics may have been propelled by the supposition that the apparatus of mathematical reasoning would open the way to deeper and more meaningful insights into the structures of economic reality. But beyond that may have stood the desire, undoubtedly present in many circumstances, to attain a higher degree of conviction of truth in relation to economic assertions.[4] Thus, it may have been thought that the importation of mathematics into economics would permit the fabrication of a well-specified mathematical argument, the conclusions of which would constitute justified knowledge. But the notion that the introduction of mathematical argument would produce knowledge where none previously existed is specious. For in the words of Volterra, a well-known mathematician, "... mathematics only produces what you feed it ... ."[5]

---

[4] See Weintraub [36, p. 98].
[5] Weintraub's translation, Ibid., p. 32.

None of this is to deny the importance and usefulness of mathematics in the formation of the hypotheses and arguments of quantified and unquantified economic model building while working through stages (ii) and (iii) of model construction. Indeed, mathematics can be and has been of considerable aid in addressing real-world situations and in constructing models to understand and explain what has occurred or might occur. But while that is so, it should be remembered that epistemological clarity in the discipline of economics requires careful attention to the earlier described creation of bridges, connections, or accordances between mathematico-economic structures on the one hand, and real-world phenomena on the other. Such bridges are essential if the structures erected are to assist in the provision of knowledge of actuality. And often standing in the way of making these connections and the resulting claims of economic knowledge are the frequently cited realities described in Chapter 1: The behavior with which economics deals is in large measure generated by sentient, feeling, and reacting individuals whose motivations are complex and possibly unstable over time. The unidirectional movement of time in individuals' lives means that tomorrow is not, and in many respects cannot be, the same as today or yesterday. Thus, mathematical models based on assumptions of ergodicity, or the idea that the forces determining economic environments, endowments, preferences, and objectives will establish and repeat fixed patterns, can sit oddly with the actual facts of human experience. And it also follows that without ergodicity, the possibilities that the future may hold are often unamenable to anticipation and analysis in terms of the frequently employed probability calculus. Clearly, when the bridges break down for these or other reasons, the fault, as earlier noted, is not with the mathematics, but with the economics to which that mathematics relates.

Another way of approaching the question of why economics has leaned in the direction of mathematics is to focus on certain categories of mathematics that have received widespread application across economic modeling. Perhaps the most prominent of these is that which deals with optimization (constrained or otherwise). Other important categories, such as that attending to systems of simultaneous equations, do not seem to have been as significant in pushing economics toward mathematics. A still less significant category in the forces directing economists toward mathematics is the theory of sets. Nevertheless, all three categories have played a role in the development of economic models: The first arises in relation to things like utility, profit, and welfare maximization, and expenditure and cost minimization; the second emerges in both static and dynamic contexts with respect to, say, the static equations describing a general equilibrium and the dynamic equations associated with tâtonnement and nontâtonnement adjustment processes and economic growth. Set theory may be viewed as a foundation supporting much of mathematics in general, including that concerning optimization and simultaneous equations and, as will be seen in the next chapter, comes to the fore when dealing with the unquantified. The optimization and simultaneous equations types of mathematics overlap in that the determination of the critical values in an optimization problem often requires the solving of systems of simultaneous first-order maximization or minimization equations; and in that the demonstration of the existence of equilibrium in a general-equilibrium system, which frequently requires the solving of a system of simultaneous demand-equals-supply equations, can sometimes be accomplished by showing the existence of a constrained maximum value of an appropriate objective function.[6]

These three categories of mathematics often arise in stages (ii) and (iii) of model construction. As presented in the previous chapter, constrained utility maximization in the model of consumer demand is a stage (iii) translation of the stage (ii) primary assumption of purchasing the most preferred basket from the options available. In the model of the perfectly competitive firm, profit maximization is a primary stage (ii) assumption. The implied cost minimization determining the optimal input mix for each level of output is part of the stage (iii) working-through-to-completion of the full model. The mathematics of simultaneity appears in stage (iii) of the general equilibrium and classical models of the microeconomy as the solution to the model's equations is sought. And the theory of sets underlies the notions of ordering, function, and their properties providing not only the basis for the mathematics of optimization and simultaneity noted above, but also a language for expressing some primary (stage (ii)) and secondary (stage (iii)) assumptions. Moreover, as Chapter 5 indicates, set theory furnishes the means for defining (a) unquantified variables and functions that might arise in stages (ii) and (iii), and (b) the manipulation of such functions in stage (iii). Of the three types of mathematics, perhaps the more interesting history of its introduction into economics and, as previously indicated, the more relevant for purposes of this chapter, is that of optimization.

One of the most important phenomena that economists explain is the making of economic decisions. And of the many analytical tools that could be brought to bear on the decision problem, the most prominent has

---

[6] With respect to the latter, see Katzner [16, pp. 311–314].

been optimization. For over 200 years, economists have been concerned to find, in a substantial number of analytical contexts from various classical and neoclassical domains to the Marxian analysis of Roemer [24, Ch. 2], the optimum solution values of vectors of decision variables, thereby discovering the attainable extrema of certain appropriately defined objective functions. The logic behind that approach is derived from the idea that in economic reality the "best" alternative from any collection of available options will often be pursued, and hence, to explain that pursuit, the necessity arises of creating a structure in which the optimal decision under the circumstances presented can be extracted. In all of this, economists are conscious of the fact that most economic decisions are inevitably constrained decisions. The finiteness of resources imposes constraints at all analytical levels, from individual consumers and firms, to industries and markets, to the economy as a whole. Such constraints may be either implicit or explicit, thus affecting the nature of the mathematics required. Indeed, both unconstrained or, respectively, constrained optimization techniques in relation to first- and second-order maximization or minimization conditions have been employed in the past. Although the appearance of optimization in economics has not, as will be indicated subsequently, gone unchallenged, it nevertheless retains a central place in the discipline to this day.[7]

The exact moment at which economists became aware, either explicitly or implicitly, of the idea of optimization and its relevance to economics is not clear. But it is possible to pinpoint what may be the first appearance of optimization as part of a mathematical model in the economics literature. That initial taste, and it was, indeed, a very small sip, was a fleeting one. For in this instance, mathematics relating only peripherally to the optimization problem seems to have crept into economics surreptitiously through the back door and was thereafter quickly expelled. The story, according to Groenewegen [8, pp. vii–viii, xxvi–xxvii] and Robertson [23, pp. 526–527], is as follows: In 1771, an Italian economist by the name of Pietro Verri published a book whose title translated into English is *Reflections on Political Economy*. The book immediately met with some success, and its initial edition was reprinted several times with various and differing annotations into 1772. One of the reprinted versions (the sixth) contained some mathematical commentary attributed to Verri's friend and

---

[7] Much of the following is taken with modifications and additions from my "The Role of Optimization in Economics," *Optimization and Optimal Control*, P. M. Pardalos, I. Tseveendorj, and R. Enkhbat, eds. (Singapore: World Scientific, 2003), pp. 141–153. © World Scientific Publishing. Reproduced with permission.

mathematician, Paolo Frisi. But a subsequent, and what was considered to be the definitive, edition of the book that was published in 1781 deleted, among other things, Frisi's contribution.

Two parts of Frisi's commentary are of interest here. First, early in his book, Verri [31, p. 19] argued,[8] without using mathematical symbolism, that "... the price of things will be in direct proportion to the number of buyers and in inverse proportion to the number of sellers." Verri then went on to suggest that the ends of the state could best be served by keeping the price as low as possible [31, p. 21]. In his commentary, Frisi approximated Verri's proportionality statement by the equation $P = C/V$, where P represented price, C the number of buyers, and V the number of sellers. To examine the properties of Verri's "minimum" price value, should the state be able to maintain it, Frisi then expressed that equation in differential form and equated the price differential dP to zero. This led him to the conclusion that the minimum (or, for that matter, any value of P) could be maintained by offsetting the changes in one of C or V by changes in the other so as to keep the ratio required for achieving the minimum (or, respectively, another value of P) intact.[9]

Later on in his book, Verri discusses the problem of obtaining maximum production with minimum labor [31, p. 68]. Frisi's commentary here asserts that this problem, when reduced to analytical terms, is an isoperimetric problem – that is, it is mathematically equivalent to the problem of finding the maximum area that can be enclosed within a perimeter of fixed length. Although Frisi provides some mathematical discussion relating to the problem as set in the context posed by Verri, he does not solve it. Nevertheless, this commentary, together with that described earlier, seems to be the earliest appearance of mathematical optimization in economics.

The broader historical context concerning the development of the mathematics of optimization at the time Verri's book and Frisi's commentary were published is worth noting. First, the use of the calculus to determine the values at which functions have maxima and minima had been worked out by Fermat 100 years earlier in the middle of the seventeenth century.[10]

---

[8] It should be noted that the following references to and quotation from Verri's work are based on the translation of the 1781 edition, which is not the same as the sixth version on which Frisi based his commentary. However, it is safe to assume that the material in question is similar in spirit, if not identical in wording, to that to which Frisi was responding.

[9] That is, $dP = [VdC - CdV]/V^2 = 0$, from which it follows that $dC/dV = C/V$. See Robertson [23, p. 526].

[10] See, for example, Kline [18, pp. 347–348].

Second, the isoperimetric problem, which was related to the principle of least action (the doctrine dating to antiquity that nature acts in the shortest, most efficient way) and Fermat's principle of least time (that light only travels along paths that take the least time), had recently been solved by Lagrange in the 1750s. In so doing, Lagrange created a general technique for dealing with such matters to which Euler subsequently gave the name "calculus of variations."[11] Because of the likelihood that there was much discussion of Lagrange's "new" method among mathematicians at the time, it is not surprising that Frisi chose to point out in his commentary the implicit presence of the isoperimetric problem in Verri's book. Third, around or shortly after the time that the first edition of Verri's book was being reprinted with annotations, Lagrange was developing what later came to be known as his multiplier method for determining the critical values of functions that have maximum and minimum values under constraints.[12] But, as will be pointed out momentarily, the mathematics of constrained optimization did not enter the economics literature for another 100 years.

It is possible that Frisi's use of mathematics to express indirectly the idea of optimization – short-lived in print though it was – inspired other, more direct, mathematical appearances of optimization in mathematical economic models.[13] Be that as it may, in 1815, Georg von Buquoy, a German economist, gave an analysis of profit maximization, with respect to the depth to which, when planting crops, fields are plowed, that was remarkably prescient of what was to come. Robertson [23, p. 527] provides a translation:[14]

Let the law according to which the value of the crop [R] depends upon the depth of plowing [x] be given by the equation $R = f(x)$, and let the law according to which costs [C] depend upon the depth of plowing be expressed by the equation $C = g(x)$. The net revenue can generally be expressed at any depth by $[R - C =] f(x) - g(x)$, from which that value [of x] can be found at which the net revenue is a maximum. And this maximum will be at that value of x at which the first derived function of $f(x) - g(x)$ disappears and at which simultaneously the second derived function becomes negative.

Although it is expressed in terms of plowing depth, this, of course, is the marginal-cost-equals-marginal-revenue statement of the necessary first-order condition for "profit" maximization, along with a statement

---

[11] Ibid., pp. 580–583.
[12] Grattan-Guinness [7, pp. 326–327].
[13] See Groenewegen [8, p. xxvii].
[14] The mathematical notation employed in this discussion has been modified slightly from the original.

of the second-order condition sufficient to ensure a maximum at the critical point.

It was the French economist Augustin Cournot [2] who, in 1838, placed the mathematics of optimization in the context of many of the economic models in which it appears today. Profit was the difference between revenue and costs, the latter both expressed as functions of output, and upon equating its derivative to zero, Cournot derived the marginal-cost-equals-marginal-revenue standard that attends virtually all of today's introductory and intermediate microeconomics textbooks. He analyzed profit maximization under perfect competition (Chapter 8) and monopoly (Chapter 5). He developed the analysis of a market with two competing firms (duopoly) who are simultaneously maximizing their own profit under the assumption that the competing firm's output remains fixed (Chapter 7). And he even explored the meaning of revenue maximization along a demand curve in terms of first- and second-order maximization conditions (Chapter 4). In all of this Cournot gives extensive accounts of the derivations and implications of first- and second-order conditions. It is with Cournot that optimization and the mathematics associated with optimization became an integral part of economic modeling.

However, up to the middle of the nineteenth century, the constraints imposed by the finiteness of resources remained implicit in mathematical models employing optimization in economics. Cournot's presentations in particular did not require specific account be taken of them. The first appearance of explicit constraints in relation to optimization occurred in 1854 with the verbal statement by Hermann H. Gossen [6, pp. 108–109], another German economist, of the first-order condition resulting from constrained maximization of utility (pleasure) subject to the (linear) budget constraint:

Man obtains the maximum of life pleasure if he allocates all his earned money ... between the various pleasures and determines the ... [proportion of income for a specific pleasure] in such a manner that the last atom of money spent for each pleasure offers the same amount of pleasure.

Then in 1871 the English economist, W. Stanley Jevons [10, pp. 99–100] wrote down the first-order mathematical equations for a slightly different maximization problem and, in Switzerland in 1874, Léon Walras [33, p. 127] spelled out both first- and second-order conditions for, among other things, that same problem.[15] Thus 100 years after Frisi, constrained

---

[15] The page references in this Jevons citation are to the fifth (1957) edition of his *The Theory of Political Economy*; those to Walras' *Elements of Pure Economics* are to the English translation of the 1926 edition.

optimization finally entered economic models in a formal, mathematical way. Today mathematical models based on optimization appear almost everywhere across the discipline.

The introduction in economic modeling of mathematical systems of simultaneous relations, frequently brought in for the purpose of determining prices and quantities, can be traced back at least to Isnard in 1781.[16] But Walras [33] was the first to write down the full general equilibrium model of the microeconomy in the mid-1870s. Walras' efforts in setting out the simultaneous equations of his general equilibrium system notwithstanding, it was not until the middle of the twentieth century that the use of simultaneous relations, apart from solving systems of first-order optimization equations, achieved some prominence in the economics literature. Clearly, then, absent the mathematics of optimization, the appearance of mathematics in economics would be far less pervasive. This suggests that if the subject-matter of economics is conducive and encouraging to the overwhelming employment of mathematics in economics, the source of that conduciveness and encouragement is, to a considerable extent, the same source that has made optimization so important in economics.

As suggested, in part, above, there are two broad domains in which optimization has appeared as an integral part of economic analysis. First, optimization has become the cornerstone of multi- or function-output models that purport to explain the behavior of individual consumers and firms, and sometimes even collections of consumers and collections of firms.[17] In this category fall such applications (some with explicit constraints and some without) as utility maximization, expenditure minimization, cost minimization, profit maximization, revenue maximization, maximization of the rate of return on invested capital, and the determination of various solutions, characterized in terms of optimization criteria, of a wide variety of games.

Second, to digress slightly from the present emphasis on explanation, optimization has been employed in non-explanatory economic models whose purpose is the depiction of a possible structure that defines an ideal that a collective or a society might want to attain. Now societies are distinct from individuals. They are made up of individuals and have an aggregative

---

[16] See Robertson [23, pp. 531–533].

[17] This is not to minimize the importance of optimization in single-output models or in models whose sole purpose is to describe a possible structure as when, for example and as noted earlier, it is employed to show the existence of equilibrium prices and quantities in a general equilibrium model – including the Marxian general equilibrium model of Roemer [20, Ch. 2].

quality that individuals lack. Societies have priorities and motivations that are generally different from those of individuals, and their behaviors fall in different spheres of activity. Although there may be analogies between them, explanations of the behaviors of individuals and societies must, of necessity, deviate from each other, at least in detail. The optimization ideals that a society might pursue include Pareto optimality, aggregate social welfare maximization, maximization of the value of national output, optimal taxation, and optimal economic growth.

It is obvious, then, that optimization has become central to the analysis of economic phenomena and a stage (ii) and stage (iii) foundation on which many economic models rest. And it was (and is) through the channel of optimization that a large portion of the mathematics employed in economics has entered (and continues to enter) the economics literature. The main issue that will be addressed in the remainder of this chapter is why has optimization become so important in economics.

Consider the first of the above mentioned domains in which optimization figures centrally in models that are constructed to explain the behavior of individual economic agents. These models all attempt to clarify what is happening in the real world. That is, they purport to give relatively accurate and seemingly satisfactory reasons why certain behavior has been or might be observed. This, in turn, implies, as suggested earlier, that there must be acceptable bridges or accordances between any particular model itself and the reality that is to be explained. For it is the presence of such accordances that permits the investigator to conclude that the model is a credible and appropriate reflection of what is actually going on. One way to establish the presence of acceptable accordances is by subjecting the observable parts of the model to empirical tests (stage (iv) in the constructive method of model building set out in Chapter 3). Not all parts of all models in economics relate to variables that are observable. Some things cannot be seen. Thus economists expend considerable energy deriving properties in relation to observable variables that follow from assumptions made with respect to unobservable variables (stage (iii)). It is the former properties that can be subjected to tests against data that have been recorded in reality.

Optimization fits into explanatory models in that it is usually reflective of what is thought to be the driving force behind the behavior of agents in them. One common motive that is often seen in the stage (i) vision as important in directing behavior in reality is self-interest. Self-interest focuses an agent's attention on the achievement of a goal that, in the eyes of the agent, lies in the interest of that agent. Rational behavior is the manifestation of general goal-oriented (not necessarily self-interested) behavior in a model. In the case of the economist's model of consumer behavior, recall, it is assumed in stage (ii) that the consumer has fixed preferences among vectors or baskets of quantities of commodities, and self-interest from stage (i) takes the form of rational behavior in that the consumer is thought of as buying the most preferred basket from those available to him. Preferences are represented in stage (iii) by a utility function with appropriate properties defined over the space of all non-negative commodity vectors. (Utility functions and the preferences underlying them are generally not observable.) And rational behavior is then expressed in the particular sense that, in making purchases, the consumer always chooses that basket that maximizes utility subject to the limitations imposed by the prices of commodities (assumed to be given) and the amount of money he has available to spend (also assumed given). It is the optimization, then, that translates the consumer's unobservable preferences into buying action. Once translated, the characteristics of the consumer's buying behavior, which are observable and which emerge from the properties of his fixed preferences or utility function through the maximization, can be determined in stage (iii) and subjected in stage (iv) to empirical tests. Clearly, optimization lies at the very core of this explanation of consumer behavior. It is no less than the representation in the model of what is thought to be the fundamental propellant that determines the consumer's decisions and brings about his purchases. Optimization plays a similar role in most explanatory models in economics.

But there are problems relating to the use of optimization in these models. To illustrate them and to recall some of the questions previously raised concerning the mathematization of economic modeling, attention will focus on the model of consumer behavior described above. Also, although they are distinct concepts and may be interpreted in different ways, it will be convenient in what follows to conflate the meaning of the terms "self-interest," "rationality," and "optimization" so that the latter two both refer to constrained utility maximization and are taken to be the representation of self-interest in the model.

The chief difficulty arises with respect to the establishment of acceptable accordances between the model and reality through stage (iv) empirical testing of the observable parts of the model. To conduct such tests, it is necessary to observe the buying behavior of the individual at different times when the prices he faces and/or the amount of money he has to spend have changed. The rate of response of observed quantities purchased to changes in any price or alterations of funds available may be characterized in terms of appropriate partial derivatives, for example, $\partial q/\partial p$ or $\partial q/\partial m$, where q, p, and m, refer, respectively, to the quantity of the commodity purchased, its price, and the money available to spend. Or alternatively, the proportional change in quantity purchased, $\partial q / q$, may be expressed as a ratio of the proportional change in price, $\partial p / p$, to provide what is referred to as the price elasticity of demand, $(\partial q / \partial p)(p / q)$. A corresponding expression may be derived for the funds available or income elasticity of demand. For any test to be successful, the behavior so observed, described, in part, in the language of partial derivatives, elasticities, or appropriate approximations thereof, has to be consistent with the corresponding characteristics predicted by the model, given the fixed preferences of the consumer in it. But, as suggested in Chapters 1 and 3, the fixed preferences of the model are a depiction of predilections in the mind of the consumer, and the economist who is testing the model has no control over them. Thus any collection of purchase data that contradicts those predicted characteristics, and which, therefore, would cast doubt on the relevance of the model, can always be explained away as a consequence of changing preferences in the consumer's mind that occurred in the interval between the observation of one data point and another, and that could not be controlled. It follows that the model cannot be falsified and remains viable as a potential explanation of consumer behavior regardless of whether the observations are consistent with it or not, and hence the ability to establish acceptable accordances through empirical testing breaks down.

Where, then, do the acceptable accordances come from? Elsewhere (Katzner [13]) it has been suggested that these are derived in part from a judgment by the investigator that the assumption content of the model is consistent with the dominant features of the cultural heritage of the particular consumer in question. The argument, stated in a more general context in Chapter 1, may be briefly summarized as it relates to the model under discussion: Mental processes are heavily influenced by the cultural milieu in which they take place (Katzner [15]). In any culture, some cultural traits are dominant over others. Since the purchases of a consumer are determined through mental processes, it is both reasonable and realistic to abstract from what are thought to be less important cultural characteristics and focus on the dominant traits of the cultural heritage of that individual in making assumptions about what motivates those purchases. In the case of the Western world, the relevant dominant trait is self-interest. That trait, according to Weber [34], was institutionalized as a central tenet of Western culture during the seventeenth century through the dogmas of certain religious texts. Self-interest as a motive remains strong and dominant today – especially in America. It is therefore thought to be appropriate and accurate to explain consumer purchasing behavior in Western societies in terms of constrained utility maximization that reflects self-interest.

It follows from this argument, of course, that in societies where optimization is irrelevant or inappropriate as a representation of the existing dominant cultural traits, it should not figure in explanations of consumer buying behavior. This, it has been suggested (Katzner [13]), is the case with Japan. According to Bellah [1], the dominant traits of Japanese culture (these were institutionalized during the Tokugawa era from 1600 to 1868) include loyalty, the necessity to fulfill obligation, and frugality. But self-interest and other motives that might be represented in terms of an optimization problem are not among them. By previous argument, then, the model of constrained utility maximization can not be used successfully to explain consumer behavior in Japan. That is, the stage (i) vision of consumer behavior in the two worlds is necessarily sufficiently different that the constrained-utility-maximization model emerging at stages (ii) and (iii) for Western circumstances is unable to explain satisfactorily consumer activity in Japan. The same is true of most explanatory models that employ optimization techniques when attempting to explain the economic behavior of Japanese agents in other contexts and in general. Additional examples of societies in which deviations from self-interested behavior seem to occur have been found by Henrich et al. [9].

For the most part, modern explanatory economics was developed by Western economists to explain Western economic behavior. As a consequence, there are not many explanatory models in the economics literature that represent the driving force behind human behavior by something other than optimization.[18] One could still argue, however, that all economic behavior (both Western and non-Western) is explainable in terms of some form of optimization as long as the objective function is appropriately modified from its Western specification to fit the situation at hand. Indeed, a mathematical theorem of this sort has been proved by Katzner [14] within the framework of the theory of choice. But applying optimization techniques as representative of the motivating propellant of human behavior when optimization cannot represent the actual force that brings about that behavior is to produce inaccurate and incorrect explanation. And this can be dangerous not only because it leads to misunderstanding, but also because economists often use their explanatory models as the basis for policy recommendations. Hence the

---

[18] A few examples have been provided by Katzner [14].

use of optimization models where unwarranted can potentially lead to considerable harm.

This provides further illustration, in addition to those of Section 3.2, of why stage (i) considerations figure so importantly in model building. Creating an explanatory model by starting at stage (iii) and ignoring in particular stage (i), as would be the case if, say, the Western model of constrained utility maximization were invoked to explain Japanese consumer behavior, can lead to irrelevance and misunderstanding. More generally, error or misrepresentation of reality at the level of stage (i) may set the construction process off on the wrong foot, destroying at the outset whatever explanatory significance the model might engender. And this destruction occurs before any stage (ii) relations are specified and any stage (iii) manipulations are undertaken.

Returning to the original question, then, optimization has become so important in economic explanations of individual behavior not because it has been empirically established that optimization is universally the engine that drives that behavior but, rather, because (i) the relevance of optimization is a consequence of the peculiarities of Western culture and (ii) models using optimization were created primarily to explain economic behavior in that cultural environment. A similar argument may be made for other areas of economics and, more generally, other areas of social science where, in the subject-matter of those areas, the notion of rational behavior is predominant. But the circumstances in which rational behavior arises are not nearly as widespread in the disciplines of social science outside of economics as they are inside.

Another difficulty, actually an entire class of difficulties, relating to the application of optimization in explanatory economic models has more to do with the form in which optimization is applied than with the application of optimization itself. For, in the absence of the ability in stage (iv) to verify empirically that any particular assumption of optimization is appropriate, and the consequent reliance on the judgment of the investigator as to whether there are the requisite accordances between a model and the reality it is intended to explain, certain aspects of some applications of optimization in economics have come under heavy criticism. These criticisms frequently have to do with whether or not the individual or individuals whose behavior is in question are actually able to know or obtain enough information to be able to optimize in the manner spelled out in the model. Two examples of such criticisms will be detailed here, each drawing attention to a perceived weakness in the utility maximization model of consumer behavior.

Simon [28], as intimated in Chapter 3, has argued that to be able to maximize utility as described earlier, the consumer has to have complete knowledge of the commodities that might make up each purchase and complete knowledge of his preferences for all possible purchases. For only then can the true maximizing choice be determined. But in most situations, the number of options is so great and the amount of information so vast, that such knowledge is beyond the capacity of the consumer to secure and manage. Faced with this difficulty, consumers do the best that they can by choosing a vector that "satisfices" or that seems to be "good enough." Thus, to restore its optimizing character, the model of consumer behavior needs to be modified by introducing certain limits on the numbers of goods and the numbers of different possible quantities of goods that can be purchased, and that have heretofore been absent.

Shackle [26, 27], as noted in Chapter 1, extends this lack of information to cover much greater territory. Among other things, and remaining in the context of the utility-maximization model, he is concerned about the time that elapses between the moment a decision to purchase is made and the consumption of that purchase which necessarily occurs later. Since the future is unknown and unknowable, the individual cannot know what his circumstances will be and what he himself will be like at the time of consumption, and hence he cannot know what his preferences will be at that moment. Something bought today may turn out to be despised or useless when the time comes to consume it. Merely restricting the numbers of goods that can be purchased and their possible quantities, while it may lead to an adequate explanation of purchasing behavior, will not necessarily yield an explanation of ultimate satisfaction. Nor is the introduction of probabilities in the context of mathematical expectation, the theory of games, or some other formal structure, very satisfactory since the individual does not have enough information at his disposal to determine those probabilities in a meaningful way either. Rather, a complete restructuring of the decision model is required in which nonprobabilistic uncertainty and the consequent ignorance in which the individual decides play a major role. Shackle [26] proposed such a model in which a concept he called "potential surprise" replaces probability and in which optimization occurs in reference to the maximization of what are referred to as "attractiveness" and, in a version due to Vickers [32, Ch. 12], "decision index" functions.[19]

---

[19] Several of these ideas, including the notion of potential surprise, will be briefly considered in Chapter 10. A more extensive discussion of Shackle's approach and his decision model appears in Katzner [12].

Taking up the second domain of optimization in economic modeling introduced earlier, in which every option under consideration characterizes an ideal that might in some way be considered desirable by a collective or a society, it is clear that the optimizations involved do not themselves need to represent something present in reality. Each model, of course, has to have appropriate associations with the real world (i.e., bridges connecting the model to observations) with respect to one or more parts or extensions of its structural components. But the optimization itself appears only as the representation of an end toward which policymakers, say, are striving or that investigators are studying. Because societies are comprised of individuals, such ends or ideals are necessarily amalgams of individual thought forms.[20] Those amalgams are constrained by institutions and, in the process of formation, are buffeted by pressures from various sources. The latter include, in part, cultural habits and political forces. Cultural imperatives weigh heavily in stage (i) and are clearly significant because, in addition to what has been said of them earlier, they largely determine what is considered to be important by the individuals in the society whose economy is at issue, and are therefore crucial inputs to the crucible out of which society's ends flow. In American society, for example, where self-interest dominates, and where success as reflected in accumulated wealth and consumption is highly respected, the emergence of the maximization of national income, economic growth, and wealth, as desirable ends is quite natural.

With respect to the study of ends by investigators, any end, related to society's ideals or not, could be employed as the basis for a standard of comparison against which an analyst might contrast actual or potential situations. But, of course, the choice of that end, if it is to reflect the values of the society under investigation, has to be sensitive to that society's cultural heritage. Regardless, in light of the role that optimization plays in explanatory models, and taking into account both the prevalence in Western societies of cultural predilections that give rise to the employment of optimization, and the fact that much of current economics was developed in the context of and to apply to Western societies, the widespread use of optimization to define desirable ends is to be expected. Thus, in addition to having been the main impetus for the extensive utilization of optimization in explanations of individual economic behavior, Western cultural forces have also been responsible to a considerable degree for the

---

[20] This is not to imply that societal objective functions can be understood in terms of the aggregation of individual objective functions.

frequent appearance of optimization in the economic characterization of collective or societal ideals.

One may conclude, then, that a significant reason why the subject matter of economics is so conducive and encouraging to the employment of mathematics in model building has to do with the importance of self-interest in the cultural background within which (Western) economic behavior takes place. That is, the use of mathematics in economics flows naturally from the subject matter of economics because (Western) economists consider the primary propellant of economic behavior to be culturally determined rationality. And the obvious way to represent that rationality in economic explanation is with the mathematical notion of optimization. Moreover, in cultural environments where rationality as defined here does not exist as the main motivating force behind economic behavior, the use of optimization and the mathematics associated with it are far less relevant. Indeed, the possibility arises that the use of mathematics in economic modeling that pertains to those cultural environments, when such models are worked out, could decline precipitously.

References

[1] Bellah, R. N., *Tokugawa Religion* (Glencoe: Free Press, 1957).

[2] Cournot, A., *Researches into the Mathematical Principles of the Theory of Wealth*, N. T. Bacon, trans. (New York: Kelley, 1960).

[3] Debreu, G., "Economic Theory in the Mathematical Mode," *American Economic Review* 74 (1984), pp. 267–278.

[4] Einstein, A. "Geometry and Experience," *Ideas and Opinions*, S. Bargmann trans. (New York: Bonanza, 1954), pp. 232–246.

[5] Gorman, T., "Towards a Better Economic Methodology?" in *Economics in Disarray*, P. Wiles and G. Routh, eds. (Oxford: Basil Blackwell, 1984), pp. 260–288.

[6] Gossen, H. H., *The Laws of Human Relations and the Rules of Human Action Derived Therefrom*, R. C. Blitz, trans. (Cambridge, MA: MIT Press, 1983).

[7] Grattan-Guinness, I., *The Norton History of the Mathematical Sciences* (New York: Norton, 1997).

[8] Groenewegen, P. D., "Introduction," *Reflections on Political Economy* by P. Verri, trans. B. McGilvray and P. D. Groenewegen (Fairfield: Kelley, 1993), pp. vii–xxix.

[9] Henrich, J., et al., "In Search of Homo Economicus: Behavioral Experiments in 15 Small-Scale Societies," *American Economic Review* 91, no. 2 (May, 2002), pp. 73–78.

[10] Jevons, W. S., *The Theory of Political Economy*, 5th ed. (New York: Kelley, 1965).

[11] Katzner, D. W., "In Defense of Formalization in Economics," *Methodus* 3, no. 1 (June, 1991), pp. 17–24.

[12] Katzner, D. W., *Time, Ignorance, and Uncertainty in Economic Models* (Ann Arbor, MI: University of Michigan Press, 1998).

[13] Katzner, D. W., "Western Economics and the Economy of Japan," *Journal of Post Keynesian Economics* 21 (1999), pp. 503–521. Reprinted in D. W. Katzner, *Culture and Economic Explanation* (London: Routledge, 2008), Essay 2.

[14] Katzner, D. W., "Culture and the Explanation of Choice Behavior," *Theory and Decision* 48 (2000), pp. 241–262. Reprinted in D. W. Katzner, *Culture and Economic Explanation* (London: Routledge, 2008), Essay 10.

[15] Katzner, D. W., "'What Are the Questions?'" *Journal of Post Keynesian Economics* 25 (2002), pp. 51–68. Reprinted in D. W. Katzner, *Culture and Economic Explanation* (London: Routledge, 2008), Essay 3.

[16] Katzner, D. W., *An Introduction to the Economic Theory of Market Behavior: Microeconomics from a Walrasian Perspective* (Cheltenham: Elgar, 2006).

[17] Katzner, D. W., A Neoclassical Curmudgeon Looks at Heterodox Criticisms of Microeconomics," *World Economic Review* 4 (2015), pp. 63–75.

[18] Kline, M., *Mathematical Thought from Ancient to Modern Times* (New York: Oxford University Press, 1972).

[19] Lawson, T., "Modern Economics: The Problem and a Solution," in *A Guide to What's Wrong with Economics*, E. Fullbrook, ed. (London: Anthem, 2004), pp. 21–32.

[20] Lawson, T., "Modelling and Ideology in the Economic Academy: Competing Explanations of the Failings of the Modern Discipline?" *Economic Thought* 1 (2012), pp. 3–32.

[21] Marshall, A., *Principles of Economics*, 8th ed. (New York: Macmillan, 1948).

[22] Mirowski, P., *More Heat than Light* (Cambridge: Cambridge University Press, 1989).

[23] Robertson, R. M., "Mathematical Economics before Cournot," *Journal of Political Economy* 57 (1949), pp. 523–536.

[24] Roemer, J. E., *Analytical Foundations of Marxian Economic Theory* (Cambridge: Cambridge University Press, 1981).

[25] Setterfield, M., "Heterodox Economics, Social Ontology, and the Use of Mathematics," in *What Is Neoclassical Economics? Debating the Origins, Meaning, and Significance*, J. Morgan, ed. (London: Cambridge University Press, 2016), pp. 221–237.

[26] Shackle, G. L. S., *Decision, Order and Time in Human Affairs*, 2nd. ed. (Cambridge: Cambridge University Press, 1969).

[27] Shackle, G. L. S., *Epistemics and Economics* (Cambridge: Cambridge University Press, 1972).

[28] Simon, H. A., *Administrative Behavior*, 2nd ed. (New York: Macmillan, 1957).

[29] Solow, R. M., "Comments from Inside Economics," in *The Consequences of Economic Rhetoric*, A. Klamer, D. N. McCloskey, and R. M. Solow, eds. (Cambridge: Cambridge University Press, 1988), pp. 31–37.

[30] Suppes, P., "The Desirability of Formalization in Science," *Journal of Philosophy* 65 (1968), pp. 651–664.

[31] Verri, P., *Reflections on Political Economy*, trans. B. McGilvray and P. D. Groenewegen (Fairfield: Kelley, 1993).

[32] Vickers, D., *Money Capital in the Theory of the Firm* (Cambridge: Cambridge University Press, 1987).

[33] Walras, L., *Elements of Pure Economics*, W. Jaffé, trans. (Homewood: Irwin, 1954).

[34] Weber, M., *The Protestant Ethic and the Spirit of Capitalism*, trans. T. Parsons (New York: Scribner, 1958).

[35] Weintraub, E. R., *General Equilibrium Analysis: Studies in Appraisal* (Cambridge: Cambridge University Press, 1985).

[36] Weintraub, E. R., *How Economics Became a Mathematical Science* (Durham, NC: Duke University Press, 2002).

5

Models and Measurement (or Lack Thereof)

For present purposes, measurement may be regarded as the assignment of numbers to non-numerical manifestations or instances of a property of objects. Thus, as an illustration, various unquantified "longnesses" of specific articles are measured as their quantified length. The assignment of numbers to such manifestations is called a *scale*. Different categories of scales or measures preserve and reflect different kinds of information concerning relationships among the various manifestations of the property. The four main measure types are (i) nominal measures which only give a unique numerical name to each manifestation and contain no further information; (ii) ordinal measures that are nominal measures reflecting certain ordering relations among the manifestations;[1] (iii) interval or cardinal measures that are ordinal measures such that the numerical value of combinations of manifestations is the sum of the numerical values of the manifestations that are combined;[2] and (iv) ratio measures that are cardinal measures having the same meaning for the zero value regardless of the particular scale employed.[3]

It should be noted that since the numerical values of a variable that is only ordinally measured reflect nothing more than the underlying ordering relation defined among the possibly unmeasured manifestations to which

---

[1] For example, if object A has more longness than object B, then the length of object A is greater than that of object B.

[2] For example, the combined length (measured longness) of object A lined up end to end with object B is the sum of the length (measured longness) of A plus the length (measured longness) of B.

[3] Thus the length of an object without longness is zero regardless of whether it is measured on an inches or centimeters scale. Temperature, say, is measured on a cardinal, not ratio scale since the meaning of zero degrees changes upon switching from the Fahrenheit to the centigrade scale. That is, the "warmness" associated with zero degrees is below the freezing point of water on the former and exactly at that freezing point on the latter.

those numerical values relate, the numerical values themselves have no content and significance other than that present in the underlying ordering relation. This means that upon applying any continuous, increasing transformation[4] to a collection of ordinal, numerical, variable values results in a new set of ordinal, numerical, variable values that contains the same information as the old collection, and that one set of ordinal, numerical values is as good as any other. That is, the selection of one such collection of ordinal variable values is arbitrary. In the case of a cardinally measured variable, only positive linear transformations ($ax + b$, where x is the variable and $a > 0$ and $b \gtrless 0$ are real constants) are admissible because only those transformations preserve the meaning of the sum of variable values in terms of the combination of underlying manifestations. And with ratio measured variables, the positive linear transformations must be such that $b = 0$ in order to maintain the fixity of the zero-variable-value position.

The differences between nominal, ordinal, cardinal, and ratio scales can be illustrated by considering certain characteristics implied by their definitions. Think of two pieces of wood whose longnesses are measured in terms of inches. Suppose piece R is two inches long and piece S is ten inches long. Consider the following statements: (i) R and S have different lengths. (ii) S has greater length than R. (iii) The length of S is eight inches longer than that of R. (iv) The length of S is five times as long as that of R. Since longness, in fact, is measured as length on a ratio scale, all four statements are valid. If only the first three were meaningful (as would be the case with temperature scales such as Fahrenheit or Centigrade), then length would be a cardinal (not ratio) measure of longness. When just (i) and (ii) hold, the scale is ordinal. And with (i) alone it is nominal.

Model building in physical science frequently introduces measures early on. And once measures of appropriate property manifestations are determined, they may be used to define variables, and models involving those variables can be built and studied. Thus, for example, having scales on which to measure properties like height (length) and weight, models involving functions that relate, say, the weights of individuals (one variable) to their heights (a second variable) can be constructed and investigated. Note that both height and weight are measured on independent scales. Such relations between them (that is, between the scale values) can, as a rule, take on any relevant characteristics and assume any appropriate shape.

---

[4] An increasing transformation of a set of numerical variable values is a transformation such that if one value in the original set is greater than or equal to another, then the corresponding transformed values maintain the same greater than or equal to relation to each other.

However, transferring this general procedure into model building in economics often runs into difficulties. Indeed, it has already been remarked in Chapter 1 that many of the issues economists are called upon to address concern phenomena that seemingly defy attempts to represent them numerically. And without measures of the relevant variables, economists have tended to deal with the unquantified as though it were quantified or, as also noted in Chapter 1, to invoke questionable proxies in place of the actual variables of interest, or to ignore the phenomenon entirely in their models. This, in turn, has led to one aspect, again as set out in Chapter 1, of the absence of epistemological parity of economics with the physical sciences.

There are many questions that fall in the lack-of-adequate-measures-and-therefore-ignored category. This is true not only in economics, but also across the social science spectrum in general. For example, economists have a well-developed model of consumer behavior (mentioned in earlier chapters) resting squarely on the notions of utility and maximization.[5] But what is it about specific personalities in their relation to preferences and hence utility that leads them to purchase commodities in certain observed patterns? Culture, social class, and education, through preferences, also have an impact on utility and consumption patterns. How? Why do "waves of fashion" arise, and in what ways do they influence utility and hence demand? In relation to the firm and employment, it is well known how costs depend on factor prices and the latter on the demand and supply of factors themselves. But there is no model to elucidate why one profession is, say, "respectable" and another is not. Nor is there much theoretical understanding of the responses of participants in labor management disputes to the vague political, social, and psychological pressures under which they operate. Similarly, the standard model of firm behavior describes how valuable goods are created at minimum cost and maximum profit. But there seems to be no room for the notion that the firm is also a social unit capable of generating "well-being" for its employees

---

[5] It should be noted that the utility function in this model, like many functions in economics that are taken to be ordinally measured, rests on a notion of ordinality somewhat different from that characterized in the relatively recent literature, e.g., Pfanzagl [29, p. 29]. In confluence with Pfanzagl's notion, ordinality here means that the utility function is a real-valued function representing a preference ordering having the property that any increasing transformation of it also represents that ordering. Similarly, increasing transformations of an ordinal variable in economics usually implies no change in the underlying order or meaning of the variable's values. But these notions of ordinality differ from Pfanzagl's in that arithmetic operations may be performed on the utility-function and variable values. See p. 194 and Katzner [26].

and society as a whole in addition to money income for those employees and profit for the firm's owners.

Some years ago, Friedrich Hayek [15] complained about the tendency he observed in economics to disregard as unimportant and irrelevant that which, at the time of inquiry, did not appear to be amenable to measurement. Economists seemed to believe that, in confluence with Kelvin's famous but dubious dictum,[6] the only way to live up to the scientific requirements of economic analysis was to work with numerical measures even when knowing they captured only a small portion, if that, of the important facets of the issue at hand. By this standard, wrote Hayek [15, p. 3], "... there ... may well exist better 'scientific' evidence for a false [i.e., incorrect] theory, which will be accepted because it is more 'scientific,' than for a valid explanation, which is rejected because there is no[t] sufficient quantitative evidence for it." He then went on to say [15, p. 5], "I prefer true but imperfect knowledge ... to a pretence of exact knowledge that is likely to be false. The credit which the apparent conformity with recognized scientific standards can gain for seemingly simple but false theories may ... have grave consequences."

Since Hayek's warning, however, matters in economics have only moved in a direction in which he probably would not have approved. For in addition to the general omission of important elements because numerical measures of them are not known, it has now become commonplace in certain areas to introduce, as suggested above, what many would regard as the non-quantifiable and partially quantifiable (e.g., ordinally measured) by treating them as if they were fully quantifiable (i.e., at least cardinally measured).[7] Such fully quantified scales may be called "false measures." Thus, for example, Boulding [8, p. 32] includes variables representing "virtues," "vices," and "goodness" in a fully quantified mathematical equation, Azzi and Ehrenberg [5, p. 33] do something similar with the "expected value of afterlife consumption," and so does Akerlof with the

---

[6] "... when you can measure what you are speaking about and express it in numbers you know something about it; but when you cannot measure it, when you cannot express it in numbers, your knowledge is of a meagre and unsatisfactory kind: it may be the beginning of knowledge, but you have scarcely in your thoughts, advanced to the stage of *science*, whatever the matter may be" (Kelvin [33, p. 80]).

[7] That is, non-quantified or ordinally quantified variables appear perhaps along with cardinally or ratio quantified variables in the same analysis. No distinction between or discussion about the nature of the quantification of the variables is given, and standard mathematical techniques usually reserved for at least cardinally quantified variables are applied throughout. For present purposes, the absence of any discussion of measurement is taken to imply that in those analyses all variables are treated as if they were fully quantified.

"quality" of an automobile [1, p. 490] and a person's "reputation" [2, p. 754]. Becker and Lewis [7] maximize a utility function (subject to constraint) with respect to fully quantified "child quality" and other variables. In addition, all of the literature on efficiency wages (and related issues) and some of that pertaining to the principal–agent problem employs fully quantified mathematical models in which the questionably quantifiable variable "effort" plays a major role.[8] Another aspect of what might be called this misuse of measurement in economics is the previously noted appearance of fully quantified proxy variables in place of and as "approximations" of the variables for which no measures (ordinal, cardinal, or ratio) or only "fractional" or "incomplete" measures are available. Kalt and Zupan's [18, p. 287] substitution of a particular rating scale (based on voting) for a senator's "ideology," Fair's [11, pp. 52–58] replacement of an individual's wage by his or her occupation and education, Barro's [6, p. 432] use of the number of revolutions and coups, and the number of political assassinations, as indicators of a country's political stability, and Helliwell and Putnam's [16, p. 297] "measures" of social capital illustrate the phenomenon. In practically all such cases the authors make no attempt to justify the measurement they employ. Shackle [32, p. 360] complained bitterly about these practices: "Economics has veritably turned imprecision itself into a science: economics, the science of quantification of the unquantifiable...."

The problems that arise when misusing measurement in these ways have been discussed in general in Chapter 1. To be more specific here, using false measures, that is, say, handling unquantified or only ordinally quantified variables as if they were at least cardinally quantified has the potential of excoriating all meaning from whatever model is constructed. The point is important enough to merit a concrete illustration. Suppose the variable e (representing, say, effort) is only ordinally quantified in the sense of n. 5 on p. 103 and the model contains the function $f(e) = -e^2$ on the domain $\{e : -\infty \le e \le \infty\}$ which, according to the model's specifications, is to be maximized. It is easily seen that this function has a unique maximum at $e = 0$. But since e is only ordinally measured, any increasing transformation applied to it contains the same information and is appropriate for use in place of e in the model. And utilizing the transformation $T(e) = -\lambda^{-e}$, where $\lambda > 1$, results in $F(e) = -\lambda^{-2e}$, for which a maximum does not exist. Hence the meaning and significance of a model based on the maximization

---

[8] Currie and Steedman [9], for example, argue that effort can, at best, only be ordinally quantified.

of a function with respect to a variable that is explicitly or implicitly taken to be cardinally quantified when, in fact, it is only ordinally measured, is called into question. The Becker–Lewis model cited above is subject to this criticism. Further illustrations in which the meaning of models is compromised appear in Katzner [23]. The issue will be attacked from a different angle in Chapter 9.

The difficulty with employing proxies is, as noted earlier, that the relation of a proxy to the variable that is supposed to be represented by the proxy is usually unknown. And without that information, the model loses its connection to the underlying characteristics of the phenomenon under investigation and to the primary assumptions of the model employed to study that phenomenon. That is, the link to the first two stages of model construction set out in Chapter 2 is severed. This leaves the model without a firm foundation on which its meaning and explanatory significance rely.

Models employing non-quantified and non-quantifiable variables appear, albeit informally presented or described, throughout the social sciences. For a political scientist to claim that different types of political systems produce different career patterns (Apter [4, p. 163]), or for an anthropologist to write that the established modes of action and belief to which we refer as a people's customs are something they have made out of experience (Goodenough [12, p. 63]) is tantamount, in either case, to asserting the existence of a model containing a relation between two non-scalable entities. Paraphrasing Parsons on social behavior, Homans [17, p. 958] is more direct: when two men are interacting, variables characterizing the behavior of each man are functions of the variables characterizing the behavior of the other. Even in economics, where the non-quantified tends to be ignored or improperly measured, witness the debate between Gerschenkron and Hirshman over the non-quantifiable relation between ideology and economic systems (see Eckstein [10, Ch. 9]). There is no reason why models containing unmeasured variables cannot be employed more in economics to explain phenomena that involve significant elements (several examples have been provided earlier) for which measures are not known or knowable.

That the models involving unquantified variables described earlier are formulated in non-mathematical terms does not mean that their essence cannot be expressed with mathematical precision. The remainder of this chapter provides a relatively informal demonstration of that fact and, more generally, that mathematical and scientific analysis does not necessarily imply or contain measurability.[9] It does so by furnishing mathematical

---

[9] For more rigorous argument and applications see Katzner [21, 24].

techniques for handling unquantified variables at stages (ii) through (iv) of the model construction process. Thus mathematical argument need not involve only quantifiable elements and a lack of ability to measure is no barrier to the conduct of rigorous scientific inquiry. To refuse to consider what does not appear scalable, to represent it by dubious proxies, or to employ false measures is in serious danger of leading to entirely fallacious representations of reality and, as a consequence reflecting Hayek's warning cited on p. 104, to harmful policy recommendations. Perhaps it was the particular evolution of mathematics into its present form, or the enchantment of economists with only certain aspects of it, which induced them to try to fit numbers everywhere and to turn their backs on important phenomena simply because no sensible way of attaching numbers could be found. But whatever the reason, there is little doubt that the result has contributed significantly to the narrowness of view under which economists now labor.

It should be kept in mind that in any inquiry, the selection of a specific model has to be based on the analytic approach to structuring reality adopted by the investigator. In particular, taking a model's structure as the stage-(ii)-and-stage-(iii) foundation of an analysis reflects a commitment to that approach. That is, certain underlying questions – such as (a) what are the properties of observed elements that will appear as variable values in the model, (b) are the real-world relations, and hence those appearing in the model, thought to be invariant over time, and (c) are observed values, and hence those determined by the model, perceived to be dependent on the path those values took to arrive at their observed state – are presumably already answered in the characteristics of the structure the investigator employs. And this is so regardless of whether or not appropriate measures are available. The examples of modeling techniques presented subsequently indicate how analysis can proceed after commitment to an approach involving elements that are not capable of measurement.

Briefly, the following exposition begins with variables and relations between them. A simple simultaneous relations model in which all variables are unquantified is presented and, after a composition operation is introduced for manipulative purposes, conditions are given under which unique solutions exist and can be expressed as functions of parameters. Next, periodic relations (i.e., relations with lagged variables) are defined and explored for stationary paths and stability properties. The latter requires a digression into the idea of convergence in an unquantified setting. At this point, an analogy is drawn with the standard multiplier analysis of macroeconomic theory. Finally, some attention is directed toward the problems of optimization and empirical testing. Since general analysis and proofs can be found elsewhere,[10] discussion here is often intuitive, motivational, and suggestive. A fully specified example and a more detailed discussion of the use of these techniques will be provided in Chapter 7.[11]

5.1 Simultaneous Relations

When quantifiability is lacking, and thus arithmetic and other numerical operations are inapplicable, the passage from stage (i) to stage (ii) in model construction requires considerations that parallel those that arise when full measures of the relevant variables are available. It is natural to begin with the notion of sets. A set, call it X, is a collection of not-necessarily-quantifiable discrete and distinct objects. Except for discreteness and distinctness, no restrictions are imposed on these objects. There is nothing to prevent them from being collections of other objects or entire systems of relations (defined below). The elements (objects) of X are denoted by x. Primes, bars, asterisks, superscripts, and subscripts on x always specify particular objects of X. To illustrate one way of putting sets together, suppose agreement has been reached on a comprehensive list of I fundamental values, such as "fairness" or "honesty," that individuals may hold. Let value i (where $i = 1, \ldots, I$) have n_i manifestations $v_{i1}, \ldots, v_{in_i}$. Each manifestation is assumed to be distinct and satisfactorily defined in terms of certain primitive words accepted as the basic language of discourse. Any particular individual's collection of values could then be described as a vector containing one manifestation of each value, say, $(v_{13}, v_{27}, \ldots, v_{I2})$. Thus the set X of all possible combinations of human values consists precisely of all vectors x obtained from the $v_{i1}, \ldots, v_{in_i}$.

The variable "values that a human being might hold" may now be defined as the variable ranging over X. It is often written as x – the same symbol used to represent the elements of X. This is a perfectly valid method of characterizing stage (ii) variables in general: first specify the set X over which the variable runs; then define the variable as that variable which may assume as values the objects of X.

Stage (ii) relations among variables are also easily obtained. Let X and Y be sets whose associated variables are x and y. Then any collection of pairs

---

[10] Ibid.

[11] The rest of this chapter is taken with modifications and additions from my "On Not Quantifying the Non-Quantifiable," *Journal of Post Keynesian Economics* 1, no. 2 (Winter, 1978–79), pp. 113–128. © Taylor and Francis. Reproduced with permission.

(x, y), where x is in X and y is in Y, is said to specify a (binary) relation or relationship between x and y. For example, if X and Y are the same set of people and the relation under consideration is "sisterhood," then (x^0, y^0) is a pair in the relation if and only if x^0 and y^0 are sisters. In a second illustration with different X and Y, if x were to denote values that voters (i.e., persons) may hold as defined above, and y were to vary over vectors of traits that characterize personalities of candidates in an election, then the statement that individuals with certain kinds of values vote for candidates with particular personalities may be represented by a relation. The pair (x^0, y^0) is in the relation provided the values of the individual voting, x^0, and personality of the candidate, y^0, stand in the given relationship to each other.

Whenever a relation between x and y has the property that to each x in X there corresponds exactly one y in Y, it is called a *function* or *functional* relation. The functional requirement states that two pairs such as (x^0, y^0) and (x^0, y'), where $y^0 \neq y'$, cannot appear in the relation. Functions are often written

$$y = f(x),$$

where f is the symbolic name of the relation. Thus, the sentence, "The political personality for whom an individual votes [y] is uniquely associated with or determined by the values of the voter [x]," may be abbreviated as $y = f(x)$ as long as y and x are properly defined. In this case x is called the *independent* and y the *dependent* variable. If there were a second independent variable, z, and if x and z were functionally related to y, then

$$y = f(x, z),$$

that is, for every x in X and z in some Z, there is a unique y in Y.

It is important to emphasize that neither the notion of function nor the symbolism

$$y = f(x),$$

or

$$y = f(x, z),$$

requires that the variables x, y, and z be scalable. Both are perfectly valid in non-numerical, set-theoretic contexts. Of course, quantitative methods – in particular, arithmetic operations and the calculus of both infinitesimal and finite differences – are not applicable without measurement, and alternative analytical tools must be found. These are introduced shortly.

Consider first, however, the problem of formulating a stage (ii) conceptual model to understand or explain an observed phenomenon. Suppose that phenomenon appears as the manifestation of two variables, x and y, and in conjunction with a manifestation of a parameter, z (a variable thought to vary independently of the phenomenon but that still influences the observed manifestations of x and y). Suppose the model is hypothesized to consist of two distinct and independent functional relations:

$$y = f(x, z),$$

$$x = g(y, z).$$

(5.1)

In moving to stage (iii), two questions immediately arise. In the first place, is it logically possible to conceive of f and g in force together, or are they contradictory? In other words, given a value for z, does there exist at least one pair (x^0, y^0) satisfying both relations simultaneously? This is equivalent to asking if the hypothetical structure defined by (5.1) is internally consistent. Second, does the model (5.1) determine a unique x^0 and y^0 for each specification of the parameter z; that is, does (5.1) imply a functional relation between z and "solution" values of (x, y) from (5.1)? If so, knowledge of f, g, and z is sufficient to permit determination of (x, y) and hence to explain the phenomenon. Clearly, an affirmative answer to the second question implies an affirmative answer to the first, but not conversely.

These ideas may be illustrated with an analogy drawn from quantitative elementary algebra. For this illustration, take x, y, and z to be scalar, numerical variables. Let z be fixed and suppose f and g represent straight lines in the real Euclidean plane as pictured in Figure 5.1. As drawn, the simultaneous occurrence of f and g appears at a single point (x^0, y^0). In this case system (5.1) is internally consistent and has a unique solution; it is called *determinate*. If g were discarded, then f would still be an internally consistent structure, but it could not identify a unique point. The system is *underdetermined*. If a third relation were added that does not pass through (x^0, y^0) – say, h in Figure 5.1 – no point could satisfy all relations simultaneously and the system would be *overdetermined*. When variables are quantifiable and relations linear, there are two conditions which, if satisfied, guarantee that (5.1) is exactly determinate: (a) the number of variables and relations is the same; and (b) f and g are neither parallel nor coincident lines in the plane.

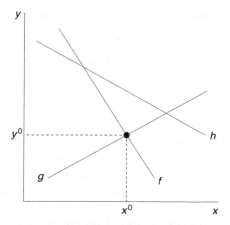

Figure 5.1. Simultaneous linear relations

When measurement is not possible, different conditions may be given, which ensure that unique solutions exist and hence that (5.1) is internally consistent. But before these are derived, techniques for manipulating relations in stage (iii) must be introduced. These serve to compensate, in part, for the loss of addition, subtraction, multiplication, and division in the non-quantifiable world.

First, with x, y, and z as variables, two functions, say,

$$y = r(x),$$

and

$$x = s(z),$$

can always be combined to form a third

$$y = q(z),$$

where

$$q(z) = r(s(z)).$$

That is, q is obtained by substituting $s(z)$ for x in $r(x)$. This elimination of variables procedure is often called the operation of *composition*. It is used extensively in the following.

Second, to assert that the functional relation

$$y = b(x, z)$$

has an *inverse* with respect to x means that there exists another functional relation

$$x = c(y, z),$$

such that

$$y = b(c(y, z), z).$$

Thus, given z and starting with any y^0 in Y, if one first applies c to obtain an x^0 in X and then applies b to revert to Y, one always obtains the original y^0. The inverse of b with respect to x is precisely c. Functions with inverses are often referred to as *invertible* and have very specific properties that are not pursued here.

Note that neither the combination (composition) of functions nor their inversion (i.e., the existence of their inverses) rests in any way on the presence of numerical scales. Both may be abstractly conceived in algebraic or set-theoretic terms.

Returning to (5.1), suppose f has an inverse with respect to the parameter z, namely,

$$z = u(x, y). \tag{5.2}$$

After the second relation of (5.1) is used to eliminate x, (5.2) becomes

$$z = \xi(y, z), \tag{5.3}$$

where

$$\xi(y, z) = u(g(y, z), z). \tag{5.4}$$

If ξ in (5.3) has an inverse, γ, with respect to y, then

$$y = \delta(z), \tag{5.5}$$

where

$$\delta(z) = \gamma(z, z).$$

Finally, when (5.5) is substituted into the second relationship of (5.1),

$$x = \lambda(z), \tag{5.6}$$

where

$$\lambda(z) = g(\delta(z), z).$$

Equations (5.5) and (5.6) express solutions of (5.1) as functions of the parameter z. The argument is valid whenever f and ξ have appropriate inverses. A similar conclusion could have been reached if g had had an inverse with respect to z and a function corresponding to ξ also had had the proper inverse. These ideas are easily generalized to larger systems involving any number of relations, variables, and parameters (Katzner [21, Sect. 5.1]).

Recall that to use the model of (5.1) to explain an observable manifestation of (x, y) associated with some z, the model has to be determinate, that is, the solution values for that z obtained from (5.5) and (5.6) have to be unique. This, of course, is guaranteed since δ and λ are functions. Moreover, even if (5.1) could be solved in both of the ways described above (first inverting f or first inverting g), using the two methods the two solutions would be identical. To see why, let (x', y') and (x'', y'') be the solutions of (5.1) for the same z^0 obtained from the two different procedures. Then

$$y' = f(x', z^0),$$

$$x' = g(y', z^0),$$

and

$$y'' = f(x'', z^0),$$

$$x'' = g(y'', z^0).$$

Because the inversion of f with respect to z applies at both (x', y') and (x'', y''), combining equations (5.3) and (5.4) in the two situations yields, respectively,

$$z^0 = \xi(y', z^0) = u(g(y', z^0), z^0)$$

and

$$z^0 = \xi(y'', z^0) = u(g(y'', z^0), z^0).$$

Recall ξ is assumed to have an inverse with respect to y. It follows as in (5.5) that

$$y' = \delta(z^0),$$

and

$$y'' = \delta(z^0).$$

But from the definition of inverse, δ is a function, and hence two distinct values of y cannot both correspond to z^0 under δ. Therefore

$$y' = y''.$$

Similarly, $x' = x''$.

Regardless of whether the above conditions for solving (5.1) are met, solutions of (5.1) may still exist. With or without solutions, "cycles" are also a possibility. Let the positive integers, denoted by the subscript t, distinguish between inputs and outputs. Think of (5.1), for example, as taking output $t - 1$ and placing it back in the system as input $t - 1$ to produce output t. Thus (5.1) may be rewritten in the form

$$y_t = f(x_{t-1}, z),$$

$$x_t = g(y_{t-1}, z).$$

(5.7)

Suppose the parameter z is fixed. Then, given an initial input (x^0, y^0), a sequence $(x_1, y_1), (x_2, y_2), \ldots, (x_t, y_t), \ldots$, is generated as t moves across $1, 2, \ldots$. It is still required that x_t be in X and y_t be in Y for every t.

A solution of (5.7) is a pair $(\bar{x}, \bar{y})$ where $\bar{x}$ is in X, $\bar{y}$ is in Y, and

$$x_t = x_{t-1} = \bar{x},$$

$$y_t = y_{t-1} = \bar{y},$$

for all $t \geq 1$. In other words, start (5.7) at a solution and it remains there. Clearly $(\bar{x}, \bar{y})$ is a solution of (5.7) if and only if it is also a solution of (5.1). Under certain conditions, convergence (to be defined in the next section) of an arbitrary sequence (x_t, y_t) obtained from (5.7) implies the existence of at least one solution. A cycle is a finite sequence of pairs $(x_0, y_0), (x_1, y_1), \ldots$, repeating itself over and over again in the same order. Should X and Y each contain a finite number of elements, exactly one of the following holds: every pair (x', y') with x' in X and y' in Y is (a) a solution of (5.7); (b) in exactly one cycle; or (c) an element of at least one sequence generated by (5.7) which converges to a solution. Further properties of cycles in the finite case have been explored elsewhere (Katzner [21, Sect. 5.3]).

When quantification is possible, these structures are often used as a basis for organizing and understanding reality. The general equilibrium and classical models of a perfectly competitive economy mentioned in earlier chapters are sophisticated illustrations. The former views the economic structure as describable by a system of simultaneous relations reflecting the hypotheses that, given exogenous preferences, endowments, and technologies, (i) all consumers are buying outputs and selling factors so as to maximize utility subject to their budget constraints; (ii) all firms are producing and supplying outputs and hiring inputs so as to maximize profits; and (iii) supply equals demand in all markets; the latter is a system of linear equations with fixed production coefficients. Economic equilibrium is a point that satisfies all relations simultaneously (see, for example, Katzner [25]).

In the non-quantifiable world, it is possible to distinguish between political structure and political system by thinking of the former as a system of simultaneous relations and the latter as determined by it (Katzner [19]). Less formal examples may be found in Pareto [27], Parsons [28], Apter [4], and elsewhere. In principle, at least, all static phenomena involving simultaneously interacting elements can be modeled in this way. The sufficient conditions guaranteeing solutions (viz., that the number of relationships be equal to the number of variables, and that appropriate inverses exist) can be used as a basis for checking internal consistency and, of course, the same conditions could also be brought to bear were x, y, and z to be cardinally quantified in the particular application under consideration.

5.2 Change Over Time

An alternative, though related, perspective for viewing reality focuses on transformation over time. The discussion centering around (5.7) has already hinted at such a possibility. It is now appropriate to consider the dynamic approach more specifically. To do so, however, requires a preliminary discussion of convergence.

Consider a set X of objects or variable manifestations and a sequence $x_1, x_2, \ldots, x_n, \ldots$ of those manifestations contained in X. When the elements of X can be measured, convergence is often defined in terms of ordinary Euclidean distance. That is, the sequence converges to x^* if, for every real number $\varepsilon > 0$, it is possible to go far enough out in the sequence so that the distance between x^* and any remaining term is smaller than ε. Although sets with many of the properties of Euclidean distance are easily specified even in cases where quantification is absent, a more general and transparent route is followed here.

Suppose the objects of X exhibit to varying degrees a particular property α. Introduce a reflexive and transitive ordering relation, ρ_α, among them indicating the extent to which each satisfies α.[12] Thus (x', x'') is in ρ_α if and only if x' displays property α at least as strongly as x''. To illustrate, the set of possible collections of human values discussed at the beginning of the previous section could be ordered to show which combinations of values make it easier for the individual to earn the respect of others in society. Since ρ_α is taken to be reflexive and transitive, it induces an equivalence relation[13] partitioning X into mutually exclusive and exhaustive equivalence classes. All elements within an equivalence class exhibit α to the same degree. In general, the existence of ρ_α implies neither ordinal nor cardinal measurement in the sense in which these terms are commonly used.[14]

Generally, any number of relevant properties might be identified during the course of an investigation. The collection of countable unions and finite intersections of all equivalence classes obtained from them defines a topology for X. In this context, the standard topological characterization of convergence applies: $x_1, x_2, \ldots, x_n, \ldots$ *converges* to x^* provided that for any set T containing x^* in the topology it is possible to go far enough out in the sequence for all remaining terms also to be in T. There are particular situations in which it might be desirable to think of convergence as "closeness" in the sense that, as n grows, x_n and x_{n+1} become more and more alike with respect to the relative strengths of the properties they exhibit.[15] But in any particular case, it is always possible that exceptions to such a rule may be present.

It should be noted that the use of sets of ordering relations defined over the same class of objects is not new in social science. Riker and Ordeshook [30, pp. 308–311] begin their discussion of voting with the assumption that on every issue the voter orders the collection of all candidates according to his feelings about the candidates' positions on that issue. For each issue, then, there is one ordering of candidates per voter. By contrast, Robinson [31] shows how orderings of a collection of archaeological deposits by the frequency of appearance of artifact types (one ordering for each type) can aid in determining the overall chronological order of the deposits. Clearly,

---

[12] Recall that ρ_α is *reflexive* if $x \rho_\alpha x$ for all x in X. It is *transitive* whenever, for all x', x'' and x''' in X, the pair $x' \rho_\alpha x''$ and $x'' \rho_\alpha x'''$ implies $x' \rho_\alpha x'''$.

[13] A reflexive and transitive relation ρ_α is an *equivalence relation* if it is also *symmetric*, that is, for all x' and x'' in X, if $x' \rho_\alpha x''$, then $x'' \rho_\alpha x'$.

[14] Only for the special case in which X is countable will there be an ordinal scale (see Pfanzagl [29]). Of course, the availability of ordinal numbers still does not legitimize the use of arithmetic operations in the usual way.

[15] For additional notions of closeness, see Katzner [22].

either set of orderings provides a framework within which closeness and convergence may be introduced and explored.

Returning to the problem of formulating stage (ii) dynamic structures, consider a simple periodic relation of the form

$$z_t = h(z_{t-1}, p). \tag{5.8}$$

Here z and p are, respectively, a variable and a parameter defined over some sets Z and P; the subscript t indicates time; and h is the symbolic name of the functional relation linking values of z in period $t - 1$ and the parameter to values of z in period t. Again, measurement of z and p are not required for the validity of (5.8). In stage (iii), the properties of z_t as time passes are of paramount interest. These properties emerge from those of h in (5.8). That is, given a starting point z_0, relation (5.8) generates a sequence or time path of values of z that reflects the relevant properties:

$$z_1 = h(z_0, p),$$

$$z_2 = h(h(z_0, p), p),$$

.

.

.

A path through $\bar{z}$ is *stationary* whenever

$$z_t = \bar{z},$$

for all t. Were relation (5.8) to start off at $\bar{z}$, it would merely reproduce $\bar{z}$ over and over again. The existence of stationary paths depends on whether or not a $\bar{z}$ can be found such that

$$\bar{z} = h(\bar{z}, p).$$

As in the previous section, if h has an inverse with respect to p, then

$$p = w(\bar{z}),$$

for an appropriate w. And if w is also invertible, $\bar{z}$ can be expressed as a function of parameter values. Therefore, under these conditions, one stationary path is associated with each value of p.

A stationary path is *globally stable* if all other time paths converge to it (in the sense defined above). Sufficient conditions ensuring convergence of individual paths can be obtained by adapting Liapunov's "second method" for analyzing stability properties of numerical differential equations. From this perspective, convergence requires the existence of a function relating z to the real numbers and having certain specific properties. The details are beyond the scope of the present discussion (Katzner [21, Sect. 5.2]).

These results are easily generalized to more complicated relations and systems of relations. Their use as an aid in understanding and explaining observed dynamic processes in quantitative areas of the social sciences is well known. The variety of models used to explore various aspects of economic growth provide numerous illustrations (see, for example, Allen [3] and recall the macroeconomic models of Kaldor and Kalecki noted earlier). As a further illustration in the quantified world, Goodwin's model is a continuous dynamic simultaneous equation model of the macroeconomy in which activity in the labor market generates a cyclical growth path for the economy. In his words [13, p. 442], "If real wages go up, profits go down; if profits go down, savings and investment lag, thus slowing up the creation of new jobs. But the labor force is continually growing both through natural increase and through men released by technological progress. The reserve army of labor grows, wages lag behind the growth of productivity, profits rise and accumulation is accelerated back up to a high level. This in turn gradually reduces unemployment, wages rise, and so it goes on, indefinitely." On the non-quantifiable level, Hagen's [14] description of a sequence of events affecting families that leads to the emergence of innovative personalities can be reduced to a periodic relation (Katzner [21, Ch. 10]).

It is worth ending this discussion of change over time with a brief reference to the multiplier analysis of quantitative macroeconomic theory. One interpretation runs as follows: Several fundamental relations (for example, the consumption function) determine an equilibrium level of income – that is, a stationary path – as a function of various parameters (autonomous investment, marginal propensity to consume, etc.). The actual time path of income emerges from a dynamic process with sufficient properties assumed to guarantee global stability. Hence, at any moment the economy is on a path converging to the equilibrium or stationary path. But before evolution can progress very far, parameters change and the equilibrium income level shifts. The actual path must, in the course of time, change direction and move toward the new equilibrium. Thus, from this perspective, the macroeconomic world is viewed in reference to a never-ending sequence of exogenous shifts in the stable stationary path, and an actual path that is somewhat behind but always trying to catch up.

The preceding analysis of the non-quantifiable suggests that such a conception of dynamic reality does not depend on the ability to measure. Stationary and actual paths can still be defined, and the former may be assumed globally stable. Transformations in the stationary path caused by parametric variation must, in light of the global stability, ultimately draw the actual path along with it. In the absence of further parameter changes, the end of the actual path, and hence its eventual direction, are known. There is no reason why non-quantifiable experience cannot be understood and policy formulated in these terms.

5.3 Optimization

Consider any collection X of manifestations of a variable x. To build a model requiring in stage (iii) the determination of a manifestation x in X that is maximal or minimal necessitates the specification of a criterion with respect to which maxima or minima are judged. Such a criterion has to be expressed in terms of an ordering relation defined among the manifestations of X. That ordering may or may not be reflected on a numerical scale. In either case, a maximum (or minimum) would be a manifestation appearing highest up (or, respectively, lowest down) in the ordering across the set X. Frequently, maximal manifestations, say, are required to be unique. To guarantee the existence of either maxima or a unique maximum, appropriate conditions have to be imposed on the underlying ordering.[16] The same principle applies to maximization or minimization under constraints since the presence of constraints only limits the set (to a subset of X) over which the ordering is relevant. Thus in regard to the Becker–Lewis constrained maximization of utility with respect to child quality criticized above, the difficulty cited could be eliminated by constructing a model with a preference ordering across verbally-described manifestations of child quality, forgetting about utility representations and scales on which child quality can be measured, and introducing enough assumptions on the preference ordering to ensure the existence of a unique, constrained, maximal manifestation.

5.4 Empirical Testing

As pointed out in Chapter 2, the formation of models as an aid in making real phenomena intelligible is all but useless without links to

---

[16] See Katzner [21, Sect. 5.4]. Uniqueness can be assured by, for example, assuming that the ordering is linear (i.e., reflexive, transitive, antisymmetric, and total).

the visible world. Some means for passing judgment on the model's empirical relevance is absolutely essential. If there were no way to check its assumptions or implications against actual observation, model building would be little more than a sterile mental exercise. This section focuses on stage (iv) empirical testing for the explanatory competence of models that admit to the possibility of such tests.[17] When calibration is possible, a wide variety of statistical procedures are available for the job. The following suggests the not-so-surprising fact that many of them are still applicable without it.

Informal checks of non-quantifiable assertions have been used in the past. Hagen [14], for example, compares his emergence-of-innovative-personalities sequence beginning with the loss of status by families, followed over subsequent generations by their heirs' retreatism, repression, and finally the emergence of creative personalities to the historical experience of England, Japan, Colombia, and so on. He is most successful, perhaps, with Japan. The pattern of Japanese history consists of cyclical oscillations between national integration and feudal disunion. Within the turmoil created by these fluctuations, influential lords were able to defend their status; the lesser elite could not. Hagen traces the retreatism of the latter elites and the ensuing appearance of innovative persons across the years. Most recently, the Tokugawa era (1660–1867) saw the declassing of samurai, merchants, and wealthy peasants. Their descendants seem to have played a major role in the nineteenth-century modernization of Japan.

As would be true even if numerical methods were employed, the correspondence between Hagen's theory and the historical record of Japan in and of itself proves nothing. It merely provides a bridge to real events, that is, in this case the comfort of consistency with experience – at least for Japan. By contrast, the remarkable economic development in Pakistan between 1947 and 1960 cannot be explained as a result of loss of status of certain groups. Thus, comforting consistency and empirical refutation are the two possibilities. Statistical analysis of quantifiable phenomena, with all of its power, can do no more. On the other hand, the advantages of formal procedures are not to be denied. They furnish specific criteria for acceptance or rejection of assertions that reflect precisely the confidence one might have of their empirical viability. In reaching for this sort of exactness, Hagen tries to establish a statistical association in early

---

[17] Recall that, as observed in Section 3.1, models such as the demand–supply model of price determination in an isolated market and the general equilibrium model of the microeconomy can typically not be tested for their explanatory competence.

twentieth-century Japan between being an economic innovator and being a descendant of one of the declassed groups. But his data are too sparse to be consequential.

A second illustration of empirical analysis of non-quantifiable phenomena appears in Katzner's [20] model within which the quality of life an individual leads is defined in terms of abstract, unobservable, and unquantified characteristics like security, freedom, and self-esteem, and related to observable career-living situations described by several sentences of prose. Through the administration of questionnaires to two small samples of subjects, he then empirically examines the potential consistency of the model with individual subjects' thought processes. That is, he successfully tests (in a very small sample) the possibility that people might actually be able to employ, if they do not already do so in rough approximation, such a model as the basis for thinking about, and evaluating their own qualities of life.

All formal statistical analysis rests on the theory of probability.[18] And it is well known that the sample space (written X) over which probability is defined does not need quantification. The single tossing of a coin is a classic example. With two outcomes, heads (H) and tails (T), the sample space is

$$x = \{H, T\}.$$

In the absence of bias, both H and T are assigned probability $1/2$. The density function is uniform and if, say, H were to come before T, according to some accepted ordering, the cumulative distribution could be found.

The same ideas apply in general with or without measurement of the elements of X. A probability function may be defined on the appropriate subsets of X in the usual manner. The standard notion of random variable mapping X into a not-necessarily-quantifiable set Y also carries over without alteration. The probability function on X then induces one on Y. Moreover, under certain conditions (which do not imply the existence of ordinal or interval scales), density and distribution functions may also be obtained (Katzner [21, Sect. 12.2]).

Even without measurement, density functions (when they exist) can still involve numerical parameters. Thus with $x = \{x', x''\}$ unquantified and $0 \le$

---

[18] In circumstances of non-probabilistic uncertainty, the concept of probability, of course, has no meaning. It therefore cannot arise analytically, and even an unquantified analytical representation of it, whatever that might be, cannot exist. An alternative way of handling uncertainty in the non-probabilistic-uncertainty context is with the notion of potential surprise (see p. 231).

$\theta \leq 1$, the density

$$f(x,\theta) = \begin{cases} \frac{1}{2}(1+\theta), & \text{if } x = x', \\ \\ \frac{1}{2}(1-\theta), & \text{if } x = x'', \end{cases}$$

depends on θ. In this context, a version of the Neyman–Pearson lemma may be proved, which justifies the ordinary hypothesis-testing procedure for choosing between two values of θ. Furthermore, when it is more appropriate to determine θ by estimation, the standard procedures also apply (Katzner [21, Sect. 12.3]).

Finally, there are non-parametric tests appropriate for various purposes. To test for the existence of a statistical relation between two variables, the rank or τ tests for independence may be employed. Rejection of the null hypothesis suggests a connection between the variables. In other contexts the test for statistical association (attempted inconclusively by Hagen) does the same thing.

5.5 Concluding Remark

In sum, economic inquiry does not require the introduction of questionable proxies and false measures to accommodate phenomena that do not appear to be easily represented on numerical scales. Without losing any of the rigor of mathematical argument, it is possible to treat the not quantifiable as non-quantifiable at all stages of the model-building process. For explanatory purposes, internally consistent static and dynamic models can be constructed, analyzed, and subjected to empirical tests. There is no excuse, then, for using false measures and proxies, and for setting aside important issues because it is difficult to see how the variables involved might reasonably be measured.

References

[1] Akerlof, G. A., "The Market for 'Lemons': Qualitative Uncertainty and the Market Mechanism," *Quarterly Journal of Economics* 84 (1970), pp. 488–500.

[2] Akerlof, G. A., "A Theory of Social Custom, of Which Unemployment May Be One Consequence," *Quarterly Journal of Economics* 94 (1980), pp. 749–775.

[3] Allen, R. G. D., *Macro-Economic Theory* (London: Macmillan, 1970).

[4] Apter, D. E., *The Politics of Modernization* (Chicago, IL: University of Chicago Press, 1965).

[5] Azzi, C. and R. Ehrenberg, "Household Allocation of Time and Church Attendance," *Journal of Political Economy* 83 (1975), pp. 27–56.

[6] Barro, R. J., "Economic Growth in a Cross Section of Countries," *Quarterly Journal of Economics* 106 (1991), pp. 407–443.

[7] Becker, G. S. and H. G. Lewis, "On the Interaction between the Quantity and Quality of Children," *Journal of Political Economy* 81, no. 2, Pt. 1 (March/April, 1973), pp. s279–s288.

[8] Boulding, K. E., *Human Betterment* (Beverly Hills: Sage, 1985).

[9] Currie, M. and I. Steedman, "Taking Effort Seriously," *Metroeconomica* 44 (1993), pp. 134–145.

[10] Eckstein, A. (ed.), *Comparative Economic Systems* (Berkeley, CA: University of California Press, 1971).

[11] Fair, R. C., "A Theory of Extramarital Affairs," *Journal of Political Economy* 86 (1978), pp. 45–61.

[12] Goodenough, W. H., *Cooperation in Change* (New York: Wiley, 1966).

[13] Goodwin, R. M., "A Growth Cycle," in *A Critique of Economic Theory: Selected Readings*, E. K. Hunt and J. G. Schwartz, eds., (Harmondsworth: Penguin, 1972), pp. 442–449.

[14] Hagen, E., *On the Theory of Social Change* (Chicago: Dorsey, 1962).

[15] Hayek, F. A., "The Pretence of Knowledge," Nobel Memorial Lecture, December, 1974. Reprinted in *American Economic Review* 79, no. 6 (December, 1989 – membership survey issue), pp. 3–7.

[16] Helliwell, J. F. and R. D. Putnam, "Economic Growth and Social Capital in Italy," *Eastern Economic Journal* 21 (1995), pp. 295–307.

[17] Homans, G. C., "Contemporary Theory in Sociology," in R. E. L. Faris (ed.), *Handbook of Modern Sociology* (Chicago, IL: Rand McNally, 1946).

[18] Kalt, J. P. and M. A. Zupan, "Capture and Ideology in the Economic Theory of Politics," *American Economic Review* 74 (1984), pp. 279–300.

[19] Katzner, D. W., "Political Structure and System and the Notion of Logical Completeness," *General Systems* 14 (1969), pp. 169–171. Reprinted in D. W. Katzner, *Unmeasured Information and the Methodology of Social Scientific Inquiry* (Boston, MA: Kluwer, 2001), Essay 13.

[20] Katzner, D. W., *Choice and the Quality of Life* (Beverly Hills: Sage, 1979).

[21] Katzner, D. W., *Analysis Without Measurement* (Cambridge: Cambridge University Press, 1983).

[22] Katzner, D. W., "Notions of Closeness in a Non-Quantifiable Setting," *Social Science Research* 17 (1988), pp. 1–18. Reprinted in D. W. Katzner, *Unmeasured Information and the Methodology of Social Scientific Inquiry* (Boston, MA: Kluwer, 2001), Essay 5.

[23] Katzner, D. W., "The Misuse of Measurement in Economics," *Metroeconomica* 49 (1998), pp. 1–22. Reprinted in D. W. Katzner, *Unmeasured Information and the Methodology of Social Scientific Inquiry* (Boston: Kluwer, 2001), Essay 8.

[24] Katzner, D. W., *Unmeasured Information and the Methodology of Social Scientific Inquiry* (Boston, MA: Kluwer, 2001).

[25] Katzner, D. W., *An Introduction to the Economic Theory of Market Behavior: Microeconomics from a Walrasian Perspective* (Cheltenham: Elgar, 2006).

[26] Katzner, D. W., "Ordinal Utility and the Traditional Theory of Consumer Demand," *Real-World Economic Review*, Issue 67 (May, 2014), pp. 130–136.

[27] Pareto, V., *The Mind and Society*, A. Bongiorno and A. Livingston, trans. (New York: Dover, 1935).

[28] Parsons, T., *The Structure of Social Action* (2 vols.), 2nd ed. (New York: Free Press, 1968).

[29] Pfanzagl, J., *Theory of Measurement*, 2nd ed. (Würzburg/Vienna: Physica-Verlag, 1971).

[30] Riker, W. H., and P. C. Ordeshook, *An Introduction to Positive Political Theory* (Englewood Cliffs, NJ: Prentice-Hall, 1973).

[31] Robinson, W. S., "A Method for Chronologically Ordering Archaeological Deposits," *American Antiquity* 16 (1951), pp. 293–301.

[32] Shackle, G. L. S., *Epistemics and Economics: A Critique of Economic Doctrines* (Cambridge: Cambridge University Press, 1972).

[33] Thomson, Sir W. (Baron Kelvin), "Electrical Units of Measurement," in *Popular Lectures and Addresses* v. 1 (London: Macmillan, 1891), pp. 80–143.

6

Issues Relating to the Construction of Models from Scratch[1]

In this and the following chapter, the threads of preceding discussion will be brought together to throw light on the actual construction of an explanatory model. Recall that in Chapters 2 and 3 model construction was conceived of in terms of five successive steps or stages: (i) formulate an initial image of the subject of inquiry; (ii) develop a preliminary model based on that image; (iii) operationalize the model; (iv) empirically test the model when appropriate; and (v) judge the model's cogency and relevance. Although model building can begin at stage (iii) as long as the first two stages have already been completed in some other venue, the present chapter considers in greater detail the process of construction that is associated with the first two stages. This will often involve the extraction of variables and relations among them from the amorphous reality of the observed phenomenon under investigation. That extraction requires considerations relating to the manner of abstraction that are both subtle and fundamental to the outcome of the inquiry. Chapter 7 will provide a concrete illustration of the full construction process.

To see what is involved, consider the distinction between arithmomorphic and dialectical concepts due to Georgescu-Roegen [4, pp. 43–47]. First, in certain cases, the human mind is perfectly capable of sharply delineating the boundaries of an idea. The result is an *arithmomorphic* concept. Such concepts, regardless of whether or not they are quantified, have the property that they can be clearly distinguished and separated from all others. They are distinctly discrete and there is no overlap

---

between them and their opposites. The velocity of a moving object is an arithmomorphic concept as is the weight of a pot of water and the length of a train. When measures are not available, non-quantifiable ideas such as the notion of a human being or a country, also have expressions in arithmomorphic form. An arithmomorphic representation of the former is so-called economic man.

On the other hand, there are concepts whose boundaries human powers seem unable to clearly and precisely define. Exact characterizations are either arbitrary in that they do not conform to standard notions or are extraordinarily difficult to employ. Where, for example, does one quality of experience leave off and another begin? Democracy and non-democracy are two different ideas, each with a variety of shades of meaning and, what is more important, with certain shades of democracy overlapping certain shades of non-democracy. Concepts such as these may be referred to as *dialectical*. Dialectical notions are distinct, though not, as their arithmomorphic counterparts, discretely so. Each is surrounded by its own penumbra of meanings. Any dialectical concept is distinguishable from all others (including its opposite), since no two penumbras, although possibly overlapping, can be identical. But, although impossible with arithmomorphic concepts, a country can be both a democracy and a non-democracy at the same time.

Now models, as they usually appear in economics, are clearly based on arithmomorphic concepts. In relation to the five-stage process of model construction envisaged here, such models are created in stage (ii) and manipulated in stage (iii) according to rules that are well known to economists. But in dialectical contexts, since a thing can be both A and not A at the same time, the same formal manipulative rules for constructions and deductions in terms of models do not apply. In particular, deductive logic can not be employed because it requires the discrete distinction of the objects on which it operates. One may still, however, make assumptions and reason with dialectical ideas, as the following passage due to Russell shows:

Not only are we aware of particular yellows, but if we have seen a sufficient number of yellows and have sufficient intelligence, we are aware of the universal *yellow*; this universal is the subject in such judgements as "yellow differs from blue" or "yellow resembles blue less than green does." And the universal yellow is the predicate in such judgements as "this is yellow".

(Russell [12, p. 12])

Dialectical reasoning can be checked in at least two ways (Georgescu-Roegen [4, p. 337]). The first is by use of the ancient Socratic method:

systematic questioning of all aspects of argument. The second is by working through arithmomorphic similes. Dialectical reasoning can often be likened to various arithmomorphic arguments, although none of these test arguments is ever capable of replacing the original in its entirety. Error uncovered by either the Socratic method or the employment of deductive logic in an arithmomorphic simile clearly casts doubt on the original dialectical reasoning. But even though it provides a certain comfort and satisfaction, a lack of detection of error does not imply correctness.

In stage (i) of model building as previously specified, the phenomenon under investigation is observed, an initial image of it is formulated, and what appear to be its significant and relevant characteristics are noted. Of course, this initial image depends on the objective the investigator has in mind. Three possibilities were described in Chapter 2: Interest could center merely on developing an explanation of how a particular phenomenon might be structured. In that case, the image will encapsulate in a preliminary way the means by which certain elements abstracted by the investigator's perception of the phenomenon may be represented, and how they relate to each other or fit together. Alternatively, if attention relates to observed outcomes in a single- or multi-outcome framework, the image emerges from the kinds of considerations set out on pp. 35–39 that arise from observing economic behavior or the consequences of that behavior. Because economic phenomena are not primarily physical objects and generally have to do with human decision making, elements related to the decisions made, and the decision-makers' consequent behavior, this image and these characteristics are necessarily dialectical in nature. In actuality, for example and as observed earlier, there is usually no such thing as the single, unique price of a good.[2] Rather, any commodity usually has an entire penumbra of prices at which it is sold. Moreover, because of the great variety of forms in which commodities normally can be produced, the line marking the "end" of one commodity and the "start" of another is often difficult to determine. Thus in saying that certain goods are sold in certain markets at certain prices, the underlying conceptual referents of "goods," "markets," and "prices" are purely dialectical. Other examples of dialectical concepts are the preferences of an individual, the technology of production, and the various forms of competition that may appear in markets, etc.

In moving from stage (i) to stage (ii), model building in economics abstracts from such concepts to secure discretely distinct (arithmomorphic) notions that are then converted into variables. The variety and

---

[2] See also Bausor [1] and Mirowski [10].

richness of having such things as multiple prices and commodity variations are lost as the former is reduced to a single price and the latter is conflated to a single generic commodity. And it is in reference to these kinds of variables and concepts that the relations of models are defined and manipulated. As will be seen in this chapter, the relations themselves may be viewed as abstractions from underlying dialectical processes. In this sense, models in economics may be described as arithmomorphic similes extracted from a dialectical base.

6.1 Arithmomorphic Abstraction

Consider a dialectical idea such as the price of good x, and suppose, in stage (ii), the arithmomorphic notion of the price of x is drawn from it. Suppose further that the arithmomorphic price of x is permitted to range over all non-negative real numbers. Thus the arithmomorphic variable called "price of x" is obtained. An arithmomorphic variable, then, is defined by extracting an arithmomorphic concept from a dialectical one and specifying the collection of discretely distinct realizations or values that the concept may possess.

Although the variable "price of x" is quantitative, there is nothing in the construction of an arithmomorphic variable requiring that measurement be possible. For present purposes it is worth providing an illustration, in addition to that of Chapter 5, of a non-quantified arithmomorphic variable. From the dialectical notion of the form of competition in the market for x, extract an arithmomorphic counterpart as follows: On 3-by-5 cards, say, write down descriptions of each of the various forms of competition that may appear in the market for x – one description on each card. Take these descriptions to be discretely distinct even though the prose on each card may appear to be imprecise and not well defined. Assume that the relevant group of investigators agrees that this collection of descriptions is appropriate for the purpose at hand. Then the arithmomorphic variable "form of competition in the market for x" may be defined as that which takes on as values the description on each of the 3-by-5 cards in the collection. The variable "values that a human being might hold" described in Chapter 5 could be thought of in these terms. Another example of such a variable (and one employed in the next chapter) is the (set of) activities in which an employee engages while at work. Each of its variable values, too, may be thought of as a description written on a 3-by-5 card.

The question of whether the 3-by-5 cards in a given collection of variable values can be supplanted by numbers that meaningfully measure the descriptions on them in some way is a separate matter. Answering it requires formalisms that are entirely different from those employed in the analysis of the particular economic phenomena under scrutiny. Measuring the descriptions on 3-by-5 cards implies that all of the important and relevant information on the cards is encapsulated in certain abstract properties, and that the specific form in which those properties arise in the description on any one card permits that card to be replaced by a single number, or vector of numbers, conveying the same information as on the card.[3] For example, if each card described a person of a certain "oldness," and if oldness were all that mattered, then a number representing the age of the person described could possibly be substituted for the description on the card. The formal conditions under which such replacement is valid in general are complex. To be able to measure ordinally, say, requires the presence of a reflexive, transitive, and total ordering relation defined among the 3-by-5 cards such that the interval topology, based on the equivalence classes generated by this ordering, has a countable base. The details and the requisites for other forms of measurement are not considered here.[4] Suffice it to say that the more information on the card that is not reflected by the number assigned to the card, and the more the extraneous information entrapped by the number itself, the less meaningful the measure. Thus the price of x is not a good measure of the quality of the commodity x since the price of x contains information having nothing to do with the quality of x, and there are many aspects of the quality of x that need not be mirrored in its price. In any case, it has already been noted that measurement is not a prerequisite of model building, and none is assumed in present discussion. Arithmomorphic variable values then, are generally viewed as descriptions on 3-by-5 cards that are discrete and distinct, and may or may not be meaningfully represented numerically.

Suppose now that the variables and relations of a model have been distilled in stage (ii) from their dialectical foundations of stage (i). (The actual extraction of arithmomorphic relations from a dialectical base, which may constitute part of the process of moving from stage (i) to stage (ii), will be considered in the next two sections.) Several issues concerning the properties of the spaces of variable values, the meaning of the relations defined on them, and the apparatus for the manipulation of these relations still have to be discussed. In the next few paragraphs each is considered in turn.

---

[3] An expanded discussion may be found in Katzner [6, Sec. 2.2].
[4] See, for example, Pfanzagl [11].

Specification of spaces of variable values (the sets over which the variables range) and the properties these spaces are to possess is one of the important elements in proceeding from stage (i) to stage (ii). Indeed, Hofstadter [5, pp. 611–613] has suggested that the proper choices in this regard may be crucial to the solution of many real problems. Economists, however, have tended to ignore the issue. When variables are quantifiable, the relevant spaces are almost always taken to be Euclidean. Other possibilities are seldom considered, notwithstanding the proven usefulness of non-Euclidean spaces for analyzing the physical world. As of now, non-quantifiable spaces have hardly been employed in formal analysis in economics, and there is still much to learn about them. One specification of such a space has been given by Katzner [6, Sects. 3.2 and 3.3]. In any case, the specification of the space over which a variable ranges contains implicit theoretical statements about the characteristics of the variable itself.

Also implicit in the specification of spaces and their properties are conventions for the stage (iii) manipulation of the variable values. The weakest convention possible is a scheme for classification. Somewhat stronger is the designation of order, that is, the imposition of an ordering relation among the elements of the space.[5] Thus in the example of the next chapter, values of the variable "activities in which a worker engages while on the job" could be classified by certain "rule sets" and ordered according to their impact on output. With enough quantification present, the arithmetic operations of addition, subtraction, multiplication, and division provide still further manipulative tools.

It should also be noted that although an infinite number of descriptions on 3-by-5 cards can never be written down, infinite collections (both countable and uncountable) of such cards can certainly be imagined. Economists and other social scientists do so all the time (Katzner [6, Sec. 7.2]). Infinite sets of non-quantifiable elements may be accepted in the same sense that infinite sets of numbers are employed in quantitative contexts: Since human limitations render it impossible ever to obtain more than a finite number of observations on any variable, such sets exist only in the minds of investigators and have no basis in reality. In this way, the set of all values of the variable "activities in which a worker engages while on the job" is thought of as a possibly uncountable set in the model of the next chapter.

---

[5] As previously suggested, specification of order alone does not, in general, imply (ordinal) measurement as the term is commonly used (Pfanzagl [11, pp. 75,79]).

Turning to the stage (ii) relational structures of models, arithmomorphic relations among arithmomorphic variables are frequently expressed as mathematical functions. And, recall from the previous chapter, the definition of function does not rely on measurement: Let x and y be two variables defined over sets called, respectively, the domain and range. (These may actually be vectors of variables such as $x = (x_1, \ldots, x_J)$ and $y = (y_1, \ldots, y_I)$.) Then the function f, often written as

$$y = f(x), \tag{6.1}$$

is a rule which assigns to each element of the domain a unique element in the range. The extraction of such a function from the dialectical base out of which it is formed is considered in Section 6.3. When x and y are not quantifiable, f is defined by listing the value of y that is associated with each of a finite number of values of x.[6] This is the meaning of the functions involving non-quantified variables in the model of the next chapter. In the full measurement case, f may be characterized by listing a finite number of associations between values of y and values of x, or by summarizing them in Equation (6.1) and specifying the properties of f, or in a specific formula such as

$$y = f(x) = x + 2.$$

In the latter two instances, an infinite number of pairs (x, y) are typically accounted for.

Suppose, for a moment, that a particular expression of (6.1) has been proposed as a stage (ii) function for a model representing some real phenomenon that is thought of for analytical purposes as unchanging over time. Now it can not be claimed that every person is committed to that expression as relevant for representing for all time the reality in question. Individuals are always free to choose the functions they think are suitable at each encounter. Different persons can come up with different interpretations and different stage (i) visions of the phenomenon, and hence different variables, different variable definitions, and different functional relations to describe the same thing. Moreover, there is no reason why someone could not invoke one function today and employ an entirely different one tomorrow. This is because each individual interprets reality and creates his stage (i) vision by making inductive inferences from past

---

[6] In spite of the fact that infinite sets of unquantified variable values can be conceived, functions of unquantified variables can only be defined with respect to a finite number of them.

experience. These understandings are one's own and can never be conveyed to another. For two persons to arrive at the same interpretation and vision, then, they must have the same experiences and must make the same inferences from them – an unlikely occurrence in the absence of negotiation or similar training. And for a single individual to maintain through time a specific function or model as appropriate, his own experiences in the interim have to be sufficiently neutral for him to perceive no significant alteration in the real phenomenon in question and his original vision. The upshot is that the arithmomorphic relations (quantified or unquantified) of any model are always subject to modifications and replacements, and such is the case even if the dialectical foundation from which they spring were to remain constant. Thus the analysis of a given phenomenon by two independent persons or at two separate times can not guarantee the same conclusions in advance. Model building, then, can not be said to provide an absolute standard against which the conclusions of other types of analyses can be compared.

It remains, in this section, to consider the rules that are employed in stage (iii) for manipulating the relations of models. These rules turn on the principles of deductive logic. Although deductive logic has no relevance in the underlying dialectical base of the analysis, its force upon application in arithmomorphic abstractions is well known.

The most fundamental operation that can be performed on functions is composition or elimination of variables by substitution introduced in the previous chapter. Recall that two functions f and g, say

$$y = f(x) \qquad \text{and} \qquad x = g(z),$$

may be combined into h by eliminating x:

$$y = h(z),$$

where

$$h(z) = f(g(z))$$

and h is referred to as the composition of f and g. To be useful, function composition must exhibit two characteristics: It must be closed, that is, the composites it produces must always be functions, and it must be associative.[7] The simplest algebraic structure conforming to these

---

[7] For example, if $w = e(y)$, $y = f(x)$, and $x = g(z)$ are three functions, then associativity of function composition means that eliminating first y and then x gives the same result as eliminating x first and then y.

properties is called a *semigroup*.[8] Hence the least that can be postulated about the functions of a model is that they are elements of a semigroup under function composition.[9]

Additional techniques for manipulating functions may also be introduced. Inverting functions to obtain inverses (as described in the previous chapter) and partial inverses is a possibility (Katzner [6, Ch. 4]). In the quantifiable case, functions may also be added, subtracted, multiplied, divided, differentiated, integrated, and so on. Clearly, each insertion of a new manipulative rule complicates the algebraic structure required to support the model.

It should be emphasized that the postulation of a semigroup structure does not imply the presence of ordinal, cardinal, or ratio measures. First of all, the conditions for the existence of such measures are not all met by semigroup structures. And second, the functions of the semigroup may express the substantive relations of the model rather than the relations required for the construction of numerical scales. Thus the convenience of numerical representations, with their attendant arithmetic tools of manipulation, is not necessarily available. What is at hand are the discrete variable values and the functions relating them, the operation of composition for manipulating functions which is closed and associative, plus any other elements such as inverses that may be introduced for analytical purposes. All dialectical facets of thought have been exorcised.

6.2 Time and Change

As far as human capacity to sense nature is concerned, there is no such thing as an "instant of time." Rather, time is perceived as a series of imprecise and overlapping durations in which the future becomes the inexactly felt present and then slips into the past. It is a dialectical concept (Georgescu-Roegen [4, pp. 69–72]). The idea of instants of time (or discretely distinct time periods) all lined up one after the other is an arithmomorphic abstraction. It permits identification of the linear continuum as the standard reference for keeping track of the movement of time. The use of dynamic equations (differential or otherwise, thought of in reference to either logical or historical time[10]) in models depends on it.

---

[8] A semigroup is a nonempty set on which a closed and associative operation has been defined.

[9] See Mirowski [10].

[10] The distinction between logical and historical time noted in Chapter 1 occurs at the arithmomorphic level after abstracting the notion of time from its dialectical base.

Time and change are tightly interwoven; one can hardly be discerned without the other. Change, unobservable at an instant of time, is capable of detection only over durations. Although the distinction between sameness and change rests ultimately in the beholder, judgments as to whether a change has actually occurred turn on the relation of the thing in question to its "other." Change can only appear in contrast to the environment in which it is set. And because there are no clear-cut boundaries delineating where it begins and ends, change, like time, is dialectical in character (Georgescu-Roegen [4, pp. 63,69]).

One way of describing change at stage (i) of model building is with the notion of process (Georgescu-Roegen [4, pp. 213–215]). A process involves something happening, i.e., certain events or alterations taking place over time within the milieu of a wider class of happenings. Each process is defined by the subset of happenings that make it up. All remaining events constitute the process environment. The process itself can be understood only in the context of the relationship between the happenings that constitute the process and its environment. These two collections of occurrences dialectically overlap each other.

To extract an arithmomorphic analytical representation of a given process and move to stage (ii), that is, to reduce change to motion or displacement as described earlier, an arithmomorphic boundary partitioning reality is drawn between the process and its environment. (Figure 6.1 provides a schematic illustration.) Included in this boundary is a specification of the finite (arithmomorphic) period of time over which the process is considered. Neither occurrences entirely within the process nor entirely within its environment can be seen. Only arithmomorphic objects crossing the boundary that remain unchanged over time as they cross are capable of observation. Thus the analytical representation of the process consists of the record of boundary crossings over the interval of time in question. Elements crossing from the environment to the process are called *inputs*; those passing from the process to the environment are *outputs*. (In Figure 6.1, only one input arrow and one output arrow are drawn. These are intended to represent schematically all inputs into and outputs from the process.)

Observe that in taking the arithmomorphic analytical representation of a process to be an arithmomorphic record of boundary crossings, all intentions of analyzing what goes on within the process must be given up. Of course, it is always possible to peer "inside" the process by drawing a second arithmomorphic boundary and dividing the original process into two subprocesses, so that the output of one subprocess provides part or all of the input for the other. (In Figure 6.2, subprocess II receives input

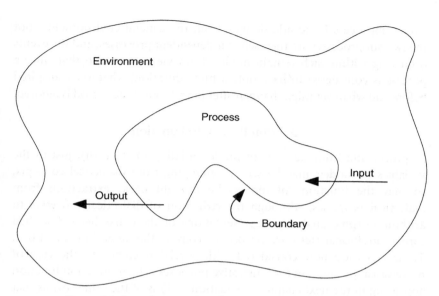

Figure 6.1. Boundary crossings for a process and its environment

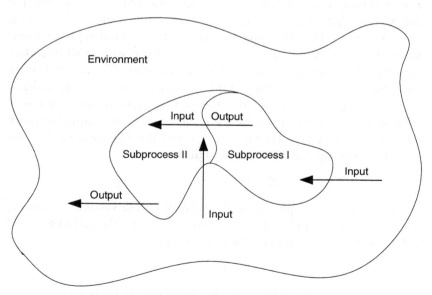

Figure 6.2. Boundary crossings with two subprocesses

from subprocess I and additionally from the general environment.) But the two subprocesses are themselves independent processes, and the events occurring within each remain hidden from view. Note also that since a process is considered to have only a finite duration, whatever transpired before and whatever might happen after the relevant time period is ignored.

6.3 From Process to Function

In proceeding from stage (i) of model building to stage (ii), just as the variables of models may be seen as emerging from dialectical concepts, so may the functions of models be thought of as extractions from dialectical processes. Although the reduction of dialectical processes to arithmomorphic analytical representations of them has been described earlier, additional steps are needed to convert the latter into functions. These steps are now considered with special reference to the case of neoclassical production for illustrative purposes. The production function appearing in the next chapter as equation (7.1) is of the same sort as that derived here.

Let an arithmomorphic analytical representation of a dialectical process be given and suppose the interval of duration is $\{t : 0 \leq t \leq t^0\}$, where t is a real (arithmomorphic) variable representing time. (It is often convenient to use the term "process" synonymously with its arithmomorphic analytical representation.) Thus the process (that is, its analytical representation) starts at $t = 0$ and ends at $t = t^0$. The first step is to thin all boundary crossings to not-necessarily-quantifiable arithmomorphic entities. If there are J distinct arithmomorphic input-boundary-crossing variables indexed by $j = 1, \dots, J$, and if $x_j(t)$ denotes the value of input variable j at time t (that is, an input boundary crossing at t), then the vector of input boundary crossings at t is $x(t) = [x_1(t), \dots, x_J(t)]$, and the collection of all input boundary crossings for the duration of the process is

$$X = \{x(t) : 0 \leq t \leq t^0\}.$$

Similarly, with $y_i(t)$ representing the value of output variable i at time t, where $i = 1, \dots, I$, and with $y(t) = [y_1(t), \dots, y_I(t)]$ the complete set of output boundary crossings for the process appears as

$$Y = \{y(t) : 0 \leq t \leq t^0\}.$$

The pair (X, Y) is one arithmomorphic description of the process.

The arithmomorphic representation of a process as the culmination of all input and output boundary crossings encompasses several special instances that are worthy of brief mention (see Georgescu-Roegen [4, pp. 215–217]). To begin with, some inputs might enter the process and, like catalysts in a chemical reaction, subsequently exit without noticeable change. This can be captured by the statement that

$$y_i(t+k) = x_j(t),$$

for appropriate i and j, and some positive real number k. In another instance, some entering inputs could be completely "used up" by the process and never exit as outputs, while certain exiting outputs produced by the process may have no counterpart as entering inputs. Lastly, inputs might be modified or only partially used up by the process, and hence exit in a somewhat different form from that in which they entered. Here the entering inputs may be regarded as different variables from the exiting outputs. These special cases find illustration in the production process of growing corn, in which land is often described as an input that is unchanged by the process; rain as an input that is completely used up; ears of corn as an output that does not appear as an input; and an entering spade that exits with increased wear, an input that is modified by the process.

It is also possible in a production process to divide inputs into two categories (Georgescu-Roegen [4, pp. 219–234]): those that are flows per unit of time (such as seed and fertilizer in the corn example) and those that are "agents" that use or act on the flows (like labor and shovels). One might also wish to recognize the differences between stocks and flows. But such distinctions are not worth pursuing in the present discussion.

Of course, a process need not always be depicted by the same pair (X, Y), although only one pair can be observed for every process. Conceptually, for any given process, different input values of the same variables at the same times – that is, different sequences of input boundary crossings – would generally give rise to different sequences of output boundary crossings or output variable values. Let $\mathcal{X}$ be the set of all conceivable sequences, X, of input variable values, and $\mathcal{Y}$ be the collection of all possible sequences, Y, of output variable values. Then the complete arithmomorphic analytical representation of the process is the collection of ordered pairs $f(X, Y)$, where X is in $\mathcal{X}$, Y is in $\mathcal{Y}$, and the ordered pair (X, Y) is in $f(X, Y)$ provided that Y is the unique output sequence when X is the input sequence. (In reference to the neoclassical production function, it would be necessary to add a condition of efficiency or maximization in the specification of f.) If relations such as f are to be the functions employed in a model, then the distillation from the original dialectical process stops here.

Otherwise, the next step in reducing a process to a function such as the typical production function is to focus attention on one of the output variables and ignore all others. Dropping the subscript on y, let $y(t)$ now represent the value of the selected output variable at time t. Define Y as before but now with respect to the scalar $y(t)$. Keep $x(t)$ and X without change and write f in its more typical functional form

$$Y = f(X).$$

However, f is not the same sort of function that is usually employed in economic analysis. That is because X and Y actually contain, respectively, vectors of functions of t and a (scalar) function of t. These functions are denoted by the previously introduced symbols $x(t)$ and $y(t)$. Thus f is really a mapping of functions x into a single function y, or

$$y = f(x),$$

where the functional argument t, though present, has been excluded to simplify notation (Georgescu-Roegen [4, p. 236]).

Occasionally, these kinds of functions are taken as the stage (ii) relations in models by economists. More often, however, ordinary functions are employed, as is usually the case when focusing on production. The final step in securing the latter kind of function is to make assumptions about the nature of the $x(t)$ and $y(t)$. Indeed, appropriate specification of $\mathcal{X}$ and $\mathcal{Y}$ is capable of turning f into either static or dynamic form. If, for example, it were supposed that

$$x(t) = x(t') \qquad \text{and} \qquad y(t) = y(t'),$$

for all t and t', and for all $x(t)$ in $\mathcal{X}$ and $y(t)$ in $\mathcal{Y}$, then all functions $x(t)$ and $y(t)$ are constant functions, and the function f becomes an ordinary function of (not-necessarily-quantifiable) arithmomorphic variables that are independent of time. This may also be written as

$$y = f(x),$$

where x and y are now interpreted as ordinary time-independent vector and scalar variables.

It is clear, then, that the arithmomorphic functions typically employed by economists in models may be viewed as extractions from dynamic, dialectical processes. Following the above mentioned path in the case of neoclassical production, the initial process is diluted to a static, technical structure that merely indicates possible (efficient) ways to combine inputs into outputs. Evidently, the deletion of time precludes serious discussion of change.

6.4 Limits and Power

It is worth concluding this chapter with a few comments about the limits and power of model building as explanation in economics. In regard to the former and confirming the "falsity" of models described in Section 3.3, it is clear that the results obtained by building a model are necessarily somewhat removed from actual life. There is no way to avoid this. Deviation from reality necessarily derives from the loss of stage (i) dialectical content required for the construction of stage (ii) arithmomorphic models. A portion of this loss is a consequence of the fact that only certain very specific elements of the characteristics of the phenomenon at issue and the stage (i) vision are captured in the arithmomorphic variables employed. All remaining variable-type characteristics of dialectical reality are forfeited. Recall the earlier example that the market price of a good is an abstraction from the many different prices of the good that appear in a variety of different venues. Moreover, additional losses of dialectical content emerge from the extraction of stage (ii) arithmomorphic functions from stage (i) processes. As an illustration, a production function usually involves abstractions from many different kinds of labor and the fact that the quality of labor that individuals provide can vary from day to day. Still further losses come from such abstractions as the representation of the driving force behind human economic behavior as, say, maximization. Since every one of these abstractions is at least a little arbitrary, and since none of them can be verified as the "true" appropriate representation of reality, the model is, to a degree, capricious and some distance away from describing and explaining the actual phenomenon. It is not only that the specific assumptions of some models are better than others. Rather, it is that all such sets of assumptions (each of which serves as the basis for a separate model) are constrained by the greater-or-lesser arbitrariness imposed so as to be able to build models in the first place.

Note that measurement is not at issue here. The same problem of the relationship of the real world to the constructs, axioms, and implications of a model turns up regardless of whether or not the variables employed may legitimately be represented by numbers. Limits on the meaningfulness and appropriateness of certain numerical quantifications are certainly not the same thing as limits on the use of models. However, to the extent that arbitrariness in quantification is present, such limits have to be taken into account. Thus, in addition to questioning the appropriateness of the abstractions of a particular model, it is also possible to ask about the appropriateness of using abstract measures in the investigation of actuality.

A second limitation of model building as explanation in economics is derived from the previously discussed fact that demonstrating the existence of solutions of the static or dynamic equations of a model establishes the abstract existence of such entities in the model but can never establish the existence of such entities in reality. Recall, for example, to show the existence of equilibrium in a model of a market is not to demonstrate the existence of equilibrium in a real market. Economists often fill such a gap between what is shown to exist in a model and what is seen to exist in reality by interpreting the latter as the former. In other words, the market price and quantity abstracted from the dialectical base that would be "observed" by looking at an actual market at any moment would be identified as an equilibrium in a model of the market determined by the interaction of demand and supply.[11] This, then, permits the assertion that the model explains what is seen.

Thus, to the extent that a model derives and employs abstract entities such as equilibrium, interpretation of these entities is often essential if the links between the model and actuality, i.e., the bridges mentioned earlier, are to be established. Neither the model itself nor the real phenomenon under investigation typically gives clues or standards for determining what these interpretations should be. And of course, different interpretations may yield different explanations of the same thing. The arbitrariness of interpretation, then is a significant limitation on the use of model building as explanation in economics.

In addition to the above limitations, model building also faces the problem noted above that the meanings of the relations of a model are not absolute and unchanging over time: One is not committed to the same understandings of them each moment they come up.

It should be emphasized that all of these limitations emerge solely from the particular discipline that model building imposes on our thought processes. Thus the issue in stage (v) of the relevance of a model in understanding and explaining economic reality derives, in part, from the things that have to be thrown out, the concessions that have to be made, and the arbitrariness that has to be imposed in order to proceed from

---

[11] Recall the discussion on pp. 42–43. As pointed out there, there are other well-known interpretations. For example, the observations may be thought of as lying on a "dynamic" time path that is converging to equilibrium.

dialectical foundations and arrive at the abstractions of stage (ii) where the formal building of a model can begin. A particular reason for caution over the significance of the relations of a model may be attributed to the abstraction procedure, which results in functions that are deceptively well defined. Lastly, the frequent necessity for interpretation of entities shown to exist emerges from the development of the model required in stages (ii) and (iii) as a basis for achieving explanation.

Finally, apart from understanding and explanation, what can be said in favor of the use of model building in economics? To be sure, model building may always be employed in constructing arithmomorphic similes to look for error in dialectical reasoning. But it also has a broader application in the building of arithmomorphic metaphors or analogies to understand and explain dialectical experience. Recall that metaphors and analogies in economics serve as both an instrument of thought and as a device for communicating meaning (McCloskey [9]). Their force lies in that they transfer the sense of one person's vision to another. They are figures of communication in which one thing, say thing *A*, is compared to a different thing, call it thing *B*, by speaking of *A* as if it were, or as if it were something like, *B*. Thus, for example, a market operates as if to equate demand and supply. Economic analysis is heavily metaphorical and analogical, and model building provides one way of developing metaphors and analogies.

And these metaphors and analogies are powerful – powerful in a larger sense than, as described in Chapter 2, an ability to explain in detail. They permit an analyst to focus his thoughts in a concrete and precise fashion on variables and relations that seem important by current professional standards.[12] Models and the conclusions drawn from them often constitute an "ideal type" or mental construction that isolates what are thought to be "fundamental" forces of reality for study by themselves in the absence of the "secondary" and still less important forces also thought to be present.[13] Hence the investigator can gain an understanding of the ideal system functioning alone as a "first step" in his exploration of reality.

The metaphors and analogies also provide standards for judging real-world behaviors; that is, for example, standards for deciding whether actual firm or consumer behavior could be, in fact, maximizing. Lastly, the metaphors and analogies are relatively easy for those who wish to

---

[12] Current professional standards are determined by a complex social and historical interaction exhibited in the work of present and past economists involving, in part, the techniques of analysis themselves.

[13] This, of course, is Mäki's position on the admisibility of "false" models described in Section 3.3.

pursue similar analyses within the model building framework to modify and extend as new techniques, new concepts, and new assumptions are introduced.

But model metaphors and model analogies are still extractions from dialectical perceptions of reality. They are abstract. They often contain entities shown to exist in the model that serve as the basis for the interpretation of reality. And so on. Hence such metaphors and analogies can only be regarded as very crude "approximations" of the real world. Marshall was similarly circumspect in his view of the demand–supply analysis of an isolated market:

> The theory of ... equilibrium ... of demand and supply helps indeed to give definiteness to our ideas; and in its elementary stages it does not diverge from the actual facts of life, so far as to prevent its giving a fairly trustworthy picture of the chief methods of action of the strongest and most persistent group of economic forces. But when pushed to its more remote and intricate logical consequences, it slips away from the conditions of real life.
>
> (Marshall [8, p. 461])

Why is model building as a general approach so compelling and appealing to economists? One reason is the power (described above) of the metaphors and analogies it is able to produce. Moreover, in the arithmomorphic contexts in which it is set, model building has rendered errors in deductive reasoning easier to detect; it is thought to have deepened understanding; and it has increased the simplicity, elegance, and generality of argument. It has provided a clear and precise way of organizing thoughts and it has made available the efficient language of mathematics for use in developing and reporting research (Debreu [2, p. viii], [3, p. 275]). And, most consequential, it has led to what are considered to be meaningful and relevant arithmomorphic results.

An important example of the significance and success of model building as explanation in economics is the previously noted widespread acceptance of the demand–supply model of an isolated market by both economists and the general public as the basis for understanding and explaining how a market works. When the "price" of gasoline, say, increases in the real economy, that change is typically understood and explained as the result of an increase in the market demand for, or a reduction in the market supply of gasoline. No one, of course, has ever seen the relevant demand and supply curves. Nevertheless, most everyone is comfortable and satisfied with the explanation.

Citing the fact that the subject does not have a unique, rigorous, logical structure, Kline characterizes mathematics as "... a series of great intuitions carefully sifted, refined, and organized by the logic men are willing and able to apply at any time" (Kline [7, p. 312]). These intuitions have had an enormous impact on economics, largely entering our discipline through model building. Even though mathematics may be internally inconsistent, even though the correct foundation for it may never be determined, and even though it is incomplete, mathematics has still been effective in various fields – and no one knows why (Kline [7, p. 7]). Mathematics, after all, has been instrumental in sending man to the moon. In the guise of model building, it has been employed throughout economics. Perhaps one of the most important accomplishments of mathematical model building in economics is the demonstration of the possibility of coherence in a world of individuals motivated solely by their own self-interest.[14] While not as spectacular as placing a man on the moon, this may still be regarded as progress.

References

[1] Bausor, R., "Time and Equilibrium," in *The Reconstruction of Economic Theory*, P. Mirowski, ed. (Boston, MA: Kluwer-Nijhoff, 1986), pp. 93–135.

[2] Debreu, G., *Theory of Value* (New York: Wiley, 1959).

[3] Debreu, G., "Economic Theory in the Mathematical Mode," *American Economic Review* 74 (1984), pp. 267–278.

[4] Georgescu-Roegen, N., *The Entropy Law and the Economic Process* (Cambridge, MA: Harvard University Press, 1971).

[5] Hofstadter, D. R., *Gödel, Escher, Bach: An Eternal Golden Braid* (New York: Basic Books, 1979).

[6] Katzner, D. W., *Analysis without Measurement* (Cambridge: Cambridge University Press, 1983).

[7] Kline, M., *Mathematics: The Loss of Certainty* (New York: Oxford University Press, 1980).

[8] Marshall, A., *Principles of Economics*, 8th ed. (New York: Macmillan, 1948).

[9] McCloskey, D. N., "The Rhetoric of Economics," *Journal of Economic Literature* 21 (1983), pp. 481–517.

[10] Mirowski, P., "Mathematical Formalism and Economic Explanation," in *The Reconstruction of Economic Theory*, P. Mirowski, ed. (Boston: Kluwer-Nijhoff, 1986), pp. 179–240.

[11] Pfanzagl, J., *Theory of Measurement*, 2nd ed. (Würzburg-Vienna: Physica-Verlag 1971).

[12] Russell, B., "Knowledge by Acquaintance and Knowledge by Description," in *Mysticism and Logic and Other Essays* (London: Allen & Unwin, 1959), pp. 209–232.

---

[14] This is the import of the proof of existence of equilibrium in a Walrasian general equilibrium system.

7

An Example:
The Efficiency of Organizational Forms[1]

It is now appropriate to provide an example of model construction in economics that illustrates previous discussion. To display fully the depth and significance of the use of models in analysis and explanation, it is necessary that the example be both detailed and complete. Furthermore, to be able to emphasize the power of model building independently of quantification (remember that arithmomorphic extraction does not imply measurement), the example focuses almost exclusively on non-quantifiable entities. The particular example under consideration is a model whose objective is twofold: The first is to describe the possible structure of an economic entity so as to explain its characteristics and how it might operate and, as a by-product to explain the single collection of observed variable values that the entity produces. The style of the model's output clearly places the model in the single-output category. As an analytical edifice in and of itself, then, the explanatory competence of the full model does not admit of empirical tests. However, the second objective is to extend the model to permit the derivation within its framework of behavioral functions subject to multiple observations over time, and that, therefore, are capable of empirical estimation and test. In this context, the style of the model's outputs has changed and the model moves into the multi-output category. Discussion begins with some general introductory, motivating, and suggestive remarks that are prior to stage (i) of model building and to distinctions between dialectical and arithmomorphic ideas.

For a long time economists have believed that certain ways of organizing firms are more efficient than others. Adam Smith, for example, thought

---

[1] This chapter is taken with modifications and additions from my "The Efficiency of Organizational Forms," *Économie Appliquée* 40 (1987), pp. 539–564. Published by the Institut de Sciences Mathématiques et Economiques Appliquées, Paris. Reproduced with permission.

that a firm producing pins in which employees specialized in straightening wire, cutting wire, making points, etc. would be more efficient than one in which each worker produced complete pins by himself alone.[2] However, recent approaches to this problem (e.g., Beckmann [1], Calvo and Wellisz [3], Sah and Stiglitz [16], and Williamson [18, 19]) have tended to de-emphasize the technological aspects of production and center instead on certain social relations among individuals in the firm. These social relations arise in that some workers are above other workers in the firm's authority structure; they are significant because it is the social interactions between those above and those below that seem to be responsible for coordinating effort and seeing production through.[3]

The ways in which a supervisor and subordinate interact socially on the job depend in part on such organizational matters as whether the two arrive at work decisions through mutual discussion or whether the supervisor makes all relevant decisions and tells the subordinate what to do. In other words, they depend on the specific activities of production in which the supervisor and subordinate respectively engage. Each circumstance is accompanied by its own range of possible social interactions between them. The particular collection of social interactions that arise in any one case is an indicator of how well the supervisor and subordinate are getting along. When the two have difficulty in getting along, their social interactions tend to impede the smooth functioning of the firm and lower its productivity. Thus the pattern of lines of authority and the social interactions and productive activities that go with it impacts the production process and the firm's output behavior, and makes for efficiency or inefficiency of an organizational form.

With these considerations in mind, and in addition to the standard input, production output, price, and profit variable values that emerge in many models of the firm, the single output of the model in the example presented later in this chapter also includes the work activities selected by employees in doing their jobs and the rules they issue constraining the activity selection of any subordinates they may have. With respect to the model's structure, the example discusses two kinds of organizational efficiency, each founded on a distinct approach to dealing with conflicts among employees arising along hierarchical lines. First, the firm may take

---

[2] Smith [17, pp. 4, 5].

[3] It is the coordination and accomplishment of the activities of production alone, without direct reliance on a price mechanism for guidance, that Coase regards as the distinguishing feature in the economist's notion of a firm [4, pp. 388, 389].

these conflicts as given and try to overcome their effects by incurring administrative costs, or second, it may attempt to cause the conflicts to disappear by hiring only certain kinds of individuals. The notion of efficiency emerging from the former is based on the idea that different forms of organization require different social interactions and different productive activities. Hence different sorts of conflicts come up and different costs of administration are needed to surmount them. This kind of organizational efficiency is the better known of the two and leads to comparative statements indicating that under certain conditions, an organization of one form is more efficient than that of another. The concept of efficiency arising from the latter also derives from the fact that the different patterns of social interactions occurring in different organizational forms spring from different allocations of productive activities among employees. But here, putting people with the right characteristics in the right jobs eliminates the conflicts that impede the smooth functioning of the firm. Taking such an approach to efficiency, the allocation of activities accompanying "internal equilibria" in certain ideal organizational forms (ideal, that is, with respect to the nature of the people employed) turns out to be "internally Pareto optimal." Thus the development of the complex mesh of activities and social interactions that support the organizational structure of the modern business enterprise does not, by itself, necessarily lead to allocative waste.

The presentation begins with a stage (i) discussion of a dialectical vision of various organizational forms. Next, in passing to stage (ii), an arithmomorphic model is extracted from the vision, which lends itself to the analysis and explanation in structural terms of the two kinds of efficiency described earlier. In developing the model at the level of stage (iii), the efficiency of organizational forms is considered from both points of view. Since the model is of the single-output variety, it cannot, in and of itself, admit to a stage (iv) empirical estimation or test of its explanatory competence. Rather, its observable output is identified with actual observation of the entity being explained. Nevertheless, the model will, as previously noted, be extended to incorporate several behavioral functions that have the potential to be tested. The actual empirical testing of those functions, however, is beyond the scope of present considerations and is therefore ignored.[4] But the presentation still ends with an acknowledgment of the possibilities for such testing, a discussion of the possibilities for another kind of partial testing of the model's explanatory

---

[4] Empirical testing of models with unmeasured variables has been discussed at the end of Chapter 5, and in greater detail and with a detailed example by Katzner [7, Chs. 12–14].

competence, and a stage (v) judgment of the model's cogency, relevance, and usefulness. Although many of the ideas presented have significance that extends beyond the normal limits imposed in an analysis of the firm, no effort is made here to cross over these boundaries and expand discussion into more general territory.

Before proceeding, it should be recalled that the operationalization process of stage (iii) does not require that the model be developed in a manner that creates the possibility of empirical estimation or empirical tests. The additions in that stage, of course, will vary over models designed for different purposes. In some instances, for example, the operationalization at stage (iii) may involve, as indicated earlier, the assumption of certain functional forms. But in the case of the model at present under discussion, the operationalizations of Sections 7.3 and 7.4 introduce new concepts and assumptions to complete and carry out the purpose of the inquiry.

7.1 Preliminaries: Stage (i)

Recall that in stage (i) of model construction, initial images are formulated. In the present case, these images, as previously suggested, reflect single-output variable values and may be thought of as drawn from observations of organizational patterns within real firms. Although abstraction is necessarily involved, the images may still be considered to be largely dialectical in character.

According to Ouchi, an organization is "any stable pattern of transactions between individuals or aggregations of individuals" [13, p. 132n]. Implicit in this conceptualization is a configuration of information flows among participants that supports the pattern of transactions and permits the organization to function. Ouchi's definition is very broad; yet it is useful for present purposes. Clearly, collections of markets may be understood as organizations. Firms, too, are organizations since they may be viewed as consisting of implicit transactions among individuals or groups.[5] Similarly, governments, universities, hospitals, etc., are also organizations. Although only organizations that may be conceived of as firms are considered subsequently, these still may take on a variety of forms. A sampling appropriate for subsequent discussion is as follows:

Imagine a firm producing output from given inputs in which all implicit transactions are made explicit through markets. Each employee is a sub-firm: he buys the things he uses in markets, does his job, and sells

---

[5] Williamson [19, pp. 8,9].

what he has done in another market to another employee. The difference between his receipts and costs is his pay. The firm consists of all of its sub-firms (employees) and the market relations among them. Together they convert those items taken to be the firm's inputs into that identified as its output. There is no authority structure and no social interaction among employees beyond what is necessary to complete transactions. The market network serves as the coordinating instrument which, in the firm, ensures that production is accomplished. The human characteristics of the individuals involved, together with the environmental factors of the markets defining the firm, require that all transactions be based on complex contingent claims contracts that are costly to write, execute, and enforce.[6] These contract costs (which include the costs of gathering sufficient information to be able to write, execute, and enforce the contracts) are the coordination or organizational costs of production. Such an arrangement is referred to here as the *market* organizational form for the firm.

All other forms of organization introduced subsequently are hierarchical in that most of the market transactions are absorbed into an authority structure with individuals higher up having status and jurisdiction over persons below. Hence the Smithian invisible hand, or the market process that in the market form of organization coordinates employee behavior based on self-interest, is replaced by other "invisible hands," now non-market processes, that coordinate self-interest-motivated behavior within the internal organizational structure of the firm. The only explicit market transactions remaining are those linking the firm to the markets in which it buys its inputs (such as labor) and sells its output. The cost of market transactions (i.e., the cost of contracts) is replaced by the cost of administering the organizational form. Thus the cost of organization or coordination arises from a different source. The instrument of the non-market invisible hand that coordinates social interactions so that production gets done is an important factor in determining the nature of the organizational form in question, along with the administrative cost incurred.

The present view of production takes into account, in addition to inputs and technology, the specific people involved in the production process and what they do and do not do while on their jobs. Individuals, after all, are hired to perform particular tasks within the limits of general rules, and are left with considerable freedom to determine how they structure the activities in which they engage. A salesman, for example, has to decide how to

[6] Williamson [19, p. 9].

approach and deal with prospective buyers; a carpenter may have to choose the order in which wood is cut and nailed together. Hence with the same technology and numerical input quantities, output can vary significantly according to whether the rules are reasonable and provide the employee sufficient flexibility to make appropriate decisions, the extent to which the relevant individuals are willing to follow the rules and make decisions that are in the interest of the firm, and the extent to which the rules foster cooperation within the firm. Cases in which output has lagged at certain times due to non-technological internal problems even in the most well-supplied and technologically advanced firms are observed often.[7] At the opposite extreme, productivity has been known to soar during periods in which other social arrangements obtained.[8] These issues can only be considered by drawing the boundary of the production process somewhat differently from that of the standard production function that is only concerned with the conversion of physical and labor inputs into output. Thus, in what follows, an attempt is made to include a small part of the social interaction naturally occurring among employees. Non-labor inputs are treated in the traditional fashion. But such things as activities of employees, rule structures, influence, cooperation of workers, and incentive schemes are introduced. Both individuals and the firm itself are taken to be maximizers.

Three non-market forms of organization are described below: the bureaucracy, the clan, and the military. Following convention, the class of all bureaucratic forms could be subdivided into its own distinct categories. The U-form and M-form bureaucracies to be considered later are examples of the latter.

A *bureaucracy* is an hierarchical organizational form in which those higher up, in addition to providing direction, also monitor and evaluate the performance of those below.[9] Upon leaving the labor market and joining the firm, the employee's pay increases and promotions depend on his performance. Good performance is rewarded; poor performance is punished. Of course, the presumption is that all employees respond to these incentives, which constitute the coordinating instrument of the bureaucracy. The cost of administering a bureaucracy includes the costs

---

[7] One of the more notorious examples centers around the famous strike at General Motors' Lordstown plant. At the time, this plant was supposed to be the technological showcase for the American automobile industry. But in 1972 things went awry (see Rothschild [15, Ch. 4] and O'Toole [12, pp. 89–93]).

[8] The Eagle Project at the Data General Corporation would appear to illustrate the point (see Kidder [9]).

[9] Ouchi [13, p. 134].

of monitoring and evaluating individuals below by individuals above. For convenience, the cost of the incentives themselves (i.e., the incentive payments to employees) are included as a part of production, not administrative, costs.

Two kinds of bureaucracies may be identified.[10] The *unitary* or *U-form* bureaucracy is organized in the traditionally functional manner. Thus sales, manufacturing, finance, and other functional units all lie directly under a chief executive or director. The units directly beneath the director in the *multidivisional* or *M-form* bureaucracy are themselves U-form divisions each responsible for their own routine operations. In the M-form structure, the director is concerned only with strategic decision-making for the entire firm and is not involved with day-to-day problems. Observe that these two types of bureaucracies are defined solely in terms of their pattern of lines of authority. In both cases, the instrument that coordinates social interactions is the same as that for the bureaucracy in general, namely a system of monetary and promotional incentives.

Unlike market forms and bureaucracies, a *clan* is a hierarchical form in which all individuals are socialized into the firm in such a way that their goals become identical to those of the firm.[11] When the goals of the firm and of all employees are the same, individuals naturally act in the best interests of the firm. Hence it is no longer necessary to monitor and evaluate the performance of each person. Moreover, rewards based on performance become irrelevant. Wages and promotions can be distributed according to non-performance criteria such as numbers of years of service and numbers of dependents. And, of course, the administrative costs of monitoring and evaluating performances disappears. In place of these expenses are substituted the costs of socializing new recruits and of maintaining the sense of community and commitment on the part of employees. Thus conformity of goals is the instrument coordinating social interactions in a clan. The clan form of organization is often considered to be a trait of some Japanese firms.[12]

Moving away from the clan, and apart from monitoring and evaluating performances and socialization so that goals conform to those of the firm, individuals may also be induced to cooperate by other means. The exercise of personal persuasion and leadership is one possibility. The use

---

[10] See, for example, Williamson [19. Ch. 8].
[11] Ouchi [13, p. 132].
[12] Ibid.

of dominance and manipulation as in the armed forces is another.[13] Thus with little in the way of monetary or promotional incentives, and with little similarity between his goals and that of the organization, an employee may still be willing to carry out tasks as directed from above. An hierarchical form in which all individuals follow instructions in this way will be called a *military*. The coordinating instrument here is the exercise of "influence," in one form or another over employees. As with the clan, the military form of organization does not incur the administrative costs of monitoring and evaluating performances, but it must expend funds to enforce and enhance the legal codes, customs, and traditions from which its ability to influence the behavior of individuals derives.[14] Although few organizations in the free world have such characteristics (professional football or other sports teams and armies are examples), it is nevertheless instructive to consider the military as a distinct organizational form.

The information flows required to run non-market organizational forms have both production and administrative components. To illustrate the origins of the former, imagine that the process of making production decisions differs across non-market organizational forms as follows: In a bureaucracy the department head, division manager, and president have the responsibility for decision-making.[15] Sometimes, to arrive at decisions, they may consult with subordinates, perhaps achieving a partial or complete consensus, and sometimes no consultation is initiated. For clans, everyone throughout the pyramid of authority who will feel the impact of a decision is directly involved in making it. Discussions continue until a consensus about the correct decision to take is achieved.[16] In militaries, the primary responsibility for decision-making rests with those at the top of the pyramid. Discretionary decision-making at lower levels is strictly and progressively limited.[17] Consultation with subordinates is unlikely in arriving at decisions. Although in all three cases of bureaucracies, clans, and militaries information flows from the bottom to the top of the pyramid and directives flow in the opposite direction from the top to the bottom, the content and pattern of these flows has to vary across organizational

---

[13] Janowitz [6, p. 43].

[14] It is not necessary to monitor performances in a military because employees believe that the cost to them of not cooperating is so high (e.g., the sacrifice of one's entire career) that they do not consider non-cooperation as a viable alternative.

[15] See Ouchi [14, p. 43].

[16] See Ouchi [14, p. 44].

[17] See Lang [10, p. 852].

forms because the decision-making processes in each clearly have different informational requirements.

The information flows needed to conduct administration also vary over non-market forms of organization. In bureaucracies they arise because supervisors have to monitor and evaluate the performances of their subordinates. In clans they come about through the socialization of new recruits and the maintenance of a sense of community and commitment. And in militaries they derive from the enforcement of legal codes, customs, and traditions.

In an ideal world in which assumptions of certainty and full information are imposed, the imperative to collect information for organizational and administrative purposes disappears and the cost associated with organization and administration in each organizational form drops to zero. Without uncertainty, the only information needed by the market form of organization is the values of prices that are supplied by the markets free of charge. The necessity of contingent claims contracts evaporates and, along with it, all costs of organization. For bureaucracies, clans, and militaries, "ideal" individual participants react in perfect confluence with the organizational structure so that monitoring and evaluating performances, socialization and maintaining a sense of commitment, and enhancing legal codes, customs, and traditions, respectively, are no longer necessary. Thus information for administration, indeed, administration itself is not required, and all administrative costs are eliminated. Discussion will return to this point in Section 7.4.

7.2 The Model: Stage (ii)

Stage (ii) extracts from these considerations an arithmomorphic model whose structure, either by itself or as the basis for determination of the single-outcome produced by the model, serves as a framework for exploration and explanation of the issues raised earlier by the questions initially set out and by the discussion of stage (i). In presenting this model, the derivations of often unquantified arithmomorphic concepts, variables, and functions from their corresponding dialectical thought-forms described in Chapter 6 are not repeated. Rather, all such derivations are taken as having already been accomplished, and discussion begins with these concepts, variables, and functions in their arithmomorphic form. Recall that the assumptions introduced at this stage have been referred to as primary assumptions. The model is drawn from Gintis and Katzner [5] and Katzner [8].

Begin with the assumption that the structure of authority in the firm exists in pyramidal form. That is, at each level of authority there is at least one employee. Every employee k (where $k = 1,\ldots,K$) has exactly one immediate superior or supervisor and all employees except those at the bottom end of a line of authority in the pyramid have at least one subordinate. There may be more than one subordinate at the level immediately below k (in which case k is the supervisor of each) and there may be more than one employee at more than one level below k (in which case k is superior in authority to all of them). Two or more employees with the same supervisor are co-workers. Situated at the top of the pyramid is the director who is designated by the symbol $k = 0$. The director may also be thought of as a chief executive, board of directors, or as a combination of both.

Each employee k supplies labor time z_k to the firm. During time supplied the employee performs activities a_k, which fall within the terms of his work contract.[18] These activities involve social interactions among employees and are limited by the technological imperatives of production. It is not required that the a_k be quantifiable: The only restrictions are that each "value" of a_k be capable of distinct, discrete, verbal description, and that the set of activities, A_k, over which a_k may range also be subject to similarly precise definition. (This is an example of what was previously contemplated as an unquantified arithmomorphic variable.) Apart from the boundaries on the activities in which k may engage as described in his work contract, the set A_k will be further confined by restrictions imposed by persons above k in authority. That is, in addition to performing activities, each employee provides rules that constrain the activities (i.e., limit the activity sets) of all workers (not only immediate subordinates) below him in authority. For example, suppose person k is hired to build timing devices for certain products. A multitude of ways of doing this may be contained in his activity set A_k. But for reasons of marketing, availability of materials, productive efficiency, or just to fit the specification of the products for which the timing devices are intended, individuals above k in authority may induce him to follow specific courses of action by prescribing rules that eliminate various activities in his A_k. These rules are completely characterized in terms of the constraints they impose.

---

[18] The definition of an activity would normally include a statement or an implication regarding the length of time necessary to perform the activity. This, in turn, suggests a relation between z_k and a_k. The latter relation, however, is beyond the scope of present discussion and will be ignored.

More precisely, if k is above k' in authority and if $R_{kk'}$ is a set of rules issued by k for k', then $R_{kk'}$, is defined as a subset of $A_{k'}$, or $R_{kk'} \subseteq A_{k'}$. To illustrate the structural properties of rules, consider three employees k, k', and k'', where k is above k' in authority and k' is above k'' in authority. Now employees at different levels of authority usually have different production-related concerns and responsibilities that (a) lead them to impose different rules at different levels on those below them in the authority structure, and (b) require those above them at different levels of authority to prescribe different rules for them. It is a consequence of (a) and the fact that k' and k'' are likely to have different activity sets that $R_{kk'}$ and $R_{kk''}$ are typically not identical. And from (b), it is not necessary that $R_{kk''} = R_{k'k''}$, although the two rule sets need to be consistent in that they leave k'' with an activity or activities in $A_{k''}$ to perform, that is, $R_{kk''} \cap R_{k'k''}$ has to contain at least one element. In general, the furnishing of rules may be thought of as an activity that is independent of all other activities and singled out for special attention. Rules may be so restrictive as to dictate exactly what must be done (i.e., select a single element from the employee's activity set) or they may allow for considerable flexibility and choice. In any case, rules are assumed to be obeyed. Rules also have to be adapted to the technology of production and the capabilities of the individuals for whom they are intended.[19] Moreover, as in the case of the three employees discussed above, the collection of rules imposed on any employee k' by all those above him in authority must necessarily be consistent or, in other words, $\cap_k R_{kk'}$ has to be non-empty, where the intersection is taken over all k above k' in authority. It is from this intersection (which is contained in $A_{k'}$) that k' will eventually select an activity to perform in carrying out his job. Let r_k denote the collection of sets of rules – one set $R_{kk'}$ for each person k' below him – issued by person k. When k has no subordinates, the symbol r_k has no meaning. Write $a = (a_1, \ldots, a_K)$ and $r = (r_1, \ldots, r_K)$. The director's rules, r_0, are presumed given.

To provide an illustration of the manner in which rules may be issued, suppose, in an automobile manufacturing firm, the vice president for production gives an immediate, subordinate manager instructions (a rule) to produce a car of a certain design. This will clearly limit the activities of the manager. But it may or may not limit the activities of employees further down the authority structure on the production line. The manager interprets the instructions of the vice president in terms of his own

---

[19] Rules, of course, may be altered in response to such things as technological innovation or improvements suggested from below.

activity set and issues more specific rules that limit the activities of those immediately (and possibly further) beneath him in authority. It follows, of course, that a person at any given level of authority cannot convey to a level below him a rule that conflicts with the rules he has received from above, that is, conflicts with the manner in which his own activity set has already been restricted.

The output of the firm, x, depends on quantities of labor time and non-labor inputs purchased by the firm, as well as on rules for subordinates and activities (consistent with rules received from above) supplied by employees. This production function may be written mathematically as

$$x = f(y, z, a, r), \tag{7.1}$$

where $z = (z_1, \ldots, z_K)$ and $y = (y_1, \ldots, y_I)$ is an I-vector of quantities of non-labor inputs. Actually, since r only serves to limit the values that a can take on and does not affect output directly, it need not be listed as an argument of f. But retaining r in the production function introduces no difficulties and at the same time provides convenience that is useful below. In the currently standard textbook treatment, y and z are picked by the firm on the basis of profit maximization and a and r are ignored. The present approach maintains the criterion of profit maximization on the part of the firm as the basis for selection of y and z given values for a and r, and, in addition, a and r are thought of as determined by employees through the (constrained) maximization of their individual utility functions.[20] Of course, the choice of a and r reflects and describes the relevant social interactions among the employees of the firm.

Let the firm pay each employee k a wage w_k according to the incentive function[21]

$$w_k = W^k(a_k, r_k), \tag{7.2}$$

where $k = 1, \ldots, K$. Non-monetary incentives, such as the possibility of promotion and guaranteed long-term employment, are not considered. The firm's profit function which, given a and r, it maximizes to secure

---

[20] The presence of real capital assets among the components of y could be taken to imply that the model, in making y a decision variable, is determining an instantaneous, optimum capital structure for the firm. Analytically, that raises the question as to whether employees' choices of activities and rules (a, r) can be expected to remain constant throughout the lives of the assets. But this problem is set aside and disregarded in subsequent discussion.

[21] The determination of W^k and its relation to the labor market is not considered here.

values for y and z is

$$\pi(y,z,a,r) = p_x f(y,z,a,r) - \sum_{i=1}^{I} p_i y_i - \sum_{k=1}^{K} w_k z_k, \qquad (7.3)$$

where p_x denotes output price, and p_i the price of non-labor input i. To keep matters simple, p_x and the p_i are taken to be determined in perfectly competitive markets and the director is assumed to be paid out of profit rather than provided a wage.[22]

The nature of the incentive functions W^k selected by the firm (or its director) deserves comment. On one hand, the W^k may be constant functions associating the same wage to all (a_k, r_k). Alternatively, those values of $(a,r) = (a_1, \ldots, a_K, r_1, \ldots, r_K)$ that enhance the productivity or profitability of the firm may be assigned a higher wage by the W_k. In the latter case, however, suppose that for fixed values of $p_x, p_1, \ldots, p_I$, y, and z, output is higher at (a', r') than at (a'', r''). If profit is also to be higher at (a', r'), then it is necessary that the firm set the W^k so that the additional wages paid employees at (a', r') over those paid at (a'', r'') is less than the additional revenue received at (a', r'). Were this not the case, then the most productive (a, r) need not be the most profitable, and hence moving to increase productivity might reduce profitability. Formally, the collection of incentive functions $\{W^k\}$, one for each employee $k = 1, \ldots, K$, is said to be *profit-efficient*[23] whenever

$$f(y,z,a',r') \geq f(y,z,a'',r'')$$

if and only if

$$\pi(y,z,a',r') \geq \pi(y,z,a'',r''),$$

for all y, z, a', a'', r', and r''. Profit-efficient incentives, then, have the property that productivity increases due to changes in (a,r) always are translated into larger profit. Note that in addition to incentives that provide wage raises that are smaller than resulting revenue increments, all collections of constant incentive functions are also profit-efficient.

To capture the idea that leadership and influence may be exercised by supervisors in their provision of information, training, encouragement,

---

[22] For the case in which a y_i is a real capital input, the corresponding p_i will be a periodic running cost, i.e., an amortized dollar amount whose capitalized value equals the investment needed to purchase the input.

[23] This definition of profit efficiency, although identical to the one appearing in Katzner [8], is not quite the same as that employed by Gintis and Katzner [5].

and advice to subordinates, suppose each employee k senses a goals and premise $(g\text{-}p)$ function

$$g_k = G^k(a_k, r_k), \qquad (7.4)$$

in which g_k varies over ordinal numbers that express the preferences of his immediate supervisor among vectors (a_k, r_k) as perceived by k. The G^k are taken to be given and the characteristics they might be expected to possess are not discussed. $G\text{-}p$ functions themselves do not interpret or qualify rules received from those higher up in authority, but only encourage the employee to be fully cooperative and do his job well. They are also independent of incentive functions, relying on social rather than economic pressures for their effect.

Assume employees choose values of the activities in which they engage a_k and the rules they issue r_k independently from their selection of leisure time and consumption. Ignoring the latter, let the utility function of employee k be written as

$$\mu_k = u^k(a_k, r_k, w_k, g_k), \qquad (7.5)$$

so that the roles of incentives and influences are explicit. However, substitution of (7.2) and (7.4) into (7.5) eliminates w_k and g_k from the latter and reduces it to

$$\mu_k = U^k(a_k, r_k).$$

Suppose $(a, r) = (a_1, \ldots, a_K, r_1, \ldots, r_K)$ emerges uniquely from the simultaneous maximization of $U^k(a_k, r_k)$ by each employee $k \neq 0$, subject to the constraints that every a_k is consistent with all rules imposed on k from above or, in other words, that a_k is in $\cap_{k'} R_{k'k}$ for each k, where the intersection is taken over all k' above k in authority. (Note that this symbolism involves reversing earlier notation in which k was taken to be above k' in authority.) Such an (a, r) is called an *internal equilibrium* for the firm.[24] Thus given the director's rules r_0, (a, r) is obtained from utility

---

[24] This equilibrium, like all equilibria, is present in the model but not in the real phenomenon under investigation. This is so because, apart from the fact that the equilibrium is a mental construct and cannot, therefore, be a part of the phenomenon, (a) the model in which the equilibrium appears only approximates reality due to the model's abstractness, and (b) the model is static whereas the real world is dynamic. Even if the model were dynamic and the equilibrium arose in the model as an "equilibrium path," it would still be a mental fabrication and (a) would still apply.

It should also be noted that this model, with its static notion of equilibrium, ignores the possibility that the firm might accept lesser profit now in order to realize greater profit in the future.

maximization, (y, z) is secured from profit maximization as described earlier, and the firm's output and profit are determined from (7.1) and (7.3). The values obtained of each of the variables a, r, y, z, x, and π, constitute the single observable output of the model and can be identified with actual observations of their values. The collection of all internal equilibria generated as the director's rules vary and (y, z) remains fixed is denoted by $\mathcal{E}$. Note that $\mathcal{E}$ contains the internal equilibria arising when the director's rules are such that they impose no effective constraints on the activities of any worker.

7.3 Administrative Cost Efficiency: Stage (iii)

In stage (iii), the model is operationalized by introducing new elements and assumptions so as to be able to focus on the specific matters at issue. For now there are two: allocative efficiency and administrative efficiency, both of which relate directly to the characteristics of the structure of the firm as set out in the previous section. With respect to the former, the stage (ii) model is sufficiently rich to encompass all of the organizational forms described in Section 7.1 except the market form in which each employee is a sub-firm. (Of course the market form does not have a hierarchical authority structure and can not, therefore, fit in.) The instruments required to coordinate social interactions and hence production in bureaucracies, clans, and militaries are all present in that incentive, utility, and g-p functions have been included. In an idealized or perfect environment, differences among these organizational forms are accounted for by differences in the characteristics of the incentive, utility, and g-p functions pertaining to the individuals employed in each case. Indeed, the notions of (ideal) bureaucracy, clan, and military will be defined abstractly by imposing certain restrictions on these functions later on (Section 7.4). This will permit their allocative efficiency properties to be studied. But before following this route, attention is focused first on administrative efficiency. The stage (iii) assumptions brought in to examine both forms of efficiency are what have been referred to earlier as secondary assumptions.

Fix y and z and suppose there exists a unique internal equilibrium $(\hat{a}, \hat{r}) = (\hat{a}_1, \ldots, \hat{a}_K, \hat{r}_1, \ldots, \hat{r}_K)$ that maximizes $\pi(y, z, a, r)$ over $\mathcal{E}$. Then the utility-maximizing selection by workers of any other (a, r) in $\mathcal{E}$ is not profit-maximizing. Of course, if the director believes that workers, when left alone, are likely to choose $(a, r) \neq (\hat{a}, \hat{r})$, he can always issue rules that confine individual choice options in such a way as to increase profit beyond $\pi(y, z, a, r)$. At the extreme, he could even force workers to choose from the single-element sets $\{(\hat{a}_k, \hat{r}_k)\}$, thereby ensuring compliance with profit-maximizing behavior. However, the more confining the director's rules, the more workers have to gain (in terms of their own utility) by violating them. Hence, for the director to proceed in this way, he must establish an administrative mechanism to ensure that his rules are carried out. (A similar problem arises in the relationship between any supervisor and his subordinates, but this complication is not pursued here.) The administrative mechanism and the assumptions necessary to deal with it constitute, respectively, the new stage (iii) feature and the stage (iii) secondary assumptions introduced to operationalize the stage (ii) model in relation to administrative efficiency. Their connections to stage (i) of the model-building process are apparent in the discussion of Section 7.1.

Suppose the director does not want to post rules that, in the absence of violations, would lead workers to the profit-maximizing internal equilibrium $(\hat{a}, \hat{r})$.[25] Assume, however, that he nevertheless hires the extra administrative resources required to achieve $(\hat{a}, \hat{r})$. The actual resources needed would depend on the choice (a, r) in $\mathcal{E}$ that workers would make when the director's rules by themselves do not bring forth $(\hat{a}, \hat{r})$. The cost of these resources is called the *administrative* cost of the firm and is described symbolically by the function $C(a, r)$. Clearly, $C(\hat{a}, \hat{r}) = 0$ and $C(a, r) > 0$ for all other (a, r) in $\mathcal{E}$. It is assumed that $C(a, r)$ is sufficient to ensure that workers perform $(\hat{a}, \hat{r})$ for each (a, r).

The net profit accruing to the firm if the director were to ensure indirectly the selection of $(\hat{a}, \hat{r})$ as described above is

$$\pi(y, z, \hat{a}, \hat{r}) - C(a, r), \tag{7.6}$$

where y and z are given and (a, r) is the internal equilibrium that would arise given the director's rules. Only when

$$\pi(y, z, \hat{a}, \hat{r}) - C(a, r) > \pi(y, z, a, r)$$

will it pay to incur the administrative cost necessary to pressure workers into maintaining profit-maximizing behavior. In general, net profit need not be maximized by pushing workers to $(\hat{a}, \hat{r})$. The director may be able to do better than (7.6) by, for example, allowing workers some flexibility in their choices (i.e., by not insisting on $(\hat{a}, \hat{r})$) and also by not hiring the full complement of resources $C(a, r)$. Net profit would be larger than (7.6) in this case if the loss from not achieving $\pi(y, z, \hat{a}, \hat{r})$ were smaller than

---

[25] For example, there may be personal or cultural constraints that make him reluctant to force workers to choose from the single-element sets $\{(\hat{a}_k, \hat{r}_k)\}$.

the savings in $C(a, r)$. Let $(\tilde{a}, \tilde{r})$ denote the internal equilibrium in $\mathcal{E}$ that arises when the director imposes no rules at all and workers are relieved of directorial constraints in the selection of their own activities and the rules they designate for their subordinates. The imposition of no rules by the director is one element in the collection of all sets of rules the director may issue that impose no effective constraints on the selection of activities and rules by any worker.

The administrative mechanisms implemented to enforce the director's rules differ for bureaucracies, clans, and militaries. In bureaucracies they take the form of an arrangement to monitor (and evaluate) worker performance.[26] Workers are said to "shirk" whenever $(a, r) \neq (\hat{a}, \hat{r})$. The purpose of monitoring is to reduce or eliminate shirking and thus increase profit. In clans, administrative mechanisms are concerned with establishing and maintaining the sense of community and commitment; and in militaries they attempt to build and preserve the ability of supervisors to influence subordinates. As indicated in Section 7.1, all of these administrative mechanisms have informational requirements that are costly to meet. The appropriate costs of information are a part of $C(a, r)$ in each case.

Recall that in all non-market forms of organization, administrative cost replaces the transactions costs that must be present and explicit if the same firm were reorganized as a collection of sub-firms each consisting of a single employee. The administrative cost of the market form, written c_m, is the sum of all market transactions costs (i.e., all contingent claims contract costs) necessary for its operation. Note that c_m is determined by the structure and pattern of the contingent claims contracts required. The selection of (a_k, r_k) by each employee (sub-firm) k is inconsequential since no employee has supervisors to constrain his activities with rules, and there is no social interaction among workers beyond that arising from the participation in market transactions.

One way to think of the efficiency of organizational forms is with reference to the $C(\tilde{a}, \tilde{r})$ and c_m. Given a firm as described in Section 7.2 having fixed quantities of inputs y and z, and a number of potential organizational forms, one form may be said to be more *administratively efficient* than another if its administrative cost when all workers are free of directorial constraints is lower.[27] Thus the market form is relatively inefficient when

---

[26] See, for example, Calvo and Wellisz [3].

[27] See Ouchi [13, pp. 132–137]. Note this definition of comparative administrative efficiency implicitly requires that administrative and production costs be separable and that the production function (7.1) be the same for all organizational forms under consideration.

the transactions costs it requires, namely c_m rise above the values of $C(\tilde{a},\tilde{r})$ from other forms. The bureaucratic form is relatively inefficient when it becomes prohibitively expensive to monitor performances. Similarly, the clan and military forms are relatively inefficient if the costs, respectively, of maintaining the sense of community and commitment, and of preserving the ability to influence are very high. The exact manner in which, for a given firm, these four organizational forms are ordered by this notion of administrative efficiency depends on the relative values of $C(\tilde{a},\tilde{r})$ and c_m where in each case once again, $(\tilde{a},\tilde{r})$ is selected by the firm's workers in the absence of rules imposed by the director.

Suppose $C'(\tilde{a}',\tilde{r}')$ represents the administrative cost of one non-market form of organization, say, where $(\tilde{a}',\tilde{r}')$ is the internal equilibrium chosen within this organizational form without directoral constraints, and let $C''(\tilde{a}'',\tilde{r}'')$ denote the administrative cost of another. Then

$$C'(\tilde{a}',\tilde{r}') < C''(\tilde{a}'',\tilde{r}'') \tag{7.7}$$

does not necessarily imply

$$\pi'(y,z,\hat{a},\hat{r}) - C'(\tilde{a}',\tilde{r}') > \pi''(y,z,\hat{a},\hat{r}) - C''(\tilde{a}'',\tilde{r}''), \tag{7.8}$$

where π' and π'' are the profit functions defined in (7.3) for the two forms, respectively, and $(\hat{a},\hat{r})$ indicates generally different profit-maximizing activities and rules in each case. That is, lower administrative cost may be accompanied by lower net profit. Thus, depending on the intended purpose, (7.6) evaluated at $(\tilde{a},\tilde{r})$ may be a more appropriate measure of administrative efficiency than $C(\tilde{a},\tilde{r})$. An obvious sufficient condition for (7.7) to imply (7.8) is that

$$\pi'(y,z,\hat{a},\hat{r}) \geq \pi''(y,z,\hat{a},\hat{r}), \tag{7.9}$$

and such will obtain if the level of maximum (gross) profit is the same over the relevant sets $\mathcal{E}$ for both forms. With (7.9) in force, lower administrative cost or greater administrative efficiency always corresponds to higher net profit.

These ideas may be applied to compare administrative efficiencies as the firm's pyramidal structure expands and changes. To do so requires that administrative cost be expressed as a function of hierarchical levels. Two employees in the firm's pyramid of authority are said to be on the same

---

Use of the latter precludes examination of the ability of an organizational form to adapt to technological change.

hierarchical level if there are an equal number of persons above each. Let a pyramid of authority for a large number of levels be given, which depicts the authority structure of the firm as it expands by adding hierarchical levels. Take the number of hierarchical levels to indicate the size of the firm. Then once the firm has decided to structure itself in such a way as to adopt a particular level, n, the optimal quantity of labor and non-labor inputs to be employed along with the size of the firm is determined. Also determined at n are the utility-maximizing $(\tilde{a}, \tilde{r})$ and profit-maximizing $(\hat{a}, \hat{r})$, as well as the corresponding function values $\pi(y, z, \hat{a}, \hat{r})$ and $C(\tilde{a}, \tilde{r})$. The latter, in particular, may be expressed as functions of n. Thus write $\hat{\pi}(n)$ and $C(n)$ as, respectively, the maximum profit and the administrative cost associated with level n. Since the number of employees usually increases at an increasing rate with n, one would expect the same to be true of $C(n)$. Hence administrative efficiency declines as n rises.[28] Moreover, the optimal firm size can be defined as that which maximizes

$$\hat{\pi}(n) - C(n),$$

provided such an optimum exists.[29]

The replacement of the market form of organization by the bureaucratic U-form in many late nineteenth century American industries (this is the nod to the empirical corroboration of stage (iv) mentioned earlier) has been explained in part by arguing that the latter had become relatively more administratively efficient than the former.[30] The subsequent switch (beginning in the early 1920s) from the U-form to the M-form as the number of hierarchical levels of the U-form grew has been interpreted similarly.[31] The rationale for the latter abandonment of the U-form in favor of the M-form as n rises is especially easy to illustrate in the present scheme. As many such explanations do, the one given here abstracts from practical considerations in order to focus all attention on the pure logic of what is involved. Consider a hierarchical firm organized as a U-form bureaucracy with administrative cost $C(n)$. Suppose the firm has the option of expanding by either adding θ hierarchical levels to its U-form or replicating itself θ times in an M-form multidivisional structure, and that in either case $\hat{\pi}$ is the same for each n. The administrative cost of the first option is $C(n + \theta)$; that of the second is $\theta C(n)$. In both instances the firm expands by enlarging θ for fixed n. Hence administrative cost expands

[28] See Coase [4, pp. 394–395].
[29] See, for example, Williamson [18].
[30] See, for example, Williamson [19, p. 133], [20].
[31] See, for example, Williamson [19, Ch. 8], [20].

(as indicated earlier) at an increasing rate with θ for the U-form, but only proportionately for the M-form. Thus it is possible for the M-form to eventually become (if it is not already) more efficient than the U-form. To the extent that the M-form equivalent of adding θ levels to the U-form is smaller than θ replications of the original firm, the M-form will become more efficient than the U-form that much sooner.

As an example suppose $C(n) = n^2$ so that

$$\theta C(n) = \theta n^2$$

and

$$C(n+\theta) = (n+\theta)^2.$$

In this case it can be shown that if $n > 4$, then for all θ where

$$\theta > \frac{n^2 - 2n}{2} + \frac{n\sqrt{n^2 - 4}}{2}, \tag{7.10}$$

one necessarily has

$$\theta C(n) < C(n+\theta).$$

Thus the M-form will be more efficient than the U-form whenever $n > 4$ and θ grows large enough to satisfy (7.10).

Precise mathematical propositions describing the formal conditions under which a bureaucracy, say, is more administratively efficient than a market form, clan, or military are not possible without much more detailed analysis of the structure of the costs that determine $C(n)$. Rather than proceed along this path, however, the next section examines the allocative efficiency of the distribution of activities among employees occurring within these organizational forms.

7.4 Allocative Efficiency: Stage (iii)

Consider, next, the operationalization of the stage (ii) model of Section 7.2 with respect to allocative efficiency. The first step is to provide idealized characterizations of the organizational forms under consideration – i.e., the bureaucracy, clan, military, and market form – in the context of the model of Section 7.2. These characterizations and the implicit and explicit secondary assumptions injected into the model with them are the new operationalizing components that, in the case of allocative efficiency, define the transition from stage (ii) to stage (iii). Now it has already been pointed out that the instruments of the non-market invisible hands that coordinate social interactions among employees in bureaucracies, clans, and militaries (namely incentive, utility, and g-p functions, respectively) are all present in the model. But rigorous arithmomorphic definitions of these organizational forms are not provided by merely noting the presence of such functions. It is still necessary to specify how individuals respond to them, or in other words, how the coordination of social interactions actually works in an ideal environment. The relevant concepts for doing so are presented next. The links back to stage (i) are clear from the discussion in Section 7.1.

An employee $k \neq 0$ is called *incentive motivated* if for all pairs of values (a'_k, r'_k) and (a''_k, r''_k) the numerical inequality

$$W^k(a'_k, r'_k) \geq W^k(a''_k, r''_k)$$

implies

$$U^k(a'_k, r'_k) \geq U^k(a''_k, r''_k).$$

He is *vertically influenced* when

$$G^k(a'_k, r'_k) \geq G^k(a''_k, r''_k)$$

forces

$$U^k(a'_k, r'_k) \geq U^k(a''_k, r''_k).$$

Incentive motivation and vertical influence mean, respectively, that individual preferences are such that employees respond in the "same direction" as that of incentives and influence.

Now recall production function (7.1). For employee $k \neq 0$ consider any two vectors (a'_k, r'_k) and (a''_k, r''_k) such that (a) output is at least as high using a'_k in (7.1) instead of a''_k, and (b) r'_k restricts all subordinates of k to subsets of their respective activity sets obtained under r''_k on which output is at least as large as it is anywhere else in the r''_k sets. Other things being equal, then, the output associated with (a'_k, r'_k) can not be less than that associated with (a''_k, r''_k). Assume that (a) and (b) hold regardless of the activities performed by the remaining employees, and regardless of the quantities of labor time and non-labor inputs hired by the firm.[32] Under these conditions, if

$$W^k(a'_k, r'_k) \geq W^k(a''_k, r''_k),$$

---

[32] The idea that in these circumstances the output associated with (a'_k, r'_k) is larger than that identified with (a''_k, r''_k) furnishes a way of ordering the collection of all vectors (a_k, r_k). See Katzner [8] and Gintis and Katzner [5]. The present "weak" version of this ordering is assumed to be reflexive, transitive, antisymmetric, and total.

or if

$$G^k(a'_k, r'_k) \geq G^k(a''_k, r''_k),$$

then W^k and G^k, respectively, are referred to as *non-decreasing*. In other words, incentive or *g-p* functions are non-decreasing provided they are set so as to reward or influence employees toward activities which do not decrease output. Similarly, employee k is said to *internalize the values of the firm* when, under the same conditions,

$$U^k(a'_k, r'_k) \geq U^k(a''_k, r''_k).$$

Thus, a socialization process has taken place leaving the employee's preferences among activities and rules coincident with the interests of the firm.

It is now possible to give abstract definitions of the notions of bureaucracy, clan, and military in idealized form. Like the standard characterization of perfect competition, these may be thought of as "ideal types" which do not usually appear in reality exactly as pictured, but which are useful for study nonetheless. The firm described in Section 7.2 is called an *ideal bureaucracy* provided that all incentive functions W^k (where $k \neq 0$) are non-decreasing and (as a group) profit-efficient, and all employees ($k \neq 0$) are incentive motivated. It is referred to as an *ideal clan* whenever all incentive functions are constant functions (and hence profit-efficient) and all employees ($k \neq 0$) internalize the values of the firm. And it is said to be an *ideal military* if all incentive functions are constant functions (and hence profit-efficient), all *g-p* functions G^k (where $k \neq 0$) are non-decreasing, and all employees ($k \neq 0$) are vertically influenced.[33] These definitions capture and formalize the essence of the concepts of bureaucracy, clan, and military discussed in Section 7.1. The *ideal market* form of organization of the firm is the market form described in Section 7.1 for the case in which all contingent claims contract costs, i.e., the administrative cost, $c_m = 0$.

Reflexivity and transitivity have already been defined in n. 9 on p. 62 and n. 12 on p. 116. A relation ρ on a set X is *antisymmetric* when, for all x' and x'' in X, if $x' \rho x''$ and $x'' \rho x'$, then $x' = x''$. It is *total* provided that either $x' \rho x''$ or $x'' \rho x'$, for all x' and x'' in X.

[33] According to these definitions, it is technically possible for the firm to be, say, both an ideal clan and an ideal bureaucracy at the same time. But such combinations of organizational forms are irrelevant for present purposes. In a clan, the emphasis is on internalization of values, regardless of how individuals might react to incentives. A bureaucracy, on the other hand, focuses on incentive motivation independently of the extent to which values happen to be internalized.

Consider now a distinct internal equilibrium (a, r) in different sets $\mathcal{E}$ for each of the idealized organizational forms described above. Such equilibria have been defined in general in Section 6.2 and hence apply directly to bureaucracies, clans, and militaries. With respect to the market form, rules do not constrain individual choices, and the selection of activities, which defines internal equilibrium here, has no impact on output and profit. All that matters is that certain quantities of goods are exchanged in the relevant markets according to the contingent claims contracts. Hence the profit of the firm, that is, the sum of the "profits" of the individual sub-firms (employees), is constant over all vectors (a, r) or, what in this case is the set of all internal equilibria, also denoted by $\mathcal{E}$. The following proposition, then, follows immediately from previous definitions.

Theorem 7.1: *Let fixed values of y and z be given and suppose the director's rules impose no effective constraints on the selection of activities and rules by any worker. Then in an ideal bureaucracy, clan, military, or market form, internal equilibrium always maximizes profit over the set of all consistent vectors (a, r), that is, over the relevant $\mathcal{E}$.*

Theorem 7.1 has several implications. First, every (a, r) in $\mathcal{E}$ that is not profit maximizing must arise because the director's rules exclude the profit-maximizing (a, r) from the options open to employees.[34] Although logically possible, one would not expect the director's rules to be so constituted. Second, assuming that the director's rules do not effectively constrain workers' choices, at internal equilibria in ideal bureaucracies, clans, and militaries, administrative cost $C(a, r) = 0$. (Recall that c_m has already been defined to be zero in the idealized market form.) Hence, according to the criteria of Section 7.3, the administrative efficiencies of (ideal) bureaucracies, clans, militaries, and market forms are all equal. In each case, individuals pursue profit maximization automatically without needing the director to dictate rules and incur administrative costs. Third, these conclusions apply regardless of whether the pyramidal structure of the firm is of the U-form or M-form variety.

Another way to study the efficiency properties of idealized organizational forms is in terms of internal Pareto optimality. Economists are quite familiar with the proposition that, under certain well-known conditions,

---

[34] The converse assertion also holds.

in a perfectly competitive economy, equilibrium is Pareto optimal. That is, given endowments, tastes, and technology, and with consumers buying output quantities and supplying factor quantities so as to maximize utility subject to their budget constraints, with firms selling output quantities and buying input quantities so as to maximize profits, and with supply equal to demand in all markets, quantities of outputs and inputs cannot be redistributed among consumers and firms to make one person better off (i.e., raising his utility) without making at least one other person worse off (i.e., lowering his utility). In this sense, the market form of organization is allocatively efficient: having perfectly competitive equilibrium inputs and outputs in all sub-firms, it is part of an economy-wide Pareto optimum. Of course the same thing is true for any organizational form whose input and output quantities are consistent with perfect competition. But as soon as the market form is discarded in favor of bureaucracies, clans, or militaries, the possibility of waste in the "improper" allocation of the activities of production within the firm arises.[35] And such is the case regardless of whether the distribution of input and output quantities across the economy is Pareto optimal. For even at an economy-wide competitive equilibrium, it might be possible (without any change in input quantities and without lowering anyone's utility) to expand output in a bureaucracy, say, by reallocating activities inside the firm. Hence it becomes necessary to ask if the coordination of social interaction in bureaucracies, clans, and militaries, which replaces coordination by markets in these non-market organizational forms, is sufficient to ensure the allocative efficiency of internal equilibrium.

Let y and z in the production function (7.1) be given. A vector $(a^0, r^0) = (a_1^0, \ldots, a_K^0, r_1^0, \ldots, r_K^0)$ is called *internally Pareto optimal in production* as long as there is no other (a, r) in the relevant $\mathcal{E}$ such that

$$U^k(a_k, r_k) \geq U^k(a_k^0, r_k^0)$$

for all $k = 1, \ldots, K,$

$$U^k(a_k, r_k) > U^k(a_k^0, r_k^0)$$

for at least one $k = 1, \ldots, K,$

$$f(y, z, a, r) \geq f(y, z, a^0, r^0),$$

---

[35] Leibenstein refers to this waste as "X-inefficiency" [11, p. 95].

and

$$C(a, r) \leq C(a^0, r^0).$$

Thus at an internal Pareto optimum, no reorganization of production in terms of activities and rules can make one employee better off, and no one else worse off, without lowering output or raising the administrative cost that pushes the firm to maximum profit. If, for example, through the imposition of rules, workers are not permitted to perform their jobs in ways in which they prefer, even though their preferred ways lead to the same output and administrative cost, then the (a, r) obtained is not Pareto optimal. Note that the director is not included in this notion of Pareto optimality and that the functions U^k, f, and C are all taken to be given.

Propositions asserting the allocative efficiency of ideal bureaucracies, clans, and militaries are presented in the following. In all cases y and z are assumed fixed and, as in the perfectly competitive economy, a non-market invisible hand allocates activities and rules so as to achieve optimality. Only the proof of Theorem 7.2 is outlined here; those of Theorems 7.3 and 7.4 are similar.[36]

Theorem 7.2: *Let the firm described in Section 7.2 be an ideal bureaucracy and suppose the director's rules impose no effective constraints on the selection of activities and rules by any worker. If $(\bar{a}, \bar{r})$ is an internal equilibrium for the firm, then it is also internally Pareto optimal in production.*

Proof: Suppose $(\bar{a}, \bar{r}) = (\bar{a}_1, \ldots, \bar{a}_K, \bar{r}_1, \ldots, \bar{r}_K)$ is an internal equilibrium (given y and z). Invoking Theorem 7.1 and the profit efficiency property that characterizes (in part) ideal bureaucracies, $(\bar{a}, \bar{r})$ also maximizes both profit and output. If $(\bar{a}, \bar{r})$ were not internally Pareto optimal, then there would exist a reorganization of production $(a, r) = (a_1, \ldots, a_K, r_1, \ldots, r_K)$ in the relevant $\mathcal{E}$ such that

$$U^k(a_k, r_k) > U^k(\bar{a}_k, \bar{r}_k), \tag{7.11}$$

for some employee k, and the levels of output and of utility of all other employees are no lower, and administrative cost is no higher at (a, r) than at $(\bar{a}, \bar{r})$. Now because the firm is an ideal bureaucracy, all employees are incentive motivated and all incentive functions are non-decreasing. But

---

[36] The proof of Theorem 7.3 is the same as that of Theorem 7.5 (or Theorem 11.2-5 in the reprinted version) in Gintis and Katzner [5]. (In each case, these proofs are located in an appendix.) See also Theorems 9, 7, and 8, respectively, in Katzner [8].

incentive motivation for the employee k in (7.11) implies

$$W^k(a_k, r_k) > W^k(\bar{a}_k, \bar{r}_k) \tag{7.12}$$

and hence by the non-decreasingness of W^k, output must be larger at (a, r) than at $(\bar{a}, \bar{r})$.[37] This contradicts the maximality of output at $(\bar{a}, \bar{r})$. Therefore $(\bar{a}, \bar{r})$ is internally Pareto optimal in production.   **Q.E.D.**

Theorem 7.3: *Let the firm described in Section 7.2 be an ideal clan and suppose the director's rules impose no effective constraints on the selection of activities and rules by any worker. If $(\bar{a}, \bar{r})$ is an internal equilibrium for the firm, then it is also internally Pareto optimal in production.*

Theorem 7.4: *Let the firm described in Section 7.2 be an ideal military and suppose the director's rules impose no effective constraints on the selection of activities and rules by any worker. If $(\bar{a}, \bar{r})$ is an internal equilibrium for the firm, then it is also internally Pareto optimal in production.*

An analogous theorem for the ideal market form of organization is easily established since (a) in this case employees (sub-firms) choose, without being subject to rule constraints, the highest level of utility that they can achieve; (b) output and profit are independent of these choices and hence automatically "maximized" over them; and (c) administrative cost is defined to be zero.

Thus, although trading the coordination of production within a firm by markets for the non-market coordination of social interactions among employees present in bureaucracies, clans, and militaries necessarily introduces social interactions where none formerly existed, it still does not force allocative inefficiencies of the activities and rules of production to which these social interactions relate. Internal Pareto optimality is a characteristic of internal equilibrium, at least theoretically, in all four idealized organizational forms. Therefore, the insertion or emergence of such organizational forms into an economy need not, as a matter of course, create new allocative waste which was not already there.

---

[37] This last step depends on the totality of the ordering defined in n. 32 on p. 164 above. For the uninteresting special case in which W^k is a constant function, inequality (7.12) by itself provides a more immediate contradiction. An alternative proof that does not use the non-decreasingness property of incentive functions can be found in Gintis and Katzner [5] as the proof of Theorem 7.3 in the original or of Theorem 11.2-3 in the reprinted version. (Again, these proofs are located in corresponding appendices.)

7.5 The Potential for Empirical Testing: Stage (iv)

In describing the stages of model construction as that has been outlined earlier, it was observed that stage (iv), the testing of a model against empirical reality, is often significantly important in assessing the competence of the model to explain, that is, its relevance to the explanation of the phenomenon under review. However, regardless of whether it is perceived as a structure elucidating the characteristics and functioning of an observed object such as a firm or is focused on observed outcomes that are represented in the single-output model style, the model of the present chapter built up until now does not, as pointed out previously, admit of empirical testing of its explanatory competence. In that regard, it is like the Walrasian general equilibrium model, Roemer's Marxian general equilibrium model, and the classical model of the microeconomy: The internal equilibrium $(\bar{a}, \bar{r})$ exists only in the model – not in a real firm. And given the profit-maximizing vector (y, z), the model is linked to reality in part by interpreting, in parallel with the Walrasian, Marxian, and classical cases, observations of real activities and rules as internal equilibria in the model. In this way the model may be said to explain those observations. That is, just as the general equilibrium fabrication, say, is useful in explaining and clarifying the operation of the microeconomy and its distinguishing features, the present model sheds light on the categorization of certain types of firms in terms of their characteristics, and their possible efficiency properties. Nevertheless, by introducing new elements it is possible to extend the model's stage (iii) development in such a manner that supplemental outputs of a different style are created. The model becomes, with respect to only this extension, a multi-output model, and one aspect of its explanatory competence becomes feasible to test.[38] In particular, the expansion of the model implies that the added model outcomes have specific properties that can be compared to characteristics of observed data, thus providing the means for a test. This expansion of the model is now briefly considered.[39]

The idea is to allow employees to become more skilled in their jobs and then derive the implications of their newly added skills for firm output and profitability. In present circumstances, the addition of new skills for

---

[38] Recall that, as indicated in n. 7 on p. 57, Brown and Matzkin [2] were able to impose testable restrictions on the general equilibrium model by expanding it to include varying initial endowments.

[39] A more detailed exposition may be found in Gintis and Katzner [5, pp. 286–288].

employee k involves the enlargement of his activity set A_k to, say, A_k^* where $A_k \subset A_k^*$. To keep notation simple, focus on employee 1. Let (y, z) be given and consider $(a, r) = (a_1, \ldots, a_K, r_1, \ldots, r_K)$ where all rule sets in the r_k are based on the activity sets $A_1^*, A_2, \ldots, A_K$. Suppose for each a_1^* in $A_1^* - A_1$, the output associated with $(a^*, r) = (a_1^*, a_2 \ldots, a_K, r_1, \ldots, r_K)$ is larger than that associated with (a, r). Under these conditions, when A_1^* is substituted for A_1 in the model of Section 7.2, employee 1 may be said to have become *more skilled* in his job. But at this point, there is no guarantee that employee 1, upon becoming more skilled, will use his new skills in doing his job (i.e., choose activities a_1^* from $A_1^* - A_1$), and that something or someone within the firm (for example, a jealous employee) will not act to subvert those new skills and thereby prevent firm output from rising. To handle the latter, call the firm *receptive to the new skills* of, say, employee 1, provided that if employee 1 becomes more skilled, then the subset of A_1^* out of which he chooses (namely, that subset constrained by $\cap_k R_{k1}$ plus the director's rules) contains at least one element of $A_1^* - A_1$. These definitions are generalized in the obvious manner to apply beyond employee 1 to all $k = 1, \ldots K$. Sufficient conditions are now set out under which more employee skills increase firm output and profitability. Proofs are straightforward; only the first is outlined.

Theorem 7.5: *Let the firm described in Section 7.2 be an ideal bureaucracy that is receptive to new employee skills, and suppose that an employee becomes more skilled. Then the output and profit of the firm increases.*

Proof: Let employee 1 become more skilled and substitute A_1^* for A_1. Then since in an ideal bureaucracy incentive functions are non-decreasing and the employee is incentive motivated, he will automatically choose an a_1^* from $A_1^* - A_1$ that increases firm output. The profit efficiency of the bureaucracy now ensures that the firm's profit rises. The argument is the same if any of the remaining employees $k = 2, \ldots K$ becomes more skilled.

Q.E.D.

Theorem 7.6: *Let the firm described in Section 7.2 be an ideal clan that is receptive to new employee skills, and suppose that an employee becomes more skilled. Then the output and profit of the firm increases.*

Theorem 7.7: *Let the firm described in Section 7.2 be an ideal military that is receptive to new employee skills, and suppose that an employee becomes more skilled. Then the output and profit of the firm increases.*

While it is beyond present scope to discuss empirical tests in detail, it is clear that even though the initial model of Sections 7.1–7.4 does not allow full tests of its explanatory competence, the potential for partial testing still exists. In particular, by expanding its stage (iii) development, the model can be tested against certain forces that bear on the firm, forces that may come from both internal and external economic sources, in order to ascertain whether the model's structure is stable and significantly explanatory against the possible changes those forces induce. The basis for one group of tests is provided by Theorems 7.5–7.7, each of which furnishes an observable behavioral function for a certain type of firm. Thus, collecting data for firms that can be identified as bureaucracies, clans, or militaries, it will be possible to see if increasing the skills of employees actually leads to greater output and profitability.

Without going into detail, it is also worth indicating how an alternative partial empirical test of explanatory competence might be set up that does not depend on the extension contained in Theorems 7.5–7.7. Let it be supposed that an external event (perhaps in the labor market) causing the firm to alter the wage incentive functions of employees, has given rise to the adoption by workers of different observed values of a and r. If those values before and after the modification in wage incentive functions, along with the corresponding observed output and input quantity values determined by the firm and its resulting profit, are linked to internal equilibrium outcomes of the structural relations of the model appropriate to the two situations, then a conclusion may be drawn regarding the effectiveness of the explanation produced by the model. Specifically, the extent to which the model explains how employees and the firm react to externally provoked movements in wage incentive functions may be revealed. That conclusion would be obtained by comparing the characteristics of the observed variable values with possible comparative static properties of the two internal equilibria (here the relevant model outcomes) that the observations before and after the changes in the wage incentive function are provisionally taken to represent. Such comparative static properties might be derivable from an appropriate stage (iii) expansion of assumption content of the model under the further assumption that, except for the wage incentive functions, the structural relations of the model have remained constant across the period of time over which the observations were recorded. To the degree that the results of such tests turn out to be consistent with the assumptions of the model and/or their implications, the potential of the model to explain the firm's structure and adjustment behavior would be enhanced.

The explanatory stability of the model over time could also be put under empirical review. Envisage a situation in the firm in which employees have chosen the a and r in such a way as to optimize their utility functions and the director of the firm will have decided on the firm's production variables y and z so as to maximize firm profit. In addition, and at the same time, suppose the director has set his rules for the firm's operation and, in the case of a bureaucracy, the incentive functions designed to sway employees in their selection of the a_k and r_k. With regard to clans or militaries, the director will also have introduced whatever measures are considered desirable to impact, respectively, employee socialization or goals and premise functions and thereby influence employee decisions regarding the a_k and r_k. Such a complex of rules, and incentives or influence-directed measures will have been ordered in such a way as to imply the firm's profit target. That target, in turn, will have been chosen in relation to maximum attainable profit as previously described. (The selection of such a target has not been discussed in the context of previous argument.)

Of course, in any particular subsequent situation, the profit target might not be realized. Two possible internal sources of disturbances exist. First, changes may occur in employees' a and r choices, induced simply by changes in their utility functions. Second, alternative variations in a and r may result from modifications in decisions handed down by the director for non-economic reasons that affect the director's rules, socialization efforts, or the firm's incentive or goals and premise functions. Such alterations, in turn, will conceivably cause ripples through the firm, with the result that the actual profit outcome may no longer meet the contemplated profit target. The question arises, then, of whether the entire set of relations of the model continues to provide a reasonable description of the activities that lead to the change in profit and the firm's adjustment, if any, to it. If the variation in firm activity appears to be explicable in terms of the explanation the model proposes, then the model is explanatorily stable over the change.

External economic sources of disturbance may emanate from changes in market conditions. They may come from competitive-induced price changes, customer demand changes, macroeconomic cyclical variations, and so on. In response to such disturbances, changes will conceivably be made in decisions at all levels within the firm. What matters here, in so far as explanatory stability is concerned, is whether such changes, as they are induced by the exogenous shocks, undulate through the firm's structure in such a way that any variations continue to be reasonably describable by the equations of the model.

7.6 Cogency and Relevance: Stage (v)

Stage (v) in the construction of models in economics requires that a judgment be made about the significance (i.e., cogency, relevance, and usefulness) of the model in explaining how efficiency might arise in the stage (i) organizational forms set out dialectically in Section 7.1.

To begin with, it has already been stated in the previous section that the model is useful in clarifying the characteristics of firm types and firm efficiency properties. In addition, the logical coherence of the model and of the analysis of efficiency it permits are evident. All parts of the model, both within and across the various stages of construction, fit closely together and support each other. The cogency of the model and its ability to explain are therefore clear.

Moreover, as pointed out at the end of Chapter 6, the abstraction required to build and develop the model necessarily leaves the model somewhat removed from the dialectical base from which it springs. But there are clear bridges to actuality in the initial stage of constructing the model. Indeed, the arithmomorphic concepts of activities, rules, influence, bureaucracy, military, clan, and the characteristics of incentive motivation and internalizing the values of the firm, etc., are all directly linked to observations of real phenomena. In addition to the potential for empirical tests mentioned above, gathering data on things like profit efficiency, incentive functions, and motivations in order to do actual testing, though also not pursued here, would confirm different kinds of bridges at the level of stage (iv) and could only strengthen the persuasiveness and relevance of the model.

Of course, it is worth emphasizing here the earlier argument that the notion of internal equilibrium is an element of the model and does not exist with respect to the actual firms under investigation. To the extent that the model is invoked in explanation, observations of (a, r) in the firm at issue would be identified with internal equilibria in the model. This provides a further bridge from the model to economic reality.

Thus, subject to the distance from reality that is inherent in the construction of any model, one may conclude that it nevertheless provides a cogent, relevant, and useful understanding and explanation of how certain kinds of internal organizations of firms can be efficient. And this has nothing to do with whatever competitive forces may exist in the markets in which the firm sells its output and hires its inputs. The notions of efficiency of the various organizational forms described here are subtle and deep, and supplemental to the standard concepts of market efficiencies of optimal input mix, optimal output produced and inputs hired, and minimum unit cost.

References

[1] Beckmann, M. J., *Rank in Organizations* (Berlin: Springer-Verlag, 1978).

[2] Brown, D. J. and R. L. Matzkin, "Testable Restrictions on the Equilibrium Manifold," *Econometrica* 64 (1996), pp. 1249–1262.

[3] Calvo, G. A., and S. Wellisz, "Hierarchy, Ability and Income Distribution," *Journal of Political Economy* 87 (1979), pp. 991–1010.

[4] Coase, R. H., "The Nature of the Firm," *Economica*, n.s. 4 (1937), pp. 386–405.

[5] Gintis, H., and D. W. Katzner, "Profits, Optimality and the Social Division of Labor in the Firm," in *Sociological Economics*, L. Lévy-Garboua, ed. (London: Sage, 1979), pp. 269–297. Reprinted as Ch. 11 in D. W. Katzner, *Analysis without Measurement* (Cambridge: Cambridge University Press, 1983).

[6] Janowitz, M., *Sociology and the Military Establishment*, rev. ed. (New York: Russell Sage Foundation, 1965).

[7] Katzner, D. W., *Analysis without Measurement* (Cambridge: Cambridge University Press, 1983), Ch. 11.

[8] Katzner, D. W., "The Role of Formalism in Economic Thought, with Illustration Drawn from the Analysis of Social Interaction in the Firm," in *The Reconstruction of Economic Theory*, P. Mirowski, ed. (Boston, MA: Kluwer-Nijhoff, 1986), pp. 137–177.

[9] Kidder, T., *The Soul of a New Machine* (Boston, MA: Little Brown, 1981).

[10] Lang, K., "Military Organizations," in *Handbook of Organizations*, J. C. March, ed. (Chicago, IL: Rand McNally, 1965), Ch. 20.

[11] Leibenstein, H., *Beyond Economic Man* (Cambridge, MA: Harvard University Press, 1976).

[12] O'Toole, J., *Work, Learning and the American Future* (San Francisco, CA: Jossey-Bass, 1977).

[13] Ouchi, W. G., "Markets, Bureaucracies, and Clans," *Administrative Science Quarterly* 25 (1980), pp. 129–141.

[14] Ouchi, W. G., *Theory Z* (Reading: Addison-Wesley, 1981).

[15] Rothschild, E., *Paradise Lost: The Decline of the Auto-Industrial Age* (New York: Random House, 1973).

[16] Sah, R. K., and J. E. Stiglitz, "The Architecture of Economic Systems: Hierarchies and Polyarchies," *American Economic Review* 76 (1986), pp. 716–727.

[17] Smith, A., *An Inquiry into the Nature and Causes of the Wealth of Nations* (New York: Random House, 1937).

[18] Williamson, O. E., "Hierarchical Control and Optimum Firm Size," *Journal of Political Economy* 75 (1967), pp. 123–138.

[19] Williamson, O. E., *Markets and Hierarchies: Analysis and Antitrust Implications* (New York: Free Press, 1975).

[20] Williamson, O. E., "The Modern Corporation: Origins, Evolution, Attributes," *Journal of Economic Literature* 19 (1981), pp. 1537–1568.

8

The Implicit Assumption Requirements of
Later-Stage Model Building

The concept of model building in explanation as contemplated here and illustrated in the previous chapter has been described in Section 3.1 to include five procedural steps in the process of model construction: (i) formulate an initial image, (ii) transform it into a model, (iii) operationalize the model, (iv) test the model when appropriate, and (v) evaluate the explanatory significance of the model, i.e., its cogency, relevance, and usefulness. It has also been suggested (Section 3.2) that in many instances of model building economists tend to ignore stages (i) and (ii) and proceed directly to stage (iii). But skipping over stages (i) and (ii), it has been argued, has serious consequences, namely, an impairment of the ability to judge the relevance and usefulness of the model under consideration. Several informal examples have been given to indicate how beginning model construction at stage (iii) can hide important assumption content that might lead the investigator to reject and discard the model on the grounds of impertinence and inadequacy. One of these illustrations was the starting of the construction of the model of consumer demand at stage (iii) with the secondary assumption of an additive utility function. It was asserted in that case (the proof has been delayed until Section 8.2 below) that additivity implied that the preference ordering underlying the utility function had the property that the individual's preference for any quantity of any commodity was independent of the quantities of all other commodities – a characteristic of individual preferences that might not seem realistic and suitable for the purpose at hand.

This conclusion points to a general principle of some importance that has been brought out earlier and is worth emphasizing again: To a considerable extent, the ability of a model to relate and explain rests on the nature of the stage (iii) secondary assumptions and what they imply at the nearer-to-reality stage (i) and stage (ii) levels. Thus model building that neglects stages (i) and (ii), and begins at stage (iii) leaves important questions concerning its acceptability somewhat in doubt.

The purpose of this chapter is to investigate in more formality and greater detail the nature of some of the assumptions at the level of stage (ii) that are implicitly introduced, that is, implied though not explicitly stated, by certain secondary assumptions when starting at stage (iii) with an operational model. In particular, the stage (ii) implications of the stage (iii) assumptions that introduce new ordering relations and various forms of function separability are explored. The secondary assumption of an additive utility function described above will be included in the discussion of the last of these topics. In general, by bringing such properties to light, the ability to judge the relevance and usefulness of a model will be enhanced.

To be more precise with respect to subsequent argument, suppose a model-building process starts at stage (iii) by specifying a single-valued, quantified or unquantified function of one or more quantified or unquantified variables. Since stage (ii) has not previously been considered, this may also be interpreted, were the process begun at earlier stages, as a function that could have appeared in some form at stage (ii) before it was operationalized into stage (iii). For the purpose of present discussion, identify the latter as the stage (ii) function. If the quantification (or lack thereof) of a dependent or independent variable of the function were thought to be the same at both stages, then the variable in the two stages would be identical. If quantification were present at stage (iii) and if it were taken to be lost in moving back to stage (ii), then the stage (ii) variable would be that which underlies its measured counterpart at stage (iii). Present concern is with the implications that are implicit in whatever properties are assumed on the stage (iii) function. These implications might possibly have been imposed on the function at the level of stage (ii) had the model building begun with the first two stages as described in Chapter 2.

The discussion that follows is necessarily quite technical. It is summarized here so that the technicalities may be skipped if desired. To present basic ideas, a model relevant to the physical world is examined first. Let a stage (iii) linear functional relation between the measured weight and measured length of material objects be postulated. Nothing else is assumed at the level of stage (iii) nor is attention paid to earlier stages. Nevertheless, pushing the linear relation back to the level of stage (ii), that function may be interpreted as relating the non-measured heaviness of objects to their non-measured longness. The stage (ii) implications that are derived from the original stage (iii) assumption, then, are that ordering relations are induced among longness and heaviness values by the numerical measures of length and weight, and that the stage (ii) function is both order-preserving and, when more than one independent variable is involved, subject to a cancellation property.

The same sorts of things carry over to economic modeling. Regardless of whether variables are quantified or not, any ordering relation assumed on the range of a function in the model-building process starting at stage (iii) induces an ordering of the vectors in the domain of definition of that function. The latter ordering is an implication of a stage (iii) assumption and can be interpreted as a property that could have been introduced at stage (ii) were the model-building process to include earlier stages. Acknowledging the induced ordering, the stage (iii) function itself could be described as order-preserving. Adding, at stage (iii), the assumption that that function takes on various forms of separability (weak, strong, additivity) to the supposition of an ordering of the range of the function implies that that function partitions the vectors in its domain into sub-vectors. Moreover, the variable values of any sub-vector are ordered by the ordering induced by that on the function's range independently of all variable values not associated with the particular sub-vector under consideration. In the case of additivity, the values of each variable are ordered independently of the values of all other variables. These, too, may be regarded as properties that might possibly have been introduced at stage (ii) and are implicitly present by dint of the assumption content at stage (iii). The existence of such properties, if unrecognized, may lead to a faulty stage (v) judgment of the model's explanatory competence.

8.1 The Problem in Physics Terms

The issues addressed here are not as serious when they arise in many instances of physical science. For example, consider a set of objects for which it is assumed that their weights (W) are proportional to their lengths (L). Thus, at stage (iii) operationality,

$$W = \alpha L, \tag{8.1}$$

where α is the (positive) constant of proportionality. Now length and weight are measured on ratio scales, and the presence of these measures already implies something about the underlying properties of the objects in terms of, respectively, their "longness" (ℓ) and "heaviness" (w). To illustrate, objects are ordered by their longnesses, and "more" longness is accorded greater numerical length on the scale that measures it. A parallel statement applies for heaviness and weight. Moreover, once the longnesses and heavinesses of the objects are measured, the constant of proportionality α can be estimated. Of course, changing the scales on which longness and heaviness are measured will change the estimated value of α. In terms of the stage (ii) specification of this model, (8.1) says, apart from the requirements due to the existence of the ratio scales, that longness is related to heaviness,

$$w = f(\ell),$$

where f is the name of the relation, and that the more longness in any one object, the more heaviness. The latter statement asserts that the relation between longness and heaviness is order-preserving: as longness increases, so does heaviness. One of the implicit assumptions of the operational form (8.1), then, is the presence of such a relation in the associated stage (ii) specification.

As a second example, suppose objects consist of two parts, 1 and 2, and that the operational specification is

$$W = \alpha_1 L_1 + \alpha_2 L_2 \tag{8.2}$$

where W is the weight of the object, L_1 is the length of part 1, L_2 is the length of part 2, and α_1 and α_2 are constants. Here, one of the implicit assumptions imposed on the stage (ii) specification is that the longness of part 1 (ℓ_1) combined with the longness of part 2 (ℓ_2) relate to the heaviness of the object (w):

$$w = f(\ell_1, \ell_2), \tag{8.3}$$

where, again, f is the name of the relation. And a form of order-preservation appears in f in that an ordering of the vector values in the domain of f is induced by the greater-than-or-equal-to ordering of weight values in its range. Of course, (8.1) may be regarded as a special case of (8.2). But the fact that (8.2) is additive implies something further about (8.3). To illustrate this in simplest form, suppose that there is a 1-1 correspondence between values of ℓ_i and values of L_i, for $i = 1, 2$. Then it is clear from (8.2) that for any values ℓ_1', ℓ_1'', and ℓ_2', if

$$f(\ell_1', \ell_2') = f(\ell_1'', \ell_2'),$$

then

$$\ell_1' = \ell_1''.$$

This last property is sometimes referred to as *cancellation*.[1] It asserts here that if two objects have equal heavinesses and if the longnesses of their first parts are the same, then the longnesses of their second parts are also the same. As before, changing the scales on which any of the longness or heaviness variables are measured will change any estimated values of α_1 and α_2.

The implications of (8.1) and (8.2) for their respective stage (ii) specifications described above cause no problems because they are consistent with what our intuition would suggest at stage (i). But, as is often the case in economics, when variables reflecting the properties of the objects under examination are not as clearly quantified or even nonquantifiable, the procedure of starting at stage (iii) becomes murky. For postulating, at the stage (iii) operational level, functional relations between such "measured" variables or between numerical "proxies" for such variables is implicitly imposing specific characteristics on the stage (ii) specification that may or may not be appropriate. (A different argument has been made above against starting at stage (iii) in general when measurement is not at issue.) For example, suppose at stage (iii), measures of security and freedom were developed and a functional relation between them in the form of (8.1) were hypothesized. Suppose further that the constant of proportionality were negative, meaning that greater security would be associated with less freedom. Then in the stage (ii) specification that underlies this relation the implication would be that certain forms of unquantified security are identified with certain forms of unquantified freedom in an order-reversing way, where the orderings are determined by the numerical measures of these variables.[2]

Of course, unlike the situation with respect to length and weight where intuition suggests clarity in specification and a meaningfulness to order preservation in that context, it is not obvious how, in the case of unquantified variables such as security and freedom, to identify concretely the underlying order-reversing relation and interpret its meaning. What values of the variable security would be associated with what values of the variable freedom? Is that association consistent with what is known or suspected about reality? Do the orderings that are involved in the order-reversing

---

[1] Without the one-to-one correspondence, the equation $\ell_1' = \ell_1''$ would be replaced by the statement that ℓ_1' is "equivalent" to ℓ_1'', meaning that both are associated with the same measured value of L_1.

[2] Fromm [2, pp. 194–197], for example, describes such a relationship without reference to numbers.

property make intuitive sense in terms of the variable values? And so on.[3] Nevertheless, deducing from the hypothesized properties of the model in question that such a functional relation is order-reversing still provides some information about what is being assumed in reference to the stage (ii) specification. That information may contribute at stage (v) to an evaluation of the appropriateness and usefulness of the original relation itself.

In the next section of this chapter, the nature of some of the characteristics imposed on stage (ii) specifications by operationally hypothesized functional properties at stage (iii) will be examined. For it is at the earlier stage (ii) that, as has been suggested, critical questions arise relating to the explanatory competence of the model under consideration. Indeed, when model-building proceeds by starting at stage (iii), it may turn out that the functional specifications involved imply assumption counterparts at what would be stage (ii) that were intuitively irrelevant or contrary to actual fact. Logically speaking, of course, these same inappropriate stage (ii) characteristics may often be interpreted as the source of the stage (iii) functional properties initially assumed.

8.2 The Problem in Economic Terms

Consider first, in the interest of generality, a real situation in which, at stage (i), two unquantified variables, say x and y, seem to be involved. Suppose also that circumstances suggest the presence of a functional relation between them. Then, for analytical purposes at stage (ii), it would be reasonable and appropriate to postulate (this would be a primary assumption) a function mapping, for example, x into y:

$$y = f(x). \tag{8.4}$$

Although the domain, call it D_x, and range, identified as R_y, of this function could be conceived as containing an uncountably infinite number of elements, in practice it is not possible to specify more than a finite number of elements of each. Moreover, when defining f in such an unquantified world, general rules of association are not available. It is therefore necessary

---

[3] Were the variables to remain in an unquantified state, then the form of the functional relation would be unique. If they were both ordinally measured, then the form of the relation would be unique up to increasing, continuous transformations of its domain and range into the reals. When cardinally measured, the form of the relation is unique up to increasing linear transformations of its domain and range into the reals. With respect to the latter two cases, the transformation applied to the domain of the function in any particular instance need not be identical to that applied to its range.

to indicate by explicit identification which value of y in R_y is to be associated under f with each value of x in D_x. And this can only be done for a finite number of pairs (x, y). Thus, in moving to the operational level of stage (iii), postulation without explicit specification of a more expansive function having nonfinite domain and range, though possible, falls in the realm of pure conjecture and, except for a finite number of functional pairs, can have no basis in experience. The same is true when both x and y are expressible in numerical form – although, in that case, f is often fully and explicitly specifiable through the articulation of a general, quantitative rule. Regardless, it follows that, when constructing a model (quantified or not), any stage (iii) assumption (made, perhaps, for analytical convenience) of a function with a nonfinite domain and range introduces a certain arbitrariness into the analysis that is more severe in some cases than in others. Subsequent discussion, however, ignores the issue and applies to both finite and nonfinite domain-range situations.

Continuing with the unquantified example of (8.4), let ordering relations $\geq_x$ and $\geq_y$ be defined on D_x and R_y respectively, that are reflexive, transitive, and total.[4] On their respective domains, these relations each generate further relations $>_x$, $=_x$, $>_y$, and $=_y$ defined, for example, as follows: For all x' and x'',

$$x' >_x x'' \quad \text{if and only if}$$
$$x' \geq_x x'' \quad \text{and it is not the case that } x'' \geq_x x',$$

and

$$x' =_x x'' \quad \text{if and only if} \quad \text{both } x' \geq_x x'' \text{ and} x'' \geq_x x'.$$

It can be shown that $>_x$ and $>_y$ are irreflexive, asymmetric, and transitive and $=_x$ and $=_y$ are equivalence relations.[5] Of course, if, for all x' and x'' in D_x,

$$f(x') \geq_y f(x'') \quad \text{if and only if} \quad x' \geq_x x'', \tag{8.5}$$

then f, as previously suggested, *preserves* order. If $x' \geq_x x''$ in (8.5) were replaced by $x'' \geq_x x'$, then f would *reverse* order. Thus, were an analysis

---

[4] Recall that a relation such as $\geq_x$ on D_x is *reflexive* when $x \geq_x x$ for all x in D_x. It is *transitive* if $x' \geq_x x''$ and $x'' \geq_x x'''$ imply $x' \geq_x x'''$, for all x', x'', and x''' in D_x. And it is *total* provided that, for all x' and x'' in D_x, either $x' \geq_x x''$ or $x'' \geq_x x'$.

[5] A relation like $>_x$ on D_x is *irreflexive* when it is not the case that $x >_x x$ for every x in D_x. It is *asymmetric* provided that for all x' and x'' in D_x, if $x' >_x x''$ then it is not the case that $x'' >_x x'$. As indicated in an earlier chapter, an *equivalence relation* is one that is reflexive, transitive, and symmetric. In terms of $=_x$, *symmetry* requires that if $x' =_x x''$ then $x'' =_x x'$ for all x' and x'' in D_x.

to start at the operational level of stage (iii) by postulating (these would be additional secondary assumptions) the existence of $\geq_y$ on R_y and f on D_x, then an ordering relation $\geq_x$ would be implied on D_x and, with respect to those ordering relations, f would be order preserving. The existence of $\geq_x$ on D_x is the implicit assumption counterpart at the level of primary or stage-(ii)-level assumptions to the secondary assumptions imposed above. And it is precisely at this point that questions arise as to whether that implied stage (ii) primary-level assumption could be consistent with, assuming they have been developed, the investigator's stage (i) understanding of the universe in which the phenomenon in view arose and with his conceptualization of the phenomenon itself. (A reverse order, not that implied by order preservation might be what the investigator thinks is required to analyze the problem at hand.) If the implied stage (ii) primary-level assumption is not consistent with that understanding, then what relevance to reality and what meaning, if any, can be attached to the stage (iii) assumption of the ordering of the elements of R_y by $\geq_y$? Of course, if the investigation starts at stage (iii) with the assumptions of f and the ordering $\geq_y$ on R_y and if no implications appropriate to stage (ii) of those assumptions are explored, then the investigator would not be aware of any lack of consistency with reality in this regard, and the stage (v) judgment of the explanatory competency of the model would not take that inconsistency into account.

These ideas apply to (8.4) and (8.5) in exactly the same way when x is a vector of unquantified variables x_i where $i = 1, \ldots, I$, that is, $x = (x_1, \ldots, x_I)$ for x in D_x. From here on it is assumed that x is such a vector and that the meaning of (8.4) and (8.5) is expressed with respect to that fact. In this latter case, further possibilities for secondary assumptions are worth considering. The illustrations presented below are all based on the standard analysis of separable preferences and their utility representations in the theory of consumer demand,[6] and will include the special case of additive utility functions discussed earlier.

Partition the numbers $1, \ldots, I$ into $N < I$ mutually exclusive and exhaustive sets: $s_1 = \{1, \ldots, i_1\}$, $s_2 = \{i_1 + 1, \ldots, i_2\}, \ldots, s_N = \{i_{N-1} + 1, \ldots, I\}$. Using this partition, divide the components of x into the N subvectors $x_{(1)} = (x_1, \ldots, x_{i_1})$, $x_{(2)} = (x_{i_1+1}, \ldots, x_{i_2}), \ldots, x_{(N)} = (x_{i_{N-1}+1}, \ldots, x_I)$. Then $x = (x_{(1)}, \ldots, x_{(N)})$ and each of the subvectors $x_{(n)}$, where $n = 1, \ldots, N$, ranges over an appropriate subdomain $D_{x_{(n)}}$ obtained by correspondingly

---

[6] See, for example, Katzner [3, pp. 27–31]. The terminology employed here is somewhat different from that used by Katzner.

partitioning D_x so that $D_x = D_{x_{(1)}} \times \cdots \times D_{x_{(N)}}$. In addition, for any n define the vector

$$x_{(\bar{n})} = (x_{(1)}, \ldots, x_{(n-1)}, x_{(n+1)}, \ldots, x_{(N)})$$

and the set

$$D_{x_{(\bar{n})}} = (D_{x_{(1)}}, \ldots, D_{x_{(n-1)}}, D_{x_{(n+1)}}, \ldots, D_{x_{(N)}}).$$

Even though the order of appearance of the x_i's may be different, for notational convenience $(x_{(n)}, x_{(\bar{n})})$ will be thought of as identical to x for any n.

Now the ordering $\geq_x$ induces an ordering on each $D_{x_{(n)}}$ which generally depends on points of $D_{x_{(\bar{n})}}$. For any n, if $\hat{x}_{(\bar{n})}$ is such a point, then the induced ordering, $\geq_{\hat{x}_{(\bar{n})}}$, is defined by

$$x'_{(n)} \geq_{\hat{x}_{(\bar{n})}} x''_{(n)} \text{ if and only if } (x'_{(n)}, \hat{x}_{(\bar{n})}) \geq_x (x''_{(n)}, \hat{x}_{(\bar{n})}), \qquad (8.6)$$

for all $x'_{(n)}$ and $x''_{(n)}$ in $D_{x_{(n)}}$. In light of (8.6), call $\geq_x$ *separable* with respect to the partition $\{s_1, \ldots, s_N\}$ whenever $x'_{(n)} \geq_{\hat{x}_{(\bar{n})}} x''_{(n)}$ implies $x'_{(n)} \geq_{x_{(\bar{n})}} x''_{(n)}$ for every $x_{(\bar{n})}$ in $D_{x_{(\bar{n})}}$ and every n. That is, for each n, the ordering $\geq_{\hat{x}_{(\bar{n})}}$ on $D_{x_{(n)}}$ does not change as $\hat{x}_{(\bar{n})}$ varies. In parallel fashion, the function f induces functions on the $D_{x_{(n)}}$ that also depend on the points of $D_{x_{(\bar{n})}}$. With $\hat{x}_{(\bar{n})}$ a fixed point of $D_{x_{(\bar{n})}}$, the induced function is given by

$$f^{\hat{x}_{(\bar{n})}}(x_{(n)}) = f(x_{(n)}, \hat{x}_{(\bar{n})}) \qquad (8.7)$$

for all $x_{(n)}$ in $D_{x_{(n)}}$. Evidently, the range of each $f^{\hat{x}_{(\bar{n})}}$ is a subset of R_y. In addition, the function f is referred to as *separable* with respect to the partition $\{s_1, \ldots, s_N\}$ provided that there exist functions g and $f^1, \ldots, f^N$ such that

(a) g maps an N-dimensional set $Z_1 \times \cdots \times Z_N$ of vectors $z = (z_1, \ldots, z_N)$ ordered by some reflexive, transitive, and total relation $\geq_z$ into R_y in an order-preserving way,

(b) each set $Z_n \subseteq R_y$ and is ordered by some reflexive, antisymmetric,[7] transitive, and total relation $\geq_{z_n}$, which is a subset of $\geq_y$,

(c) each f^n maps $D_{x_{(n)}}$ in an order-preserving way into the set Z_n,

(d) in light of their implications through the order-preserving functions $f, f^1, \ldots, f^N$, and g, all ordering relations $\geq_{x_{(\bar{n})}}, \geq_{z_n}, \geq_z$ and $\geq_y$ are consistent with each other,

---

[7] The relation $\geq_{z_n}$ is antisymmetric if $z' \geq_{z_n} z''$ and $z'' \geq_{z_n} z'$ implies $z' = z''$, for all z' and z'' in Z_n.

and

(e)

$$f(x) = g(f^1(x_{(1)}), \ldots, f^N(x_{(N)})) \tag{8.8}$$

throughout the domain D_x.

Theorem 8.1: *Let f and $\geq_x$ be defined on D_x and $\geq_y$ be defined on R_y such that, in addition to its other properties, $\geq_y$ is antisymmetric. Suppose f is order-preserving. Then f is separable with respect to the partition $\{s_1, \ldots, s_N\}$ if and only if $\geq_x$ is too.*

Proof: Suppose f is separable with respect to the partition $\{s_1, \ldots, s_N\}$. Choose an n and $\hat{x}_{(\bar{n})}$ in $D_{x_{(\bar{n})}}$. For any $x'_{(n)}$ and $x''_{(n)}$ in $D_{x_{(n)}}$, suppose $x'_{(n)} \geq_{\hat{x}_{(\bar{n})}} x''_{(n)}$. As described earlier, with f order preserving and separable, f^n is order preserving. Thus

$$f^n(x'_{(n)}) \geq_z f^n(x''_{(n)}) \text{ if and only if } x'_{(n)} \geq_{\hat{x}_{(\bar{n})}} x''_{(n)}.$$

Since this is true for any $\hat{x}_{(\bar{n})}$ in $D_{x_{(\bar{n})}}$, it follows that $\geq_{\hat{x}_{(\bar{n})}}$ is independent of $\hat{x}_{(\bar{n})}$. A similar argument holds for each n. Therefore $\geq_x$ is separable.

Assume, on the other hand, that $\geq_x$ is separable with respect to the partition $\{s_1, \ldots, s_N\}$. For each n, choose an $\hat{x}_{(\bar{n})}$ in $D_{x_{(\bar{n})}}$. Set $Z_n = R_y$ so that $Z = R_y \times \cdots \times R_y$ where Z has N dimensions, and define $f^n(x_{(n)}) = f^{\hat{x}_{(\bar{n})}}(x_{(n)})$ where $f^{\hat{x}_{(\bar{n})}}(x_{(n)})$ is the function induced on $D_{x_{(n)}}$ by f in (8.7). Since f is order preserving, so is f^n. Let $\geq_{z_n} = \geq_y$ for every n. Lastly, define g by (8.8) and take $\geq_z$ to be the relation defined by $z' \geq_z z''$ if and only if $z'_n \geq_{z_n} z''_n$ for every n, where $z' = (z'_1, \ldots, z'_N)$ and $z'' = (z''_1, \ldots, z''_N)$. Thus g is order preserving and f is separable.   **Q.E.D.**

Letting $\geq_y$ generate $\geq_x$ through f as in (8.5) with x' and x'' taken as vectors, a second result is obtained. Its proof is similar to the first part of the proof of Theorem 8.1 and is omitted.

Theorem 8.2: *Let f be defined on D_x and $\geq_y$ be defined on R_y. If f is separable with respect to the partition $\{s_1, \ldots, s_N\}$, then any ordering relation $\geq_x$ determined by f on D_x through (8.5) is also separable with respect to that partition.*

Thus when an ordering relation is defined on the range of a function, secondary assumptions like (8.8) imply, at the primary assumption level, a separable ordering of the function's domain. In the stage (v) evaluation of a model containing the secondary assumption of a separable utility function, it is necessary in this case to ask if the implied assumption of separable preferences is appropriate in light of initial stage (i) considerations.

Now suppose that R_y and the Z_n are subsets of the real line and $\geq_y$, the $\geq_{z_n}$, and $\geq_z$ are "greater-than-or-equal-to" among real numbers. Let $\mathcal{T}_x$ be the order topology defined with respect to D_x in terms of $\geq_x$,[8] and the $\mathcal{T}_{x_{(n)}}$ that with respect to $D_{x_{(n)}}$ in terms of $\geq_{x_{(\bar{n})}}$. All notions of continuity are characterized in relation to these topologies and the standard order topology for sets of real numbers. For example, if $\mathcal{T}_y$ is the latter order topology with respect to R_y, then to say that f is continuous is to say that the inverse image under f of any set in $\mathcal{T}_y$ is contained in $\mathcal{T}_x$. Continuity, of course, is another property of functions, which, when assumed at the operational level of stage (iii) as a secondary assumption, has its own implications for the collection of assumptions at the primary level of stage (ii).

Refer to $\geq_x$ as *multi-separable* with respect to the partition $\{s_1, \ldots, s_N\}$ if it is separable with respect to $\{s_1, \ldots, s_N\}$ and each of the partitions consisting of unions of $s_1, \ldots, s_N$ except $\{1, \ldots, I\}$ itself. The function f is said to be *additively separable* with respect to the partition $\{s_1, \ldots, s_N\}$ if it is separable with respect to that partition, the functions f, g, and the f^n are all continuous and

$$f(x) = g(f^1(x_{(1)}) + \cdots + f^N(x_{(N)})). \tag{8.9}$$

Observe that in (8.9), g is now a function of what has become the scalar variable z. The next two propositions provide results parallel to Theorems 8.1 and 8.2 relating these two stronger forms of separability. The proof of the second, being clear, is not given.

Theorem 8.3: *Let f and $\geq_x$ be defined on D_x and $\geq_y$ be defined on R_y such that, in addition to its other properties, $\geq_y$ is antisymmetric. Suppose f is order-preserving and continuous. Then f is additively separable with respect to the partition $\{s_1, \ldots, s_N\}$ if and only if $\geq_x$ is multi-separable with respect to that partition.*

Proof: If f is additively separable with respect to the partition $\{s_1, \ldots, s_N\}$, then repeated applications of Theorem 8.1 to partitions consisting of $s_1, \ldots, s_N$ and unions of $s_1, \ldots, s_N$ shows that $\geq_x$ is multi-separable with respect to $\{s_1, \ldots, s_N\}$.

---

[8] That is, each element of $\mathcal{T}_x$ is the union of finite intersections of sets of the form $\{x : a >_x x\}$ or $\{x : x >_x a\}$ for a in D_x.

If $\geq_x$ is multi-separable with respect to the partition $\{s_1, \ldots, s_N\}$, applying the construction in the second half of the proof of Theorem 8.1 to any partition consisting of $s_1, \ldots, s_N$ or unions of $s_1, \ldots, s_N$, the order-preserving f^n are continuous because f is continuous. Hence, for that partition, the function g can be taken to be continuous. Consider, first, the case in which $N = 3$ and focus on the following three of the associated partitions: $\{s_1 \cup s_2, s_3\}$, $\{s_1, s_2 \cup s_3\}$, and $\{s_1, s_2, s_3\}$. Distinguish among them with the superscript j for $j = 1, 2, 3$ respectively referring to each of the three partitions. As in the second half of the proof of Theorem 8.1, there exist continuous, order-preserving functions g and f^{jn} such that

$$
\begin{aligned}
f(x) &= g^1(f^{11}(x_{(1)}, x_{(2)}), f^{12}(x_{(3)})) \\[6pt]
&= g^2(f^{21}(x_{(1)}, f^{22}(x_{(2)}, x_{(3)}))) \qquad\qquad (8.10) \\[6pt]
&= g^3(f^{31}(x_{(1)}), f^{32}(x_{(2)}), f^{33}(x_{(3)})),
\end{aligned}
$$

where f^{jn} is the function f^n of (8.8) for the j-th partition, and

$$
f^{11}(x_{(1)}, x_{(2)}) = h^1(f^{31}(x_{(1)}), f^{32}(x_{(2)})),
$$

and

$$
f^{22}(x_{(2)}, x_{(3)}) = h^2(f^{32}(x_{(2)}), f^{33}(x_{(3)})),
$$

for some functions h^1 and h^2 that are continuous and order-preserving.[9] Moreover, since $f^{12}(x_{(3)})$ can be seen as a continuous, order-preserving function of $f^{33}(x_{(3)})$, and $f^{21}(x_{(1)})$ as a continuous, order-preserving function of $f^{31}(x_{(1)})$,[10] the functions g^1 and g^2 in (8.10) may be redefined

---

[9] For example, to obtain h^1, invert g^1 in the first equality of (8.10) to obtain $f^{11}(x_{(1)}, x_{(2)}) = g^*(f(x), f^{12}(x_{(3)}))$. (This may be done since order preservation and the anti-symmetry of $\geq_{z_n}$ implies the existence of the required inverse.) Next substitute for $f(x)$ using the third equality of (8.10) so that $f^{11}(x_{(1)}, x_{(2)}) = g^*(g^3(f^{31}(x_{(1)}), f^{32}(x_{(2)}), f^{33}(x_{(3)})), f^{12}(x_{(3)}))$. The right-hand side, with $x_{(3)}$ fixed at any value, may be taken to be $h^1(f^{31}(x_{(1)}), f^{32}(x_{(2)}))$. Previous assumptions imply that h^1 is continuous and order preserving.

[10] For example, invert g^1 in the first equality of (8.10) to obtain $f^{12}(x_{(3)}) = g^{**}(f^{11}(x_{(1)}, x_{(2)}), f(x))$. Then substitute for $f(x)$ using the third equality of (8.10) to secure $f^{12}(x_{(3)}) = g^{**}(f^{11}(x_{(1)}, x_{(2)}), g^3(f^{31}(x_{(1)}), f^{32}(x_{(2)}), f^{33}(x_{(3)})))$. The right-hand side, with $x_{(1)}$ and $x_{(2)}$ fixed at any values, appears as a function, call it d, of $f^{33}(x_{(3)})$, that is, $f^{12}(x_{(3)}) = d(f^{33}(x_{(3)}))$. Previous assumptions imply that d is continuous and order preserving.

as

$$f(x) = g^1(f^{11}(x_{(1)}, x_{(2)}), f^{12}(x_{(3)}))$$

$$= g^2\left(f^{31}(x_{(1)}, f^{22}(x_{(2)}, x_{(3)})\right),$$

where g^1 and g^2 remain order preserving.[11] Replacing f^{11} and f^{22} by, respectively, h^1 and h^2, and letting $q_n = f^{3n}(x_{(n)})$ for $n = 1, 2, 3$, this becomes

$$f(x) = g^1(h^1(q_1, q_2), q_3) = g^2(q_1, h^2(q_2, q_3)). \tag{8.11}$$

The solution of the functional equation defined by the right-hand equality of (8.11) (see Aczél [1, p. 312, Corollary 1]) consists of the four equations:

$$g^1(h^1(q_1, q_2), q_3) = u^1(u^2(h^1(q_1, q_2)) + u^3(q_3)), \tag{8.12}$$

$$h^1(q_1, q_2) = u^{2^{-1}}(u^4(q_1) + u^5(q_2)), \tag{8.13}$$

$$g^2(q_1, h^2(q_2, q_3)) = u^1(u^4(q_1) + u^6(h^2(q_2, q_3))), \tag{8.14}$$

and

$$h^2(q_2, q_3) = u^{6^{-1}}(u^5(q_2) + u^3(q_3)), \tag{8.15}$$

where the u^k, for $k = 1, \ldots, 6$, are arbitrary, continuous, and order-preserving functions and $u^{k^{-1}}$, with $k = 2, 6$, denotes the inverse of u^k.[12] Substituting (8.13) into (8.12) and using (8.11),

$$f(x) = u^1(u^4(q_1) + u^5(q_2) + u^3(q_3)).$$

(A parallel expression for f could be obtained from (8.11) by substitution of (8.15) into (8.14).) Recalling that $q_j = f^{jn}(x_{(n)})$ and setting $V = u^1$, $v^1 = u^4 \circ f^{31}$, $v^2 = u^5 \circ f^{32}$, and $v^3 = u^3 \circ f^{33}$ where "∘" denotes function composition,

$$f(x) = V(v^1(x_{(1)}) + v^2(x_{(2)}) + v^3(x_{(3)})),$$

---

[11] For example, take d to be the function of the previous footnote. Then from (8.10), $g^1(f^{11}(x_{(1)}, x_{(2)}), f^{12}(x_{(3)})) = g^1(f^{11}(x_{(1)}, x_{(2)}), d(f^{33}(x_{(3)})))$. Now redefine g^1 subsuming the functional symbol d in the notation g^1.

[12] Actually, Aczél's corollary asserts that the u^k are "strictly monotonic." In the present context, strict monotonicity is equivalent to the possibility of either order preservation or order reversal (i.e., (8.5) with $x' \geq_x x''$ replaced by $x'' \geq_x x'$). Now, since f and the f^{jn} preserve order, the u^k must either all preserve order or all reverse order. And in the latter case, alternative functions could easily be found that all preserve order.

so that in this case, f is additively separable with respect to $\{s_1, \ldots, s_N\}$. The proof is completed by an induction argument on N.[13]   **Q.E.D.**

Theorem 8.4: *Let f be defined on D_x and $\geq_y$ be defined on R_y. Suppose f is continuous. If f is additively separable with respect to a partition $\{s_1, \ldots, s_N\}$, then any ordering relation $\geq_x$ determined by f on D_x through (8.5) is multi-separable with respect to that partition.*

Evidently, in a manner similar to that of Theorem 8.2, when f is additively separable, the ordering relation on R_y is projected onto D_x in a multi-separable way. That is, the former secondary assumption is projected back to stage (ii) as the latter primary-level assumption.

In addition, cancellability as described earlier (several lines after equation (8.3)) is implied directly from either additive separability or multi-separability. For example, consider two vectors $x' = (x'_{(1)}, \bar{x}_{(2)}, \ldots, \bar{x}_{(N)})$ and $x'' = (x''_{(1)}, \bar{x}_{(2)}, \ldots, \bar{x}_{(N)})$ in D_x. If f is additively separable and $f(x'_1) = f(x''_1)$, then

$$g(f^1(x'_{(1)}) + f^2(\bar{x}_{(2)}) + \cdots + f^N(\bar{x}_{(N)}))$$
$$= g(f^1(x''_{(1)}) + f^2(\bar{x}_{(2)}) + \cdots + f^N(\bar{x}_{(N)})).$$

Applying the inverse of g (which exists because $\geq_z$ is antisymmetric and g, here a function of a single variable, is order preserving) to both sides results in $f^1(x'_1) = f^1(x''_1)$. Since f^1 is order preserving, it follows that $x'_{(1)} =_{\bar{x}_{(1)}} x''_{(1)}$. If, in addition, $\geq_{\bar{x}_{(1)}}$ were antisymmetric, then $x'_{(1)} = x''_{(1)}$. Likewise, with the same vectors x' and x'', if $\geq_x$ were multi-separable and $x' =_x x''$, then $x'_{(1)} =_{\bar{x}_{(1)}} x''_{(1)}$ and, in the case of antisymmetry, $x'_{(1)} = x''_{(1)}$. Thus, at the level of primary assumptions (stage (ii)), cancellability is also imposed on $\geq_x$ by an assumption of additive separability on f. And once again, in the stage (v) evaluation, the appropriateness with respect to the initial stage (i) vision of the implied multi-separability and cancellation properties at stage (ii) needs to be addressed.

The relation $\geq_x$ is *pointwise separable* if it is multi-separable with respect to the partition $\{\{1\}, \ldots, \{I\}\}$. The function f is said to be *additive* provided that it is separable with respect to $\{\{1\}, \ldots, \{I\}\}$, the functions f, g, and the f^i, where $i = n$ runs from 1 up to I, are all continuous and

$$f(x) = g(f^1(x_1) + \cdots + f^I(x_I)). \tag{8.16}$$

---

[13] See Katzner [3, p. 30].

The following two propositions are obvious consequences of, respectively, Theorems 8.3 and 8.4.

Theorem 8.5: *Let f and $\geq_x$ be defined on D_x and $\geq_y$ be defined on R_y such that, in addition to its other properties, $\geq_y$ is antisymmetric. Suppose f is order-preserving and continuous. Then f is additive if and only if $\geq_x$ is pointwise separable.*

Theorem 8.6: *Let f be defined on D_x and $\geq_y$ be defined on R_y. Suppose f is continuous. If f is additive, then any ordering relation $\geq_x$ determined by f on D_x through (8.5) is pointwise separable.*

Thus additivity, a secondary-assumptions property of f ensures that the ordering relation on D_x obtained from $\geq_y$ through f has an associated primary-level-assumption characteristic, namely, pointwise separability. The relevance of pointwise separability in relation to stage (i) considerations in models of utility maximization has already been noted in the introduction to this chapter.

Moreover, the linear form

$$f(x) = a_0 + a_1 x_1 + \cdots + a_I x_I,$$

where the a_i, for $i = 0, \ldots, I$, are fixed real numbers, is the special case of (8.16) in which the x_i (here $i = 1, \ldots, I$) are quantified in some way and g and the f^i are similarly linear. This, of course, is a very common form, appearing often throughout the social sciences. In such contexts, the $\geq_{\bar{x}_{(i)}}$ are frequently thought of as greater-than-or-equal-to among real numbers. Of course, the results of Theorems 8.5 and 8.6, along with that relating to cancellability, apply here as well.

8.3 Concluding Remark

The analysis of this chapter has provided several examples of the implications in terms of primary-level assumptions that are implicitly imposed at the level of stage (ii) by starting the model-building process at a level of analysis, stage (iii), that is more remote from the real world. The main impositions considered are arbitrarily enlarged domains, possible orderings of variable values, various forms of separable orderings, and the cancellation property. Once such properties are exposed, it becomes possible to consider their relevance to the real phenomena the model addresses as envisaged in stage (i) and, in that way, make a determination of the relevance and usefulness of the project itself. In general, however, the additions forced on the collection of primary-level assumptions of stage (ii) by the secondary assumptions in constructions that begin some distance of abstraction away from that stage may be very difficult, if not impossible, to determine. In those circumstances an evaluation of the relevance of the analysis to the reality it purports to explain will be hard to achieve. But that does not mean that the effort to reduce secondary assumptions to determine their stage (ii) level assumption counterparts should not be attempted. For that is the only way to be able to claim with some confidence that the model built or the analysis undertaken that is based upon it has relevance to the reality under investigation.

References

[1] Aczél, J., *Lectures on Functional Equations and Their Applications* (New York: Academic Press, 1966).
[2] Fromm, E., *The Sane Society* (New York: Rinehart, 1955).
[3] Katzner, D. W., *Static Demand Theory* (New York: Macmillan, 1970).

9

Ordinality and the Adequacy of Analytic Specification[1]

From the vantage point taken here, analytical economics as exemplified in Chapter 7 holds as its objective and province of argument the explanation of economic behavior, decision, and choice. Analysis within its purview may or may not assume predictive competence as distinct from explanation; and it may or may not be readily adaptable to detailed empirical description and corroboration. The methods employed can, among other things, be directed to questions of agent optimization and welfare, or to those that bear on wider issues of aggregative activity or social benefit. In analyses of this sort, economists generally and typically construct models by postulating relational structures that have specific properties. Those contemplated relations, which may or may not be well specified and may or may not be written in (ordinally, cardinally, or ratio) quantified functional form, are often reflective of deeper determinant forces. But in any case, it is well known that a number of difficulties stand in the way of such an approach.

First, it is obvious that for an analysis based on relational structures to have sustainable meaning, the structures and their properties must remain fixed throughout the investigation and over all relevant, analytically manipulative procedures. But second, questions of analytical legitimacy arise when, as suggested earlier, one or more of the variables incorporated in the argument are only ordinally measured while all remaining variables are taken to be at least cardinally quantified. In such a case, it is possible that the structures and properties assumed, if expressed only in the numerical terms of the quantified variables (ordinal, cardinal, and ratio),

[1] This chapter is taken with minor modifications and additions from my "Ordinality and the Adequacy of Analytic Specification" (with P. Skott), *Journal of Economic Methodology* 11 (2004), pp. 437–453. © Taylor & Francis. Reproduced with permission.

are dependent to a considerable extent on the scales on which the ordinal variables are measured. It follows that in the presence of such ordinality, the properties can often be altered or entirely lost upon application of certain increasing transformations of scale with respect to the ordinal variables. Thus, to cite an example similar to one presented in Chapter 5, the structure $h(y) = -y^2$, where $-\infty \le y \le \infty$ and y is only ordinally measured, has a unique maximum at $y = 0$. But with $\lambda > 1$ a fixed number, applying the increasing transformation $T(y) = -\lambda^{-y}$ to y and replacing y in h by the ordinally equivalent transformed variable $T(y)$, results in the structure $h(T(y)) = -\lambda^{-2y}$, which has no maximum anywhere.

The implications for explanatory model building are clear. If, upon completion of the model-building process up through the operationality of stage (iii), it turns out that some variable values of the model that has been constructed can, as a practical matter, only be measured ordinally, questions arise as to the significance of the model's structure, its relation to the underlying reality out of which that structure emerged through the earlier stages of the model-building process, and hence to the model's explanatory competence. The issues involved center around the assumed significance of the scale transformations that are legitimately allowable by dint of the ordinality that is present. In light of those transformations and in addition to the model's relation to the underlying reality, the meaning of the model's structures has to be interpreted in reference to the model's integrity and the maintenance of its internal consistency. Often it is necessary to accept either the unspecifiability of what are taken to be known structures and known measures, or a degree of arbitrariness in limiting the ordinally permissible scale transformations applicable to the model's variable values. These qualifications are explored in the following.

Before proceeding, it needs to be recognized that ordinal numbers as defined at the start of Chapter 5 do not admit of arithmetic operations since the underlying basis for those operations is not present. That is because to add, say, values of the numerically measured property of longness, ratio-measured as length, requires a means of combining the objects to which the numerical values of the properties adhere. Placing two pieces of chalk end-to-end permits the longness of the combined pieces to be measured as the sum of their individual lengths. With properties that can only be ordinally measured like the overall quality of pencils, there is no sensible way to combine the underlying pencils and speak of the overall quality of the combination. If on an ordinal scale, then, one pencil has ordinally measured quality 15 and the other 25, the sum $15 + 25$ has no meaning. But when economists deal with ordinality, they do not seem to have in mind so stringent a notion. In many instances, ordinal numbers to economists are ordinary real numbers to which arithmetic operations can be applied. What defines ordinality to them is only the fact, described in n. 5 on p. 103, that those numbers are unique up to continuous, increasing transformations. Applying such a transformation to each number of any set of ordinal numbers yields a new set of ordinal numbers of equivalent meaning. That is, the square, for example, of each number in a collection of ordinal numbers contains the same information as, and can therefore be used in place of, and with the same meaning as, the original numbers. This weaker concept of ordinality is the one that is invoked below.

In the present chapter, the problem of the preservation of structures and their properties across transformations of scale as set out above is taken up in some detail. At the outset, however, it should be noted that this problem does not arise in certain well-known cases, like that of the utility function in the derivation of consumer demand functions, where ordinality is characterized in terms of the weaker of the previously described concepts and appears only with respect to a dependent variable. Nor does it usually arise when cardinal or ratio scales are involved because, generally speaking, the transformations permitted in those circumstances are insufficient to cause significant alteration or loss of information pertaining to the postulated structures and their properties. In subsequent discussion, then, only scale changes with respect to ordinal scales are considered. To the extent that variables measured on cardinal and ratio scales are introduced, those scales are assumed to be fixed and no modification in them is permitted. With regard to dependent variables, only those situations in which scale changes have the potential to cause difficulties are discussed.

More specifically, the chapter begins with a general discussion of ordinality in reference to a single structural relation. Three approaches to handling that ordinality, which may arise in reference to the middle stages (ii) and (iii) of the process of model building set out in Chapter 3, are identified: The first (Approach A) is to begin with the relation in an unquantified state and then employ specific ordinal scales to translate it into numerical form. This procedure, which introduces at the start of the analysis the theoretical challenge of according meaning and manipulability to nonquantified variables according to the rules of "analysis without measurement,"[2] ensures that the original structure and its properties do not modify with ordinal scale changes. Indeed, they are independent of all ordinal measurement scales. Approach A is illustrated in Katzner's

---

[2] Recall Chapter 5. See also Katzner [7, 10].

[6, Chs. 5 and 6] implicit construction of numerical representations of individual "quality of life technologies" relating "career-living situations" to "qualities of life." The two alternative approaches are, first, to postulate the existence of a numerical function that reflects a known but unspecified underlying, unquantified structure (Approach B) and, second, to assume that that underlying structure is not only unspecified, but also unknown (Approach C). Both of these approaches, as will be argued, have serious weaknesses.

There are many studies in the economics literature that, since their authors ignore underlying structures and do not specify how their questionably quantified variables are to be measured, can be taken to exemplify either Approach B or C. To name two (more will be identified momentarily), Akerlof includes variables representing the "quality" of an automobile [1, p. 490] and a person's "reputation" [2, p. 754] in quantified mathematical equations, and Becker and Lewis [3] derive the constrained maximization of a utility function with respect to "child quality" and other variables.

After a general description and comparison of the three approaches, Approach C and one of its limitations is considered in greater detail. The chapter concludes by examining the special case in which the dependent variable of the single structural relation (with one independent, ordinally measured variable) is assumed to be measured on a ratio scale. This discussion is taken up in reference to all three Approaches A, B, and C.

The range of difficulties suggested in the foregoing have presented economists with problems that have seemed analytically intractable and have raised uncertainty regarding the use and manipulability of variables measured on differently specified scales (ordinal, cardinal, and ratio), quite apart from the knotty problem of nonquantifiability.[3] Such problems can be exemplified by reference to certain efficiency wage and other models. There the issues involved have led to controversy over the viability of the internal logic of the particular models that have been employed. For example, Currie and Steedman [4] and Katzner [9] have correctly argued (in part) that, taken on face value, efficiency wage models as presented in the economics literature (e.g., Stiglitz [14, p. 27, n. 47]) are unsustainable: Effort can only be ordinally measured, and the use in those models of some arbitrary ordinal representation of effort as an argument of the production function leaves that production function inadequately specified. Skott [12], on the other hand, argues, also correctly, that introducing an implicit

---

[3] See, for example, Katzner [9, pp. 5,6].

link between unquantified effort and (quantified) output pins down the quantified production function (relating ordinally measured effort to output) sufficiently to eliminate the problem. More specifically, the stipulated production function in efficiency wage models is conditional on the particular choice of the ordinal representation of effort, and any change in that choice will necessitate a corresponding modification in the production function. (A similar assertion is latent in Leslie [11].) However, Skott provides no details concerning the relation of that link between unquantified effort and output to the quantified production function, although his suggested procedure will be seen in what follows to be an example of Approach B. An associated controversy has arisen between Leslie [11] and Skott [13] with the latter taking a position similar to his stance on the efficiency wage case in relation to ordinally measured "education" in a model of human capital theory.[4] One of the purposes of this chapter is to make explicit Skott's implicit Approach B links between such variables as unquantified effort and output, and to examine their relation to the functions, like the quantified production function, to which they correspond. Implications are drawn not only for efficiency wage models, but also for a wider class of models in general. It will emerge that analyses that fall in the category of Approach B, like those of Approach C, carry the potential of previously unsuspected and damaging problems.

9.1 The Three Approaches

Approach A – Explicit Links. To formally characterize what has been referred to as Approach A, focus attention on functions of a single variable as described in Section 5.1. In the present case, let e and x denote unquantified or unmeasured variables[5] defined by the values or objects over which they are permitted to vary. Were e, say, to represent effort, the objects over which e varies might be verbal descriptions, each depicting a manifestation of effort thought to be relevant to the issue at hand. Denote the collections of objects that e and x may assume as values by, respectively, E and X. Take f to be a function associating to each value of e in E a unique value of x in X, and write

$$x = f(e). \tag{9.1}$$

---

[4] Leslie's argument in this regard is not so far from that of Skott. Gintis [5] also hints at something comparable.

[5] The terms "unquantified" and "unmeasured" are used synonomously in this chapter as are "quantified" and "measured."

Suppose now that e and x are capable of ordinal measurement only. Then, with respect to e, say, the objects of E are ordered according to some property such as longness, hotness, or pleasure, and that ordering, call it $\geq_e$, is fully represented on a numerical scale that is unique up to increasing (and continuous) transformations. Moreover, the ordering $\geq_e$ is reflexive, transitive, and total on E. Similar statements may be made in relation to x where, in this case, the underlying ordering is designated by $\geq_x$. Denote the measured values of e and x on the particular ordinal scales in use by, respectively, ε and χ. Then with (9.1) specified, a numerical function relating ε and χ, namely

$$\chi = F(\varepsilon), \tag{9.2}$$

is implied.[6] Clearly F depends on the choice of scales on which e and x are measured. As long as (9.1) is to be maintained as an assumed structural relation, any alteration in one or both scales, unless, in the latter case, the two alterations exactly cancel each other out, necessarily modifies F.

Now let increasing transformations T and S be applied to the scales on which, respectively, e and x are measured. Denote the new variables representing e and x by, respectively, φ and ξ so that

$$\varphi = T(\varepsilon) \quad \text{and} \quad \xi = S(\chi). \tag{9.3}$$

Then, as indicated above, F has to be altered to maintain (9.1). Write the new representation of (9.1) as

$$\xi = G(\varphi). \tag{9.4}$$

It is easy to see that, as long as appropriate inverses exist (S and T already have inverses since they are increasing), any one of F, G, S, and T can be secured from the remaining three. For example, substituting (9.4) into the right-hand equation of (9.3), and using (9.2),

$$G(\varphi) = S(F(\varepsilon)).$$

If G has an inverse, G^{-1}, then

$$\varphi = G^{-1}(S(F(\varepsilon)))$$

so that T may be viewed as the composition of F, S, and G^{-1}. That is,

$$T = G^{-1} \circ S \circ F, \tag{9.5}$$

[6] It may be noted at this point that some of the analytical problems that will be clarified in what follows turn on the question of whether the model in view and its properties are assumed to be grounded in (9.2) as opposed to (9.1).

and specification of F, G, and S determines T. Clearly, since S and T are increasing, implicit restrictions are imposed on F and G in this formulation. Alternatively, combining the left-hand equation of (9.3) with (9.4) and (9.2) gives, if F has an inverse,

$$\varphi = G(T(F^{-1}(\chi))),$$

whence

$$S = G \circ T \circ F^{-1}. \tag{9.6}$$

Similarly, $F = S^{-1} \circ G \circ T$ and $G = S \circ F \circ T^{-1}$.

Economists seem to prefer to deal with functions in numerical form rather than those in their underlying, unquantified state. Moreover, the preceding analysis suggests that functions like F ought to be constructed by specifying f and numerical measures of the values of e and x.[7] But this is not easy to do for at least two reasons. First, economists are not familiar with or comfortable dealing with the unquantified. Second, many of the techniques that they employ in their analyses render it necessary that the numerical functions under consideration be continuous or differentiable. However, as pointed out in Section 8.2, continuity and differentiability as invoked by economists usually require functions with nondenumerably infinite numbers of elements in their domains and ranges. And, although it is possible to conceive of unquantified functions with nondenumerably infinite domains and ranges,[8] because unquantified functions can be specified only by explicitly indicating which dependent variable values are identified with which independent variable values, the finiteness of our world does not permit the specification of more than a finite number of relational points under f. Moreover, the arithmetic operations needed to calculate a derivative as the limit of the slopes of straight-line segments are not available because numbers are not present. Thus to employ the approach to F described earlier, already referred to as Approach A, means that economists would have to give up analytical techniques that have been quite useful and fruitful when all variables are measured on at least cardinal scales.

---

[7] The fact that utility functions are not usually constructed in this way is irrelevant. For in that case, the variables with respect to which the domain of the utility function is characterized are ratio measured, and the application of increasing transformations to the ordinal scale on which utility is measured have no impact on the demand functions derived.

[8] Katzner [7, Sect. 7.2].

There are, however, two alternative, if somewhat less satisfying, approaches.

Approach B – Unspecified Links. What has been earlier identified as Approach B is to assume that there is an underlying function of the form of (9.1) that is known but unspecified (that is, the function is assumed to exist but its form is not articulated), that there are also known but unspecified ordinal scales on which e and x are measured, and that together they give rise to a function F in (9.2) that has certain known and fully specified properties. From the perspective of Approach B, then, analysis begins by postulating the existence of a function F that represents f and that possesses certain numerical properties, which may possibly include continuity or differentiability. But unlike Approach A, the process of specifying f and translating it into F is suppressed. Clearly the properties of F are assumed to mirror those of f, and if the full force of the properties of F are to be maintained, then any changes in scale mean that F must be adjusted to preserve f as in (9.4). Of course, the previous mathematics relating F, G, T, and S remains intact. Additive operations may act on the values of e and x because, under the definition of ordinality invoked earlier, those values are ordinary real numbers. (Were continuity or differentiability assumed of F, then f must be thought of as having a nondenumerably infinite domain and range.) This is the approach taken by Skott [12], [13] mentioned earlier. In effect, the approach surmounts the problem of nonquantifiability by assuming it away and by resting its argument on assumed, even though unspecified, ordinality.

Approach B is less satisfactory than Approach A for three reasons. First it requires greater assumption content than Approach A. In effect, both (9.1) and (9.2) must be assumed instead of having the latter derived from the former. Second, it is necessary to assume that certain things are known to exist without being able to specify what they are. Third (this arises in part from the second reason), the precise relationship between the ordinal numbers and the variable values they represent cannot be stated, and exactly what is being assumed about f and its properties is not clear. In short, a significant portion of the relationship to reality of the assumptions imposed in the model is hidden by the veil of ordinal numbers with respect to which those assumptions are expressed.

Approach C – Unknown Links. The third approach, previously called Approach C, is characterized as the same as Approach B except that both f and the ordinal scales on which e and x are measured are taken to be not only unspecified, but also unknown. The analytical content of this approach, however, raises several conceptual issues that warrant consideration before proceeding. First, it may be vaguely surmised or assumed in the explanation of certain economic conditions that an underlying, unquantified relationship exists and determines a particular outcome. (For example, a firm's reputation may influence the demand for its output.) But second, it may also be reckoned in such a case that there is no way in which ordinal scales can be meaningfully employed to numerically quantify the strength of the forces inherent in that relationship. (In the previous example, how might the quality of the firm's reputation be measured?) Third, while the general nature of those forces is thereby recognized, residual uncertainty and lack of clarity exist as to the manner in which those forces transmit their impacts to the outcome that is in view. (With respect to the example, in what precise way does the quality of the firm's reputation contribute to the demand for its output?) This, then, is one illustration of the circumstances in which Approach C might be brought into play.

It should be noted that Approach C does not suffer from the deficiencies associated with the second reason given earlier why Approach B is less satisfactory than Approach A. But it is still less satisfactory than A for reasons one and three that were stated there. Moreover, Approach C is subject to a certain kind of arbitrariness that will be explored in Section 9.2.

Comparing the Three Approaches. To further illuminate what is involved, it is worth summarizing and setting against each other the unique features of the three approaches that have now been described. In Approach A it is assumed that the relevant qualitative forces underlying and contributing to the statement of F in (9.2) as derived from the "ordinalization" of (9.1) are, for the purposes in hand, known and corralled with respect to the specific ordinal scales introduced. In Approach B the possibility is contemplated that the underlying forces and their relation to ordinal scales, though still present, need not be expressed, and that analysis could begin by directly positing F in (9.2). With regard to Approach C, however, a much higher degree of relative ignorance is assumed. Not only are the underlying forces both vague and unfettered by ordinally specified scales, but now it is reckoned that no such underlying ordinal relations that might pin them down can be known.

An alternative statement of Approach C and its relation to Approaches A and B is as follows: In both Approaches A and B the relation f is in one way or another the starting point of the argument. That is the case in Approach B because F is anchored to (the unspecified) f using the given (though unspecified) ordinal scales on which e and x are measured. But, as has been explained, that f and those scales are suppressed and the assumption is made that it is not necessary to introduce them into the analysis. In Approach C, on the other hand, F serves as its own anchor without any grounding in an underlying relation such as f and, as a result, the mathematics described earlier that relates F, G, T, and S is rendered irrelevant. Moreover, for F to remain a meaningful anchor as the scales on which the ordinal variables are measured modify (that is, to ensure the analytically relevant properties of F remain unchanged), the transformations of scale permitted have, as will be shown, to be restricted. Approach C is the focus of attention in the next section. But first it is worth presenting an example to illustrate the issues and differences involved in the three Approaches A, B, and C.

Let the variables e and x denote, respectively, unquantified effort and unquantified pleasure. Suppose there are two values of effort, e' and e'', and two values of pleasure, x' and x''. Introduce orderings of the elements of each pair in such a manner that e'' is associated with "more" effort than is e', and x'' is associated with "more" pleasure than is x'. Assume f maps $e' \rightarrow x'$ and $e'' \rightarrow x''$. Then under f, more effort corresponds to more pleasure. The latter characteristic of f, often referred to as order preservation, is the only structural property considered in this example.

Now let e and x be measured on independent ordinal scales that preserve the ordering relations among, respectively, the values of e and x. Suppose the measured values are $e' \rightarrow \varepsilon' = 2$, $e'' \rightarrow \varepsilon'' = 3$, $x' \rightarrow \chi' = 4$, and $x'' \rightarrow \chi'' = 9$. Then more effort and more pleasure are identified with higher numbers. (In the usual parlance, the values of χ are called utility values.) Furthermore, according to (9.2), f expressed in numerical form becomes, in this example,

$$\chi = F(\varepsilon) = \varepsilon^2 \tag{9.7}$$

on the two-element domain $\varepsilon = \varepsilon'$ and $\varepsilon = \varepsilon''$. Clearly, $F(2) = 4$ and $F(3) = 9$. The order-preservation property of f is reflected in F: greater effort (a higher value of ε) is associated with greater pleasure or utility (a higher value of χ). It is evident that (9.7) can only preserve this underlying ordering relation when the domain of F is restricted to non-negative numbers. Any increasing transformation that would shift the domain to negative numbers will not leave that ordering relation unchanged. From the perspective of Approach A, however, the way to ensure that, after such changes in scales are introduced, F still represents f and maintains its property of order preservation is to modify F so as to offset the scale modifications. If, say, the increasing transformation

$$\varphi = T(\varepsilon) = -2^{-\varepsilon}, \tag{9.8}$$

where $\varepsilon > 0$, were applied to the ε-scale so that $\varphi' = T(2) = -1/4$ and $\varphi'' = T(3) = -1/8$, and if S were the identity transformation (a special case of an increasing transformation), then solving (9.8) for ε and substituting the result into (9.7) gives the following expression for (9.4):

$$\xi = G(\varphi) = \left[\frac{\ln(\frac{-1}{\varphi})}{\ln 2} \right]^2,$$

where, like (9.7), $G(-1/4) = 4$ and $G(-1/8) = 9$. Clearly, the measured values of e' and e'' have become $e' \to \varphi' = -1/4$ and $e'' \to \varphi'' = -1/8$, and G preserves the same order as f since greater effort (now a larger value of φ) still corresponds to greater pleasure or utility (a larger value of $\xi = \chi$). Thus an appropriate modification of F has been made in response to the change in scale on which e is measured. A similar argument without the explicit link to e', e'', x', x'', and f applies in the case of Approach B.

However, if, as in Approach C, F serves as its own anchor in the sense previously explained (recall f is unknown), then, at least in so far as the ordinality of the measured variables is concerned, there is in that case no difference between (9.7) as above and (9.7) with ε replaced by the transformed variable $-2^{-\varepsilon}$. That is, (9.7) and

$$\chi = F(T(\varepsilon)) = (-2^{-\varepsilon})^2 \tag{9.9}$$

are equivalent formulations of the same relation in that they contain the same information. But with respect to (9.9), $F(T(2)) = 1/16$ and $F(T(3)) = 1/64$. Thus $F \circ T$ reverses order: greater effort as represented in a larger value of ε corresponds to less pleasure or utility as indicated by a smaller value of χ. Therefore, since F is the anchor and since its relevant property (order preservation) has to be preserved, application of the increasing transformation $T(\varepsilon) = -2^{-\varepsilon}$, although perfectly legitimate in terms of the ordinality of the scales involved, has to be ruled out under the methodology of Approach C. This illustrates a fundamental fact that ought to be kept in mind: When F serves as the analytical anchor, certain scale transformations of the variables involved have to be excluded if the properties of F are to be maintained as components of the structural foundation of the analysis. Part of the next section generalizes the argument and makes it more precise.

9.2 Scale Transformations under Approach C

When starting out at stages (i) and (ii) to build a model, there are two basic steps that are relevant to present considerations – first identify the variables to be accounted for, and second construct or assume relations among them. If any of the variables are ordinal variables, problems relating to that ordinality may arise at both levels.

In the process of identifying the ordinal variables, the scales on which they are measured have to be, at least implicitly, determined. That is, what version of the numbers should be used? Should they be those that present themselves by some means to the investigation, or should they be transformed in one way or another? Suppose these questions are answered first. Now let the hypothesized relations of the analysis be introduced. In the case of Approach B, these relations are reflections of known (but unspecified) underlying forces, and changes in ordinal scales cannot be permitted to destroy the representation of those forces in the hypothesized relations. In this case, then, the relations have to modify as in (9.4) with any scale changes.

Now assume, from the perspective of Approach C, that the hypothesized relations are thought to mirror unknown underlying forces. These relations and their analytically significant properties have to be kept intact because they are the only representation of those forces in the analysis. But it is still reasonable and appropriate to ask how changes in the initial choice of scales would affect the hypothesized relations, and, as described at the end of the preceding section, to rule out those scale changes that interfere with and modify the analytically significant properties. In the context of equation (9.2), say, before such interference is taken into account, all functions of the form

$$\chi = S^{-1}(F(T(\varepsilon))), \tag{9.10}$$

where $T(\varepsilon)$ and $S(\chi)$ are substituted in place of, respectively, ε and χ in (9.2), and S and T are the increasing transformations of (9.3), are potentially equivalent starting points for the analysis. Observe that (9.9) is a special case of (9.10). However, as previously indicated, the only increasing scale transformations that can be permitted are those that preserve the analytically significant properties, and hence the only functions $S^{-1} \circ F \circ T$ alternative to F that are pertinent to present discussion are those that exhibit them.[9] Were increasing transformations applied that

---

[9] Observe that $S^{-1} \circ F \circ T$ of (9.10) is different from $G = S \circ F \circ T^{-1}$, which, as indicated earlier (following equation (9.6)), always preserves the same underlying f.

did not preserve those properties, then the relevant properties associated with $S^{-1} \circ F \circ T$ would deviate from those of F. Such transformations, therefore, would have to be discarded. But ordinality by itself means that no information in the ordinally measured variables is lost by administering increasing transformations of scale to them, and hence, from this perspective, that all increasing transformations should be permissible. It follows that the more scales that have to be excluded to preserve the analytically relevant properties of F when that ordinality is imported to purported explanatory relations, the greater the arbitrariness introduced into the analysis. That arbitrariness, which, as suggested earlier, is inherent in Approach C, is a serious drawback in the construction of economic explanation.

The problem of arbitrariness arising from the necessity to discard legitimate transformations of scale in Approach C has already been illustrated in the example at the end of Section 9.1 with respect to order preservation for functions of a single variable. That argument, although easily generalized, is not developed further here.

Similar considerations apply, and again point to the limitations of Approach C, to the circumstance in which F is assumed to have a unique maximum value. For in the absence of any restrictions imposed by the necessity of preserving the properties of F, all increasing transformations of scale are permissible, and thus the possibility cannot be ruled out that maxima of F intended to be reflective of unknown underlying forces might actually not exist under some transformations of scale. Examples have previously been provided in the introduction to this chapter and in Chapter 5.

Matters are further complicated when f is a function of more than one variable since, in that case, at least one additional issue arises. To provide a simple illustration, suppose there are two independent variables. Let F be the Approach C anchor of an analysis where

$$\chi = F(\varepsilon_1, \varepsilon_2) \tag{9.11}$$

on a suitable domain, and where ε_1 and ε_2 are ordinally measured variables. Then F induces an ordering relation $\succ$ on its domain in the usual way:

$$(\varepsilon_1', \varepsilon_2') \succ (\varepsilon_1'', \varepsilon_2'') \quad \text{if and only if} \quad F(\varepsilon_1', \varepsilon_2') > F(\varepsilon_1'', \varepsilon_2''). \tag{9.12}$$

In general, the ordering $\succ$ generated by F is independent of those that define the ordinality of ε_1 and ε_2. Now, in accordance with Approach C, replace ε_1 and ε_2 in (9.11) by φ_1 and φ_2, where

$$\varphi_1 = T^1(\varepsilon_1) \quad \text{and} \quad \varphi_2 = T^2(\varepsilon_2) \tag{9.13}$$

and T^1 and T^2 are arbitrary, increasing transformations. Then F becomes

$$\chi = F(\varphi_1, \varphi_2) \tag{9.14}$$

on an appropriately altered domain. Substituting (9.13) into (9.14), the original F is modified to $F \circ [T^1, T^2]$, that is,

$$\chi = (F \circ [T^1, T^2])(\varepsilon_1, \varepsilon_2) = F(T^1(\varepsilon_1), T^2(\varepsilon_2)),$$

and $F \circ [T^1, T^2]$ induces a second ordering relation on the original domain of F as in (9.12). Clearly, these ordering relations need not be the same. To illustrate that possibility, consider the function $F(\varepsilon_1, \varepsilon_2) = \varepsilon_1 + \varepsilon_2$ and the vectors $(\varepsilon_1', \varepsilon_2') = (2, 0)$ and $(\varepsilon_1'', \varepsilon_2'') = (0, 1)$. Then $F(\varepsilon_1', \varepsilon_2') > F(\varepsilon_1'', \varepsilon_2'')$ and $(\varepsilon_1', \varepsilon_2') \succ (\varepsilon_1'', \varepsilon_2'')$. But with $T^1(\varepsilon_1) = \varepsilon_1$ and $T^2(\varepsilon_2) = 3\varepsilon_2$, the ordering of $(\varepsilon_1', \varepsilon_2')$ and $(\varepsilon_1'', \varepsilon_2'')$ under the original $\succ$ is reversed since $F(T^1(\varepsilon_1'), T^2(\varepsilon_2')) < F(T^1(\varepsilon_1''), T^2(\varepsilon_2''))$. Returning to the general situation, if the original ordering induced by F is to be preserved as an analytically significant property, then all transformations T^1 and T^2 that modify that ordering have to be excluded. Thus possible instances of the kind of arbitrariness that damaged the analytical viability of Approach C with respect to functions of a single variable can also arise for functions of more than one variable, even if F is increasing everywhere in both of its arguments.

Similar arbitrariness extends to attempts to preserve the solutions of systems of simultaneous equations involving ordinal variables under increasing transformations of scale. Except for the following illustration, the details are not pursued here.[10] The system $\chi = F^1(\varepsilon) = \varepsilon$ and $\chi = F^2(\varepsilon) = 2 - \varepsilon$, where ε and χ are ordinal scalars ranging over all real numbers, has the unique solution $\chi = \varepsilon = 1$. Applying the same increasing transformation $T(\varepsilon) = -\lambda^{-\varepsilon}$ used earlier (where S in (9.10) remains the identity transformation) results in $\chi = F^1(T(\varepsilon)) = -\lambda^{-\varepsilon}$ and $\chi = F^2(T(\varepsilon)) = 2 + \lambda^{-\varepsilon}$. The latter system has no solution since there is no numerical value of ε for which $\lambda^{-\varepsilon} = -1$.

The general point is that an analysis employing structures containing variables that are only ordinally measured must, of necessity, be grounded in unmeasured relations that lie behind the quantified relations if the

---

[10] General discussion may be found in Katzner [8, pp. 46–50].

latter relations and their properties are to have any significance. The most competent way of providing that grounding is with Approach A. And, although subject to the difficulties described earlier, Approach B respects this grounding too, albeit in a weaker sense. But when the underlying relations and scales on which the ordinal variables are measured are taken to be both unspecified and unknown as in Approach C, the grounding in unmeasured relations becomes still weaker and more tenuous, and the analysis requires the imposition of additional restrictions on the transformations of scale that may be used beyond those conditions implied by the ordinality of the measures employed. And the extent of those additional restrictions determines the degree of arbitrariness introduced into the analysis by the presence of the ordinally measured variables.

9.3 Preserving Functional Forms

It turns out that the arbitrariness inherent in Approach C, although coming from a different source, can also, under certain special conditions, extend to Approaches A and B. An important example of this extension in the case of Approach B relates to the production function in what has become known as the efficiency wage model. But before focusing attention on that function, it is necessary to consider a more general instance that derives from (9.1) and (9.2).

When x is already measured on a ratio scale, as in the case of the production function relating effort to output in the efficiency wage model, the discussion in Sections 9.1 and 9.2 applies with the obvious alterations. Indeed, since the scale on which x, or output, is measured is taken to be fixed, it is only necessary in that discussion to restrict attention to the effect of applying increasing transformations to the measured values of the remaining ordinal variables. To summarize previous argument with respect to Approaches A and B in such a context, observe that (9.2) may now be rewritten as

$$x = F(\varepsilon), \tag{9.2'}$$

where the values of ε, that is, the measured values of e, are taken from an appropriate ordinal scale. Obviously, whenever the scale on which e is measured changes, the measured values of e in E change from ε to φ, where, in the notation of the left-hand equation of (9.3), $\varphi = T(\varepsilon)$, and T is an increasing transformation. But, as before, if (9.1) is to be preserved as in Approaches A and B, since any particular value of e underlying the corresponding measured values ε and φ has not been altered by the transformation of scale, the function value $x = f(e)$ cannot modify. Hence F has to change to offset the modification of scale. Moreover, assuming appropriate inverses exist, any two of F, G, and T determines the third. That is, in particular, the reasoning behind equations (9.4) and (9.5) applies here except that now S is the identity transformation. Therefore

$$T = G^{-1} \circ F \qquad (9.15)$$

and, also as in Section 9.1, $F = G \circ T$ and $G = F \circ T^{-1}$.

It should be noted that (maintaining the perspectives of Approach A or B) if T were the identity transformation, then (9.15) or either of the above two equations following it would imply that $G = F$. Moreover, with F increasing, F itself is an ordinal scale on which e is measured and $F^{-1}(x)$ provides the measured values of $e = f^{-1}(x)$ on that scale. And this scale and the measured values on it are perfectly valid for use in analysis involving f or F.

In the case of Approach C, equation (9.2′) assumes the role of anchor. That, as has been emphasized in the foregoing argument, is the essence of Approach C. Suppose the analytically relevant property to be preserved is the form of F itself. Then changing the scale on which e is measured as in (9.10) gives (here S is the identity transformation)

$$x = F(T(\varepsilon)).$$

Since the left-hand sides of this equation and (9.2′) are fixed and equal,

$$F(\varepsilon) = F(T(\varepsilon)),$$

and, as long as F is one-to-one, it follows that

$$T(\varepsilon) = \varepsilon.$$

Therefore, under these conditions, T is the identity transformation and no changes of scale in reference to ε can be permitted. This is a rather extreme requirement that severely compromises the usefulness of analysis. Indeed, there is an overwhelming arbitrariness in the selection of F and the scale on which e is measured that cannot be mitigated by even the smallest variation in the latter scale.

Return now to Approach B and consider, for illustrative purposes, the production function of the standard efficiency wage model, namely,

$$x = F(\varepsilon L), \qquad (9.16)$$

where x represents output, ε is effort provided per unit of labor input (assumed to be measured only ordinally), and L is the quantity of labor input employed. In the formulation of (9.16) the underlying production function $x = f(e, L)$ and the ordinal scale on which e is measured are known without specification and the values of x and L are taken to be measured on known and fixed ratio scales. Furthermore, (9.16) represents $x = f(e, L)$ given the unspecified scales of measurement.

Of course, the assumption that $x = F(\varepsilon L)$ represents $x = f(e, L)$ would not be permitted under Approach A without the specification of f and explicit relationships (detailed earlier) linking the former to the latter. And such specifications have yet to be provided in the economics literature. Absent those specifications, the assumption content of the efficiency wage model in terms of the underlying reality to which it is addressed becomes murky, and questions concerning the relevance of the model to actual economic behavior come into play. Moreover, under the assumptions set out previously (and one more to be identified subsequently), to preserve in Approach B the multiplicative structure of (9.16) across increasing transformations of scale applied to ε requires, as in Approach C, restricting those transformations beyond that necessitated by dint of the ordinality of ε.[11]

To see what is involved in this last claim, let an alternate scale, φ, on which effort is measured be given, where

$$\varphi = T(\varepsilon), \tag{9.17}$$

and write the new production function implied by this scale change as in (9.4):

$$x = G(\varphi L). \tag{9.18}$$

Then combining (9.16)–(9.18) gives

$$F(\varepsilon L) = G(T(\varepsilon)L). \tag{9.19}$$

Since F is a production function, it may be assumed to be increasing (the additional assumption mentioned above). Combining this with the previously assumed increasingness of T, it follows that G is also increasing. The latter, in turn, implies that G has an inverse so that, from (9.19),

$$T(\varepsilon)L = G^{-1}(F(\varepsilon L)). \tag{9.20}$$

---

[11] A similar conclusion would obtain were (9.16) to arise with respect to Approach A (where the underlying f and appropriate scales are fully specified) and were it desired to maintain the multiplicative form of the arguments of F.

Consider combinations of ε and L such that

$$\varepsilon L = \gamma, \tag{9.21}$$

where γ is an arbitrary constant. Using (9.17), (9.20), and (9.21),

$$\varphi = \frac{G^{-1}(F(\varepsilon L))}{\varepsilon L} \varepsilon = \frac{G^{-1}(F(\gamma))}{\gamma} \varepsilon \tag{9.22}$$

Since (9.22) holds for all values of ε independently of γ,

$$\varphi = k\varepsilon, \tag{9.23}$$

where the constant k is given by

$$k = \frac{G^{-1}(F(\gamma))}{\gamma} \tag{9.24}$$

Note that, in spite of (9.24), k must be independent of γ. For if k_1 and k_2 were each associated with a different value of γ, then from (9.23), $\varphi = k_1\varepsilon$ and $\varphi = k_2\varepsilon$. Hence, because T has to remain dependent only on ε as in (9.17), $k_1 = k_2$. To show that transformations of the form of (9.23) are permissible in that they preserve the multiplicative form of F for any constant $k > 0$, observe that $\varphi = T(\varepsilon) = k\varepsilon$ and (9.16) imply

$$x = F\left(\frac{1}{k}\varphi L\right).$$

The function G may now be defined as

$$G(\varphi L) = F\left(\frac{1}{k}\varphi L\right),$$

thereby maintaining the required multiplicative form.

Thus the above assumptions reduce the admissible transformations of the effort scale to $T(\varepsilon) = k\varepsilon$. This does not mean that effort is actually measured on a ratio scale. But it does demonstrate that, to preserve the underlying structure of the standard efficiency wage production function with output determined by the *product* of effort and the amount of labor employed, the only ordinal scales that can be invoked as measures of effort are all multiples of each other. Clearly, then, the standard specification of the production function in the efficiency wage model relies on significant assumption content in relation to both an appropriate underlying structure and the choice of scale. That assumption content, moreover, injects an arbitrariness into this particular Approach-B-type analysis similar to that detailed more generally for Approach-C-type analyses above.

9.4 Recapitulation and Further Commentary

It has been suggested here that, in constructing models to explain observed economic behavior, functions of the form $\chi = F(\varepsilon)$, as in equation (9.2), where ε and χ are ordinally measured variables and where F is assumed to have appropriate properties, can be postulated as long as it is recognized that F actually represents some underlying, unquantified, and possibly unknown relation with corresponding properties. That is, the recognition of the existence of the underlying relation f without its precise specification or knowledge of it, and without precise specification or knowledge of the ordinal scales relating to it (Approaches B and C) is sufficient, if not fully satisfactory, for analysis to proceed. But degrees of arbitrariness and ambiguity, as has been seen, are involved in Approach C, which uses a function like F (rather than the underlying f) as the anchor of its analyses. Furthermore, although not intrinsic to Approach B, a certain arbitrariness and restrictiveness also creeps in when specific functional forms are imposed, as is the case with the multiplicative-argument specification of the efficiency wage production function. And to the latter arbitrariness and restrictiveness must be added the extra arbitrariness that arises from discarding the original concept of ordinality so as to be able to employ arithmetic operations in manipulating ordinal variable values. Finally, although better than Approaches B and C in principle, Approach A may not be possible to implement and, even when implementation is possible, use of the former may be analytically more tractable. In such circumstances, the best alternative may be to discard all numerical measures of e and x and proceed with f in unquantified form along the analytic lines suggested in Chapter 5.

Moreover, it should be pointed out that the deficiencies of Approaches B and C take on greater significance when, as in the present volume, explanation is the purpose of the analysis. For explanation requires an elucidation of the reasons for the observed behavior and, for the most part, this means the setting out of the assumptions that are required for the explanation to be relevant and correct. But it is clear in these cases that, because the relationship between f and F is contingent on the ordinal scales invoked, substantial information about f cannot be deduced from F and its properties alone. Thus, to specify only the latter is to leave significant and fundamental assumptions of the model, and hence of the explanation, up in the air. And therefore, what is purported to be an explanation of the observed behavior in question turns out to be, at best, rather incomplete and, at worst, no explanation at all.

References

[1] Akerlof, G. A., "The Market for 'Lemons': Quality Uncertainty and the Market Mechanism," *Quarterly Journal of Economics* 84 (1970), pp. 488–500.

[2] Akerlof, G. A., "A Theory of Social Custom of Which Unemployment May Be One Consequence," *Quarterly Journal of Economics* 94 (1980), pp. 749–775.

[3] Becker, G. S. and H. G. Lewis, "On the Interaction between the Quantity and Quality of Children," *Journal of Political Economy* 81 (1973), pp. S279–S288.

[4] Currie, M. and I. Steedman, "Taking Effort Seriously," *Metroeconomica* 44 (1993), pp. 134–145.

[5] Gintis, H., "Taking Effort Seriously: A Reply to Currie and Steedman," *Metroeconomica* 46 (1995), pp. 202–210.

[6] Katzner, D. W., *Choice and the Quality of Life* (Beverly Hills: Sage, 1979).

[7] Katzner, D. W., *Analysis without Measurement* (Cambridge: Cambridge University Press 1983).

[8] Katzner, D. W., "Analysis with Ordinal Measurement," in *Employment, Economic Growth and the Tyranny of the Market*, v. 2, P. Arestis, ed. (Cheltenham: Elgar, 1996), pp. 37–54. Reprinted in D. W. Katzner, *Unmeasured Information and the Methodology of Social Scientific Inquiry* (Boston: Kluwer, 2001), pp. 197–215.

[9] Katzner, D. W., "The Misuse of Measurement in Economics," *Metroeconomica* 49 (1998), pp. 1–22. Reprinted in D. W. Katzner, *Unmeasured Information and the Methodology of Social Scientific Inquiry* (Boston, MA: Kluwer, 2001), pp. 175–195.

[10] Katzner, D. W., *Unmeasured Information and the Methodology of Social Scientific Inquiry* (Boston, MA: Kluwer, 2001).

[11] Leslie, D., "On the Proper Use of Ordinal Variables in Labour Market Models," *The Manchester School* 63 (1995), pp. 196–205.

[12] Skott, P., "Measuring Effort," *Metroeconomica* 48 (1997), pp. 300–305.

[13] Skott, P., "On the Proper Use of Ordinal Variables – A Comment," *The Manchester School* 65 (1997), pp. 599–601.

[14] Stiglitz, J. E., "The Causes and Consequences of the Dependence of Quality on Price," *Journal of Economic Literature* 25 (1987), pp. 1–25.

10

Categories of Models

Apart from those that represent structure or outcomes alone and the single- and multi-output model types all described in Chapter 2, explanatory economic models come in many colors and shapes. Models of the consumer, general equilibrium, bargaining, economic growth, and the macro economy, to name but a few, are commonplace and well known. These models may be seen as falling into different categories according to the nature of the analytical methods or techniques required to develop structure from their assumption base. As such, the class in which a particular model falls has a significant impact on the analytical content of the stages of its construction and the overall process by which that model is built. In the examples discussed so far, the building process of models of the consumer generally involves the mathematics of constrained maximization; that of general equilibrium and the macro economy models often requires the mathematics of simultaneity; for models of bargaining the mathematics of game theory is frequently invoked; and for those of economic growth the use of the mathematics of differential or difference equations is usually a necessity. Because the category in which an explanatory model falls has such an important impact on the building of that model, it is worth considering a taxonomy of model categories in this chapter. There are numerous ways of classifying such models with respect to their assumption content and the general characteristics that that content implies. The classification scheme employed here contains three broad categories defined on the basis of abstract, general criteria that have far-reaching implications for the nature of the models they encompass. Each category is set against one that is diametrically opposed to it.

The categories in the order they will be discussed are as follows: (i) models that adhere to the tenets of methodological individualism (or just individualism) versus models that fall under the umbrella of structuralism, (ii) static models versus dynamic models, and (iii) models that assume certainty with respect to relevant data versus those that recognize and suggest ways of taking uncertainty in relation to those data into account. Also to be reviewed are several sub-categories of models, two with contrasting "opposites," contained within the above model classes. In particular, dynamic models may be divided into models based on logical time versus opposing models in which time is viewed as histori-cal.[1] Certainty models include models in which individuals have perfect information, that is, full knowledge of all pertinent analytic elements, whereas uncertainty models often postulate individuals who must make decisions in various environments of ignorance. The latter encompasses the second pair of opposing sub-categories containing, on the one hand, models that characterize uncertainty in probabilistic terms, or what is sometimes referred to as probabilistically reducible risk, along with models that rest on non-probabilistic or "true" uncertainty on the other. Moreover, the categories set out here overlap. For example, static and dynamic models can be individualist or structuralist and involve certainty or uncertainty. With respect to specific models, the traditional Keynesian-cross model of the macroeconomy falls in the structuralist, certainty, and static categories. And the Walrasian model of the microeconomy is individualistic and dynamic, and incorporates logical time, full information, and certainty.

10.1 Individualism Versus Structuralism

Before considering the notion of methodological individualism in relation to economic models, it will help to set the frame of reference by considering what has been referred to as the metaphysical theory of *mechanism* that largely directed the development of the physical sciences from the seventeenth to the middle of the nineteenth century. In that theory, the universe is made up of tiny particles, whose existence is unexplained, and which behave according to simple mechanical laws. Every physical thing is understood in terms of the configuration of the particles that make it up, and all physical behavior is a consequence of the basic mechanical laws governing the behavior of the individual particles. Like all metaphysical theories, mechanism is not empirically testable. Any physical phenomenon that does not seem to fit into the mechanism mold can be attributed to a lack of ability to come up with an appropriate mechanical model rather than to a mistaken methodological approach to reality. But

---

[1] Definitions of logical and historical time will be given on p. 218.

while mechanism is therefore compatible with any and all collections of observations that might come along, it is not consistent with all models of the physical world. For example, to think of light only in terms of waves is to abandon mechanism in favor of another metaphysical theory. Thus the adoption of mechanism as a world view restricts the kinds of models that are acceptable for understanding and explaining reality.[2]

Now, as has been suggested in Chapter 1, social science is quite different from physical science, in particular, from mechanistic physical science. It deals with thinking, feeling, reacting, and evolving human beings – not inert and changeless particles. Nevertheless, from the perspective of the social sciences, *methodological individualism* is a meta-theory quite analogous to mechanism. According to it, all social activity can ultimately be explained exhaustively in terms of individual behavior. But that behavior necessarily takes place in a context or according to rules set by environments or institutions. The emergence of environments and institutions however, cannot, in the final analysis, be reduced to the actions of individuals. That is because it is not possible to describe the initial state of nature out of which those environments and institutions grew solely in terms of individual interactions (Hodgson, [13, p. 223]). In other words, society is made up of individual agents whose existence is unexplained, and whose behavior conforms to laws in a manner that can be said to have been guided, approximately, by those agents' dispositions, their understandings of their own situations, and the institutions and environments in the context of which that behavior takes place. All social activity is understood with respect to the configurations of the agents who bring it about, and as a consequence of those agents' behavior and the interactive effects of that behavior.[3] Methodological individualism, too, is not empirically testable. If a methodologically individualistic model does not seem to reflect the social phenomenon it was built to explain, the fault can always be attributed to the inappropriateness of the model rather than to the methodological approach to reality. And while it is possible in principle to construct methodologically individualistic models to explain any and all collections of observations that might come along, non-methodologically individualistic models of the economic world may also have explanatory competence.[4]

---

[2] See, for example, Watkins [45, p. 270].

[3] Methodological individualism is distinct from philosophical materialism as described in Chapter 1 in that the former takes human behavior to be the fundamental building blocks of all social activity. The latter is concerned with the construction of human behavior from more basic material elements.

[4] Watkins [45, pp. 270–271].

It should be emphasized that non-agent elements of models classified as methodological individualistic are made up of two components: first, macro or group objects and concepts that are composed of individual (agent) objects and concepts, and second, macro behavior that is derived from or determined by individual (agent) behavior. As the phrase is construed here, methodological individualism includes both, and not just one or the other, of these elements.[5] The possibility of, say, herd effects where, by reason of absorption into the mass, individuals follow some kind of herd instinct, is precluded.

An example of a methodological individualistic model is the earlier mentioned Walrasian general equilibrium model of the microeconomy. In that model the irreducible units are consumers and firms. The quantity-of-commodity consequences of consumer and firm decisions flow through price-determining markets composed of consumers and/or firms, and their simultaneous behavior leads to a solution or equilibrium model outputs. Typically, the rules by which the markets operate to determine prices are institutionally set and do not emerge from individual action. The model is intended to explain the hidden workings of the microeconomy and its significance lies in its demonstration that the allocation of resources in the equilibrium output meets certain efficiency requirements.[6]

Although the idea of methodological individualism dates at least to Epicurus[7] and, in its physical-world manifestation, was employed as the basis for mechanism by Descartes in his *Discours* of 1637,[8] its explicit introduction into economics was probably due to Menger. In the preface to the first edition (1871) of his *Principles* (*Grundsätze*), Menger wrote [25, pp. 46–47], "... I have endeavored to reduce the complex phenomena of human economic activity to the simplest elements that can still be subjected to accurate observation, ... and ... to investigate the manner in which the more complex economic phenomena evolve from their elements according to definite principles." Evidently, Menger felt rather strongly that this was the only method for conducting economic inquiry.[9] Hayek [11, p. 6], moreover, took virtually the same position some 75 years later: "... there is no other way toward an understanding of social phenomena but through our understanding of individual actions ...." [10] And this perspective,

---

[5] Cf., Brodbeck [5, p. 286], and Sensat [35, pp. 190–194].
[6] For details see Katzner [19].
[7] Strozier [42, pp. 117–118].
[8] For example, Burtt [6, pp. 103], and Levins and Lewontin [22, pp. 1–2]. The notion of mechanism goes back beyond even Epicurus. See Strodack [41, pp. 3–4].
[9] See Menger [26, pp. 93–94].
[10] See also von Mises [27, pp. 41–43].

accepted with the same fervor of Menger and Hayek, seems to be shared by most economists today. It implies, in the final analysis, that the private economy can only be understood and explained in terms of consumers and firms; aggregate concepts, including the notion of "the economy" itself, have no independent existence or meaning apart from them.

Of course, from time to time, there appear to have been temporary lapses from the perspective of methodological individualism. The development of macroeconomic models in terms of economy-wide aggregates during the middle of the twentieth century, that is, the Keynesian revolution through the neoclassical synthesis can be interpreted in this way.[11] But the more recent search for micro foundations of macroeconomics reveals a yearning for methodological individualism that carries over into the macroeconomic arena. Indeed, evidence suggests that economists never really gave up methodological individualism even throughout their mid-century focus on macroeconomic problems.[12] There always seems to have been the feeling that, in light of the possibilities of aggregation, the whole should somehow equal the sum of its parts.[13] Moreover, with little progress made by 1967 in uncovering suitable micro foundations, Arrow referred to the persisting gap between microeconomics and macroeconomics as a "major scandal" [2, p. 734]. In any event, it is widely thought that the economics of the Keynesian revolution and the neoclassical synthesis lost its favor due, in part, to the inability to come up with appropriate micro foundations.[14]

Structuralism is the antithesis of methodological individualism. The variables and relations of models in this category are not associated with or founded on any sub-units from which they might be aggregated. According to Piaget [29, p. 5], "a structure is a system of transformations" that embodies notions of "wholeness," and "self-regulation." The transformations are laws in and of themselves. They are whole in that they are not viewed as aggregates formed from the combination of independent micro-elements. The transformations are self-regulating in that their manipulation does not produce an output that lies beyond the system. Thus, for example, equilibrium and cycles, should they be present, are outputs that exist within the models that generate them. Moreover, if the structure is contained in a larger structure, the substructure's laws are conserved and not altered by being a part of the larger structure.[15] As previously noted, the well-known

[11] Blaug [4, p. 161].
[12] Hoover [14, pp. 3–4].
[13] For example, Samuelson [34, p. 356].
[14] Hoover [14, p. 3].
[15] Piaget [29, pp. 5–14, 103–105].

Keynesian–cross model may be thought of as a structuralist model. Its basic elements are aggregates of individual consumer, individual firm investment, and individual government department expenditures. For the purposes of the model, these elements are not broken down into underlying units of, respectively, consumers, firms, and government departments. Nor do the properties of the behavior of the underlying units play any role in the model or its construction. And the simultaneous interactions among these aggregate elements determine the aggregate level of the economy's income or expenditure. The importance of the model lies in its explanation of aggregate unemployment as a consequence of aggregate expenditure falling below the full-employment level of expenditure and its explanation of inflation as a result of aggregate expenditure rising above the full-employment level. Obviously, models derived from an individualistic approach are quite distinct in form and significance from those emerging from a structuralist perspective.

10.2 Static Models Versus Dynamic Models

Static models, on the one hand, deal with the conditions under which the solution outputs or values of the model's explanatory variables do not change when acted on by various forces. That is, the solution values are in equilibrium in that the forces involved cancel each other out and the variable or solution values in question remain at rest. As a result, the passage of time is irrelevant. The supply–demand model of an isolated market described in Chapter 2 is an illustration of a static model. And the Walrasian general equilibrium model could also be viewed as static by ignoring the dynamic determination of prices from out-of-equilibrium positions.

On the other hand, dynamic models focus on forces such as motives or actions that induce change in certain model variables over time. The forces are depicted in detail and the manner in which they cause change is spelled out. Examples include the Kaldor, Kalecki, and Goodwin models cited earlier. Dynamic models, however, can recognize the nature of time in different ways.

Logical Time Versus Historical Time. In Chapter 6, it was pointed out that the notion of time employed in dynamic models is an arithmomorphic abstraction permitting the sequencing of instants or periods one after the other. With that sequencing in place, the distinction between logical time and historical time is both pertinent and important for model construction. That distinction, initially noted in Chapter 1, also divides the category of dynamic models into two non-overlapping and opposing sub-categories. It is considered now in greater detail.

Following Winston [46, pp. 32–38], who uses the adjectives "analytical" and "perspective" in place of, respectively, "logical" and "historical," the difference between these concepts has to do with the way in which time is perceived to order events. When pairwise comparisons of events are made such that any one event is considered only in a logical or putatively causal relation with other events and is said to take place before, after, or simultaneously with them, time is expressed in its logical form. Logical time, then, is not a manifestation of the real time in which human beings live. Rather, it is an abstraction that provides only a means for the sequencing of events through time without regard to the actual experiencing of them as past events, present events, or future events. It is because one may move back and forth through a sequence of such timed or dated events hypothetically, but never experientially, that Hicks [12] invoked the phrase "out of time," meaning "out of actually experienced time," to describe models placed in logical time. In the historical approach to time, however, all events are designated as belonging to one of the three groups that make up the collection of past events, present events, and future events. Here, with regard to past and future events, time order sets containing many events occurring through time at once, rather than sets having only events occurring at a single moment (or period) of time, and the basis of that ordering is solely experiential: Past events come before future events. Only present events, which lie between past and future events, are linked to a single unit of time. Moreover, to identify an event as a member of one of the past, present, or future classes, is to give it a unique experiential significance and meaning (with unique implications) distinct from that which would adhere if it were assigned to a different class. Because it focuses more on the actual experiencing of events, historical time is sometimes called "real" time and analysis based upon it was referred to by Hicks [12] as analysis "in time."

At a fundamental level, the significance of the distinction between logical and historical time is related to, though not necessarily completely dependent on, the assumed ontological status of humankind. Two different approaches to that status were described in Chapter 1. From the perspective of philosophical materialism, there may be little necessity to recognize the importance for the analysis of human behavior of the movement of historical time. In that case, however, a residual difficulty in the explanation of human behavior may arise from the impact on historical reality of haphazard shocks and unanticipatable developments.

The alternative approach is the view that human beings have cognitive capacities that go beyond, and are not solely determined by, their material parts. In other words, knowledge of all of the material facts about an individual (and his environment) is not sufficient to be able to explain his actions. This means that experience becomes a significant factor in generating, and hence explaining, human behavior. And experience, clearly, can only be properly accounted for in the context of historical time. Thus, although it is possible to remain agnostic in analytical outlook about philosophical materialism and still hold to the assumption of logical time, adherence to historical time as the setting in which human action occurs necessarily requires the rejection of philosophical materialism. That rejection could also be seen to be implied in the previous acknowledgment of the difficulties introduced to explanation by the possibility of unforeseen and unforeseeable shocks and external events.

There are three differences between logical time and historical time that are important for present purposes. First, as suggested above, time in the logical sense can be controlled. For example, an investigator explaining particular behavior that occurred at a particular past moment may, after that explanation is completed, move backward through a sequence of timed events, restart his analytical clock to explain the behavior occurring at a later past moment, and, if nothing had changed analytically in the interim between the two past moments, employ the original explanation of the behavior to explain the behavior at the later moment. Neither the values of the variables he employs nor the explanatory edifice he constructs are subject to variation simply by virtue of their existence at different actual (historical) time dates. Thus the outputs produced by his system emerge from the resolution of a fixed, often mathematical, structure having the same analytical properties at all dates. Logical time is, in other words, reversible. But the investigator has no such control of time in the historical sense. For historical time locks him in the present. Things always change from one explanatory moment to the next. The events of each moment can be experienced only once; although their effects may linger, after these events are experienced they are forever past. Thus restarting his analytical clock to explain the behavior at the later moment, if that notion has any meaning at all, necessarily leads to an entirely different analysis and a totally new explanation.[16] That is because, under the conditions implicit in the

[16] This is not to say that, in the special circumstance in which history seems to repeat itself, putting forth the same explanation at the later time is never appropriate (see n. 23 on p. 226). But as a general rule, it cannot hold up.

passing of historical time, the possibility of re-experiencing past events, in the same precise way and in terms of the same structural relations with respect to which they previously occurred, is precluded. What is experientially new or novel occurring in the interim before the clock has been restarted determines the later behavior. Thus a model purporting to explain the behavior of, say, an individual, has to be revised or rebuilt for each explanatory moment that the individual's behavior takes place.

Second, although each moment in logical time has the same properties as any other, in historical time past, present, and future moments each have their own unique properties. Uniqueness necessarily arises since all action takes place in the present, all actions of the future are yet to come, and all actions of the past are history. The implications of this fact are that each moment is associated with its own unique history and projects it own unique knowledge complex and, therefore, each decision maker has what may be referred to as a unique epistemic status at each moment. One may conclude in particular that the moment of the present has, as previously suggested, a different significance and meaning than either past moments or future moments.

Third, since an individual actor under investigation can be thought of as an investigator himself, and since the assumption of logical time permits the investigator to wander back and forth across sequences of timed events, the actor in logical time necessarily knows everything that exists and is relevant to know about the past, present, and future. His knowledge is therefore assumed to be *complete* or *perfect*, even if it is only expressed probabilistically. But in historical time the complexity of reality prevents the actor from knowing everything about the past. And, although the actor may be able to make some intelligent guesses, it is not possible for him to know anything at all about the future. Knowledge of future events, even probabilistic knowledge, is not only unknown, but also unknowable until the events are past. The question of the applicability of probability concepts under conditions of historical time and ignorance is taken up below.

The Walrasian general equilibrium model with price determination included illustrates the dynamic model employing logical time. In that model non-equilibrium prices adjust according to the excess demands present in the respective markets. Consumers and firms change the quantities of goods they want to buy and sell which, in turn, generates new prices. The process continues until equilibrium is reached. In this environment, the experience of each agent at each moment has no impact on the behavior of that agent at subsequent moments since there are no changes in the assumed forms of utility and production functions. That is, the agent always knows everything there is to know about past, present, and future preferences and technologies. The knowledge complex and the epistemic status of agents do not change from moment to moment and there is no difference between past, present, and future moments. And the fixed-through-time process of price determination can be restarted over and over without ever changing its output.

An example of a model set in historical time is Shackle's model of decision making.[17] Based on experience and the imperfect knowledge he has of the past and present, the decision maker imagines an incomplete collection of as many states of the world as he can think of that could emerge as the effects of his possible decision among the objects of choice work themselves out, and forms opinions about their possible occurrence that are expressed in the language of "potential surprise." At each decision moment, in other words, the decision maker contemplates the possibilities for future events, given the shape and texture of the history of which he is aware and as he perceives it. And he imagines the extent to which he might be surprised if certain states of the world rather than certain others were to occur. He can do this because his sense of the structure of things is historically informed by conjured relations, not necessarily stable over time, that pertain to economic affairs. Clearly, these contemplations and imaginings vary from decision moment to decision moment as the decision maker's experience and knowledge complex necessarily change in historical time. Their employment in the model of decision making developed by Shackle will be described at the end of the next section.

10.3 Certainty versus Uncertainty

A certainty environment, that is, one in which the individual or agent is assumed to have perfect knowledge of all possible eventuation, is a circumstance in which there are no doubts about its particulars. All aspects of it are unquestionably and thoroughly established. Models that fall in the certainty category clearly reflect these characteristics. In an uncertain world the available information pertaining to that world is, at least in some respects, untrustworthy, unreliable, and problematic. One area of economics in which the distinction between certain and uncertain environments is highly significant in constructing models is that of individual decision making. Although subsequent discussion of models in the certainty and uncertainty categories focuses attention exclusively on

---

[17] See Katzner [18, Sect. 4.3] for a full discussion of a simplified version of Shackle's model.

the characteristics of model building that purport to explain the making of decisions, many of the following statements and conclusions apply more broadly to other areas as well.

Ignorance is a fact of real economic life. All decision makers face decision situations with incomplete information. On the one hand, the world is so complex that the individual is unable to collect, much less assimilate, more than a small fraction of the relevant data. On the other, human beings do not possess the capacity to analyze what data they have beyond a few simplified, coarsely approximating propositions. Thus the decision context, including the set of options from which the decision maker chooses, is often imprecise and fuzzy. Moreover, even if one knew and understood everything there is to know and understand about past economic activity and present economic behavior, it would still not be possible to anticipate all future consequences of each choice option. The unexpected can, and often does, occur. For the decision maker, then, ignorance arises both from his inability to know and understand fully the past and the present, as well as from the impossibility of foreseeing the future.

The reality of ignorance, however, is only just beginning to have an impact on the economic analysis of decision making. Most models of decision making assume it away, either by supposing that there is only one state of the world and this state is completely recognizable (i.e., by supposing a certainty environment), or by postulating that there are many possible and describable states of the world all of which are fully known, and each subset of which has a (possibly subjective) probability of occurrence assigned to it. The latter apparatus is frequently employed to permit future possible values of variables to be reduced to present-value certainty equivalents (i.e., expected values).

In thinking about the making of decisions by individuals in society,[18] two general facts are immediately obvious. First, all decisions are made in environments that are characterized with respect to the individual's perceptions of (a) the possible outcomes, (b) the economic structures, and (c) the endowments that are relevant to his choice. Second, the particularities of an environment necessarily influence the means by which a decision made in that environment is reached. Not surprisingly, then, the various approaches to the building of models to explain decision making may be classified according to the environments to which they apply. In one important classification scheme, there are three primary categories of

---

[18] The present focus on individual decision making excludes decisions made in game- and social-choice-theoretic situations.

environments, each mutually exclusive of the others. These are associated with the names "certainty," "probabilistic uncertainty" (sometimes referred to as "risk"), and "non-probabilistic uncertainty." Although a general definition of the first concept has been given earlier, it is worth providing a more specific version here, along with definitions of the latter two, that relate, in particular, to the analysis of decision making.

A decision, then, is made under conditions of *certainty* provided that the state of the world, and hence the outcome of the decision that is to emerge as the decision is put into effect, is known in advance. In this case, the outcome is known in advance by virtue of the perfect knowledge the individual is assumed to have of the relations between all determining variables and functions. A decision is made under circumstances of *probabilistic uncertainty* if only the possible future states of the world (and hence the possible future outcomes) together with the (typically subjective) probabilities of those states (and outcomes) are known in advance. And a decision is made in an environment of *non-probabilistic uncertainty* when not all of the many possible future states of the world (and outcomes) are known in advance, and the probabilities of the known states (and outcomes) are unknown, unknowable, or may not exist.[19] Decision making under non-probabilistic uncertainty is also referred to as decision making in *ignorance*.

In addition to an environment, all models of decision making by individuals specify a collection of objects or options among which a choice, that is, a decision, is to be made, and either a criterion function that orders the objects of choice or a decision rule that picks out a single object of choice. The choice object selected is usually that which is "best" (assuming one exists) according to the designated criterion function or decision rule. It is the use and construction of the criterion function or decision rule that varies from environment to environment.

The numerous approaches to, and applications of, models of individual decision making under certainty are well known and need not be considered in detail here.[20] Suffice it to say that in many instances the objects of

---

[19] The distinction between probabilistic and non-probabilistic uncertainty is essentially due to Knight [21, p. 233]. Actually, the phrase "environment of uncertainty" sometimes has a slightly different meaning from that described here. Uncertain environments in this last sense are ones in which, although probabilities remain unknown, all possible future states of the world and outcomes are known in advance. Such a notion may be viewed as lying in between those of environments of probabilistic uncertainty and environments of non-probabilistic uncertainty as originally characterized above.

[20] Simon [40] provides a broad survey. To cite an example of a specific and detailed aplication, the utility-maximizing consumer is analyzed by Katzner [17].

choice are baskets of consumption commodities, quantities of outputs, or vectors of inputs; the criterion functions associated with them frequently are, respectively, utility or profit functions; and decisions are made, again respectively, by maximizing utility subject to budget constraints or by maximizing profit subject to technological and capital expenditure constraints. It should be pointed out, however, that the viability of such models has not been left unquestioned. Abbott [1, pp. 51–54], for example, has talked about the imperfectness of the knowledge that an individual has about his own utility function. Similarly, Simon [39, pp. 79–84; and 39, pp. 272–273] has concluded that, when making decisions, ignorance arising from an inability to process sufficiently large amounts of information places bounds on the capacity of individuals to know the full extent and implications of their opportunities. Hence their ability to choose is limited and they are forced to pursue "satisficing" rather than maximizing behaviors. These criticisms would appear to suggest that actual environments are not certain environments because individuals do not really know in advance some of the outcomes, or at least their evaluations of those outcomes, produced by their decisions. But whether this kind of ignorance actually leads to certainty or probabilistic or non-probabilistic uncertainty models of individual decision making depends on the particular way in which the absence of knowledge is handled. Consider, on the one hand, Radner's approach [32] to satisficing behavior, in which a manager, say, searches for improvement in the activities he supervises. Since Radner introduces a probability function as the basis for assuming that, among other things, the expected rate of improvement of each activity per unit of time depends on the search effort devoted to it, his model is clearly located in an environment of probabilistic uncertainty or risk. On the other hand, Winter's model [47] of satisficing behavior on the part of firms, which make pricing and production decisions by adopting rules of thumb such as the setting of output price by marking up from unit cost, is couched in a certainty-type environment.

Probabilistic versus Non-probabilistic Uncertainty. It is convenient to continue to refer to models of decision making in considering the distinction between models appearing in the probabilistic and non-probabilistic uncertainty categories.[21] From the point of view of the latter, since all of life's events take place in historical time, the posing of static questions that give no recognition to that conceptualization of time is

---

[21] For a more detailed and thorough discussion of decision making under conditions of non-probabilistic uncertainty, see Katzner [18].

not meaningful. For time, as previously indicated in this context, can never be started over. Rather, it is irreversible and historical: time flows in a single continuous stream along which every moment is unique. Each moment, that is, has its own peculiar history, presents its own peculiar knowledge complex derived from that history, its own peculiar institutional structures and environments, and its own totality and distribution of resource endowments. Thus the recurrence of a moment of time that has already gone by cannot happen, and phenomena that arise in historical time can never repeat themselves in exactly the same way or in the same ontological and epistemic contexts. Unique histories lead into and impinge upon unique histories that are yet to be completed. It follows that models providing explanations or understandings of any one moment, at that moment, are necessarily different from those at all other moments. To recall the Hicksian terminology introduced earlier, such models, which rest methodologically on the idea of historical time, are in time, while certainty and probabilistic models are out of time.

Throughout the passage of historical time, the present is the boundary separating the past from the future. The past, being past, is capable to a greater or lesser degree of historical description, and hence knowledge about the past can be secured. To the extent that the present is experienced and exposed, knowledge of the present is also obtainable. But such knowledge of the past and present is necessarily partial, always unique to the individual possessing it and, because the world is enormously complex, so incomplete and insufficient that it cannot usually be projected into the future probabilistically.[22] The knowledge complex an individual has of the past and present at any moment has been characterized as his epistemic status of that moment. However, knowledge, including probabilistic knowledge about the future, is impossible to secure because the future cannot be known until it is past. Both future novelty and hence

---

[22] Only knowledge of the past and present could be projected probabilistically into the future, and only in the following way: because observations of the past and present necessarily require abstraction and the omission of numerous details, it might appear that certain happenings recur in certain repeated situations. On the basis of such observations, it may be possible to extract a probability of future occurrence. That is, regardless of whether a likelihood of recurrence exists in reality or not, a probability of future occurrence of the observations might be inferred from the historical data. But it should be noted that this does not constitute knowledge of the future since the presumption is that as soon as the present moves into the past, and a new present provides a new observation, the extracted probability modifies. History, that is, does not, as a rule, establish probability distributions that are unchanging over time. In Davidson's terminology, our world tends to be "nonergodic" [7, p. 187].

the totality of future possibilities are unknowable: the unexpected may happen. Not only is the investigating economist confronted by such large gaps in knowledge, but so too are the decision makers whose behavior may be part of the subject matter of his investigation. In spite of this ignorance and the (non-probabilistic) uncertainty it imposes, these latter decision makers still imagine and guess about the future using their incomplete knowledge of the past and present. They may even build models to help organize their thoughts. In any case, such imaginings, guesses, and models may also serve as the springboards for decisions or behavior in the present. Thus an individual decision maker arrives at each moment (or period) of decision with a unique background of history and with a unique epistemic status and unique thoughts derived from that history. The environment in which he decides is also unique because it, too, has its own singular history.[23] The same environment, the same background of the individual, and hence the same decision opportunity, can never arise again.

The contrast between this vision of economic decision making and that of models of decision making under conditions of probabilistic uncertainty is quite stark. Consider, for example, the expected utility model of consumer decision making. In that case, all future possible states of the world and their probabilities of occurrence are assumed to be fully known and specified. And given his completely known and unchangeable preferences among commodity outcomes, the consumer can translate this knowledge into an expected utility function. The decision is then made by maximizing the expected utility function subject to whatever constraints are encountered. But in the context of historical time and human ignorance, history and experience are raised to a position of paramount importance, and the omniscient ability of the consumer to formulate an expected utility function is destroyed. Indeed, Hutchison [16, pp. 1–3] has argued that such omniscience is "the most criticizable and unrealistic feature of ... 'Economic Man.'"

It should also be noted that these ideas revolving around the notions of historical time, ignorance, and uncertainty are not new. According

[23] As pointed out in n. 22 on p. 225, history may, in special circumstances, give the appearance of statistically or ergodically "repeating" itself. But such repetition, if it occurs, can be perceived only after that history has unfolded, or in an ex post and not an ex ante sense. In conditions of historical time and the uniqueness of decision moments that are enshrouded in ignorance of the future, and in the context of the uncertainty that that creates, logic does not permit the assumption that the past or previously established patterns will necessarily project themselves into the future. Such an assumption is precluded by the unforseen and unforseeable outcomes that the future hides from view.

to Hutchison [15, p. 212], historical time was present in the work of Adam Smith. More recently, Marshall, Keynes, and Popper all spoke about various aspects of historical time, or the inability to foresee the future, or the impossibility of obtaining probabilities.[24] Knight [21] dealt with all three and also, as pointed out in n. 19 on p. 223, deserves the credit for distinguishing between uncertainty when probability is definable, which he referred to as risk, and uncertainty when it is not, which is what he meant by the term "uncertainty." The pervasiveness and significance of ignorance has been described in another context by Hayek [11, pp. 519–520]: "The peculiar character of the problem of a rational economic order is determined precisely by the fact that knowledge of the circumstances of which we must make use never exists in concentrated or integrated form, but solely as the dispersed bits of incomplete and frequently contradictory knowledge which ... separate individuals possess.... . It is the problem of the utilization of knowledge not given to anyone in its totality." Other authors who have taken up these and related issues include Bausor [3], Hicks [12], Loasby [23], Robinson [33], Shackle [38], and Vickers [43]. It is also interesting that the contrast between logical and historical time arose some time ago in physics when reconciling the laws of Newtonian mechanics, which are out of time, with the observation that, in real time, heat always flows from warmer to colder bodies.[25]

Consider now the meaning of the concept of probability. Although the practice of gambling, and hence the ideas of chance and frequency, were known to the ancients, the notion of probability as it is presently conceived did not emerge until the decade around 1660. And when it did it seemed to spring up in the minds of many individuals, including its legendary inventor Pascal, at once. In birthing, moreover, it came into existence in two forms, neither of which had antecedents in its prehistory, and which still persist today.[26] These two forms are often connoted by using the adjectives "aleatory" and "epistemological." Thus aleatory probability is associated with the outcomes of chance mechanisms and the relative frequencies they produce upon repeated trials, while epistemological probability is concerned with measures of degrees of belief, as warranted by evidence or judgment, that outcomes will obtain. The fact that philosophers have been unable in over three hundred years to bridge the gap between

---

[24] For example, Marshall [24, pp. 109, 347], Keynes [20, pp. 213–214], and Popper [30, pp. ix–x].

[25] Porter [31, Ch. 7].

[26] See Hacking [10, Chs. 1,2].

these two conceptualizations suggests the presence of deep and significant differences.[27]

There are alternative perspectives from which to view both forms of probability. Perhaps the dominant approach to aleatory probability is the frequentist position that the probability function $p(A)$ is the relative frequency that an outcome in the set or event A is observed in an arbitrarily large number of trials. Implicit in this definition is the requirement that the attribute defining the event A be distributed randomly over the elements of every infinite sequence of trial outcomes so that the limiting relative frequency, $p(A)$, is always the same. Observe that the frequentist notion applies only to the collective outcomes of repeated trials of a game of chance. One may say that the probability of a general toss of a fair coin yielding heads is 1/2 in the sense that after many, many trials the relative frequency of occurrence of heads approaches 1/2. But the notion of the (frequency) probability of heads on any particular toss itself is, literally speaking, not defined.[28]

The most prevalent way of thinking about epistemological probability is with respect to personal or subjective probability. In this view, $p(A)$ is a measure of the belief an individual has that an outcome in A will occur. These beliefs, and hence subjective probabilities, are revised as the individual acquires more information relevant to the possible occurrence of an outcome in A. Moreover, they have to be coherent in the sense that, based upon them, "Dutch book" cannot be made against him.[29] Clearly the subjectivist approach to probability applies to a much broader class of circumstances than does the frequentist approach. In particular, although the probability of heads in many repeated tosses of a coin is definable for both, the probability of heads on any particular toss is (literally) meaningful only for the subjectivist.

Of course, most people who apply probability to statistical decision making, or other models in their work do not take such philosophical distinctions of meaning very seriously.[30] Indeed, individuals will often think of probability as either frequency or subjective probability to suit the circumstance at hand. When it seems reasonable to conceptualize in terms of the collective outcomes of a game, one takes cognizance of the

---

[27] Hacking [10, p. 15].

[28] Oaks [28, p. 102].

[29] See, for example, ibid., pp. 106–108. An individual can have Dutch book made against him if it is possible for someone else to devise a betting strategy such that, over a sufficiently long string of bets, the individual will always lose.

[30] Hacking [10, pp. 14,15].

former. Otherwise the perception is of the latter. From this perspective, since it is relevant in either case, subjective probability may be viewed as a generalization of frequency probability. In such a context, moreover, the so-called de Finetti theorem has a significant implication.[31] For the theorem applies, in part, to situations in which an individual modifies his subjective probabilities of events concerning the outcomes of a game in accordance with the observed outcomes of repeated trials of that game. And it asserts that under certain reasonable conditions, regardless of the subjective probability of an event with which the individual starts out, if his beliefs are coherent, then, as the number of repeated trials increases, the individual repeatedly revises that subjective probability to become closer and closer to the event's observed frequency.[32] But, since, as the number of trials becomes large, the observed frequency approaches the frequency probability, the subjective probability of the event must converge to its frequency probability. It follows that given the initial subjective probability of any event in general, hypothetical translation of that event into a game environment would lead, at least in theory, to a similar convergence of subjective probability, as repeatedly revised, to frequency probability. In this sense, then, subjective probability is related to both frequency probability and replication.

However, Shackle [37, Ch. 7] has questioned the use of any notion of probability in the context of human decision making that is characterized by historical time and ignorance. His argument is threefold.[33] First, the ignorance in which decisions must be made precludes the listing of all possible outcomes resulting from the selection of each decision option. And with the potential occurrence of unknown and unknowable outcomes, the determination of the probability of any subset of known possible outcomes is problematic because it depends on the measure of the outcome space in general and, in the finite case, on the specific number of outcomes. In other words, the existence of unknown and unknowable outcomes rules out the "permanent" assignment of probability to any event.[34] One might

---

[31] De Finetti [8]. An informal statement of the theorem appears on de Finetti's p. 142. De Finetti would not agree with this implication because he does not accept the existence of frequency probability. See [8, pp. 99, 148–154].

[32] In a similar way, two persons observing the same event-generating process, who begin with different subjective probabilities of the same event, will eventually see those subjective probabilities converge to each other.

[33] Although the following is expressed in terms of frequency and subjective probability, it clearly applies to aleatory and epistemological probability in general.

[34] Shackle [37, p. 49]. To illustrate, suppose there are three candidates in an election and suppose an individual's subjective probabilities of each of them winning are 1/4, 1/4, and

think that a possible way to avoid this difficulty is to assign probabilities (they would have to be subjective probabilities) to some subsets of known outcomes, and then to lump all remaining outcomes (the number of which is unknowable), into one set and assign probability to it so that the probability of all outcomes combined is unity. But such an approach still does not permit a permanent assignment of probabilities (recall the example of n. 34 starting on p. 239), and this lack of permanence may, according to Shackle, hide analytical features of the decision problem that turn out to be significant. The use of subjective probabilities also raises the issue, to be further considered below, of how the subjective probabilities of the subsets of known outcomes are determined.

Shackle's second objection applies mainly to frequency probability and that portion of subjective probability that relates to it. Since the decisions in which Shackle is interested take place in historical time, each moment of decision is unique and can never reappear in exactly the same way again. Decisions, that is, are "self-destructive" in that they change the nature of future states of the world or outcome configurations and the epistemic statuses of the decision makers, and thereby destroy forever the possibility of their being repeated. This being so, the replication required for frequency probability does not exist, and hence the concept itself cannot be employed in such a context.[35] Thus, for example, it would have been meaningless for the purpose of making a decision about whether or not to fight, for Napoleon to have asked in advance about the probability of his winning the battle of Waterloo. For, were he to have won the battle, he would not have had to fight it again, and, were he to have lost, he would not have been able to fight it again.

The third difficulty with the use of probability under conditions of historical time and ignorance raised by Shackle is addressed solely to subjective probability and the source from which it comes. For to be able to assign relevant subjective probabilities in a particular decision situation, the decision-maker has to employ knowledge that he has obtained appropriate to that situation from what he has learned and experienced in the past. That

---

1/2. Now, at a later date, a fourth candidate, until then unknown and with a positive (subjective) probability of winning, decides to enter the race. Then, because probabilities sum to 1, the probabilities assigned to the original three candidates must change.

[35] Ibid., pp. 55–57. Knight [21, p. 226] made a similar argument some forty-five years earlier. Although observations of the past can give the false impression of replication, that replication, even if mistakenly accepted, still cannot be projected into the future (remember nn. 22, 23 on pp. 225, 226). Thus the determination of the probability of occurrence of a future event from apparent, previous replication is not possible.

knowledge need not be knowledge of frequencies, but it is knowledge all the same. However, under conditions of historical time and ignorance where, as suggested earlier, unknown and unknowable outcomes and unique decision moments are present, Shackle argues that sufficient knowledge to assign subjective probabilities is never available. Knowledge of future outcomes cannot be secured in advance, and knowledge of present and past outcomes is too replete with errors and gaps. And this is so even if the first two difficulties cited above did not happen to arise. Thus the assignment of subjective probability values to outcomes or sets of outcomes is not meaningful because there is no way to come up with suitable assignments.[36] Accepting the Shacklean perspective, only the non-probabilistic uncertainty category of models is relevant for explaining the making of real economic decisions.

At any rate, to replace probability in decision making where it does not apply, Shackle [36, p. 443], in 1939, proposed a formalization of the previously noted idea of surprise that he called potential surprise.[37] The *potential surprise* of a set of outcomes A is the surprise the individual imagines now that he would experience in the future if an outcome in A were to occur.[38] Shackle's argument, as partly outlined above, implies that this concept relies for its definition on considerably less knowledge than does probability. Indeed, it is definable even when probability, due to the difficulties brought on by the presence of historical time and ignorance, is not. Shackle [37] went on to develop a non-probabilistic uncertainty model of decision making that employed the notion of potential surprise. In that model, each object of choice is assigned a positive and a negative possible outcome value with each outcome value linked to a potential surprise value. The actual assignment is determined as that configuration of these four elements – the positive outcome value and its associated potential surprise value together with the negative outcome value and associated potential surprise value – which, in relation to the choice object in question, stands out most in the decision-maker's mind. The decision maker then selects a choice object according to a criterion defined with respect to these stand-out outcome-potential-surprise assignments.[39]

---

[36] Shackle [37, p. 60]. See also Vickers [44, pp. 9, 85–87].

[37] It should be noted that there are other indices of surprise based on probability. But these bear no relationship to Shackle's construction. See Good [9].

[38] See Katzner [18, Ch. 2]. The actual surprise the individual feels in the future if an element of A actually occurs bears no necessary relation to the presently contemplated potential surprise of A.

[39] See also Katzner [18, Sect. 4.3].

References

[1] Abbott, L., *Quality and Competition* (New York: Columbia University Press, 1955).

[2] Arrow, K. J., "Samuelson Collected," *Journal of Political Economy* 75 (1967), pp. 730–737.

[3] Bausor, R., "Time and the Structure of Economic Analysis," *Journal of Post Keynesian Economics* 5 (1982–83), pp. 163–179.

[4] Blaug, M., "Kuhn vs. Lakatos, or Paradigms versus Research Programs in the History of Economics," *Method and Appraisal in Economics*, S. Latsis, ed. (Cambridge: Cambridge University Press, 1976), pp. 149–180.

[5] Brodbeck, M., "Methodological Individualisms: Definition and Reduction," *Readings in the Philosophy of the Social Sciences*, M. Brodbeck, ed. (London: Macmillan, 1968), pp. 280–303.

[6] Burtt, E. A., *The Methodological Foundations of Modern Physical Science*, 2nd ed. (London: Routledge and Kegan Paul, 1932).

[7] Davidson, P., "Rational Expectations: A Fallacious Foundation for Studying Crucial Decision-Making Processes," *Journal of Post Keynesian Economics* 5 (1982–83), pp. 182–198.

[8] de Finetti, B., "Foresight: Its Logical Laws, Its Subjective Sources," H. E. Kyburg, Jr., trans., in *Studies in Subjective Probability*, H. E. Kyburg, Jr., and H. E. Smokler, eds. (New York: Wiley, 1964), pp. 93–158.

[9] Good, I. J., "Surprise Index," in *Encyclopedia of Statistical Science*, v. 9, S. Kotz and N. L. Johnson, eds. (New York: Wiley, 1988), pp. 104-109.

[10] Hacking, I., *The Emergence of Probability* (Cambridge: Cambridge University Press, 1975).

[11] Hayek, F. A., "The Use of Knowledge in Society," *American Economic Review* 35 (1945), pp. 519–530.

[12] Hicks, J. R., "Some Questions of Time in Economics," in *Evolution, Welfare, and Time in Economics*, A. M. Tang, F. M. Westfield, and J. S. Worley, eds. (Lexington: D. C. Heath, 1976), pp. 135–151.

[13] Hodgson, G. M., "Meanings of Methodological Individualism," *Journal of Economic Methodology* 14 (2007), pp. 211–226.

[14] Hoover, K. D., *The New Classical Macroeconomics* (Oxford: Basil Blackwell, 1988).

[15] Hutchison, T. W., *On Revolutions and Progress in Economic Knowledge* (Cambridge: Cambridge University Press, 1978).

[16] Hutchinson, T. W., "Our Methodological Crisis," in *Economics in Disarray*, P. Wiles and G. Routh, eds. (Oxford: Basil Blackwell, 1984), pp. 1–21.

[17] Katzner, D. W., *Static Demand Theory* (New York: Macmillan, 1970).

[18] Katzner, D. W., *Time, Ignorance, and Uncertainty in Economic Models* (Ann Arbor, MI: University of Michigan Press, 1998).

[19] Katzner, D. W., *An Introduction to the Economic Theory of Market Behavior: Microeconomics from a Walrasian Perspective* (Cheltenham: Elgar, 2006).

[20] Keynes, J. M., "The General Theory of Employment," *Quarterly Journal of Economics* 51 (1937), pp. 209–223.

[21] Knight, F. H., *Risk, Uncertainty, and Profit* (Boston, MA: Houghton Mifflin, 1921).

[22] Levins, R. and R. Lewontin, *The Dialectical Biologist* (Cambridge: Harvard University Press, 1985).

[23] Loasby, B., *Choice, Complexity and Ignorance* (Cambridge: Cambridge University Press, 1976).

[24] Marshall, A., *Principles of Economics*, 8th ed. (New York: Macmillan, 1948).

[25] Menger, C., *Principles of Economics*, J. Dingwall and B. F. Hoselitz, trans. (New York: New York University Press, 1981).

[26] Menger, C., *Investigations into the Method of the Social Sciences with Special Reference to Economics* (earlier published under the title, *Problems of Economics and Sociology*), F. J. Nock, trans. (New York: New York University Press, 1985).

[27] von Mises, L., *Human Action: A Treatise on Economics* (New Haven, CT: Yale University Press, 1949).

[28] Oaks, M., *Statistical Inference: A Commentary for the Social and Behavioural Sciences* (Chichester: Wiley, 1986).

[29] Piaget, J., *Structuralism*, C. Maschler, trans. and ed. (New York: Basic Books, 1970).

[30] Popper, K. R., *The Poverty of Historicism* (New York: Basic Books, 1960).

[31] Porter, T. M., *The Rise of Statistical Thinking, 1820–1900* (Princeton: Princeton University Press, 1986).

[32] Radner, R., "Satisficing," *Journal of Mathematical Economics* 2 (1975), pp. 253–262.

[33] Robinson, J., *History versus Equilibrium*, Thames Papers in Political Economy (London: Thames Polytechnic, 1974).

[34] Samuelson, P. A., *Economics*, 11th ed. (New York: McGraw-Hill, 1980).

[35] Sensat, J., "Methodological Individualism and Marxism," *Economics and Philosophy* 4 (1988), pp. 189–219.

[36] Shackle, G. L. S., "Expectations and Employment," *Economic Journal* 49 (1939), pp. 442–452.

[37] Shackle, G. L. S., *Decision, Order and Time in Human Affairs*, 2nd ed. (Cambridge: Cambridge University Press, 1969).

[38] Shackle, G. L. S., *Epistemics and Economics* (Cambridge: Cambridge University Press, 1972).

[39] Simon, H. A., *Administrative Behavior*, 2nd ed. (New York: Macmillan, 1957).

[40] Shackle, G. L. S., "Theories of Decision-Making in Economics and Behavioral Science," *American Economic Review* 49 (1959), pp. 253–283.

[41] Strodack, G. K., *The Philosophy of Epicurus* (Evanston, IL: Northwestern University Press, 1963).

[42] Strozier, R. M., *Epicurus and Hellenistic Philosophy* (Lanham, MD: University Press of America, 1985).

[43] Vickers, D., "On Relational Structures and Non-Equilibrium in Economic Theory," *Eastern Economic Journal* 11 (1985), pp. 384–403.

[44] Vickers, D., *Economics and the Antagonism of Time: Time, Uncertainty, and Choice in Economic Theory* (Ann Arbor, MI: University of Michigan Press, 1994).

[45] Watkins, J. W. N., "Methodological Individualism and Social Tendencies," *Readings in the Philosophy of the Social Sciences*, M. Brodbeck, ed. (London: Macmillan, 1968), pp. 269–280.

[46] Winston, G. C., "Three Problems with the Treatment of Time in Economics: Perspectives, Repetitiveness, and Time Units," in *The Boundaries of Economics*, G. C. Winston and R. F. Teichgraeber III, eds. (Cambridge: Cambridge University Press, 1988), pp. 30–52.

[47] Winter, S. G, "Satisficing, Selection, and the Innovating Remnant," *Quarterly Journal of Economics* 85 (1971), pp. 237–261.

11

Conclusion

The task of science, it was stated as the present point of view at the beginning, is to explain. Explanation is a human activity and is to be distinguished, on both philosophical and practical grounds, from description. To describe a thing or a complex of events is to state what it is. To explain the thing is to discover the purported reason for its being, the purported causation that makes it what it is and, to the degrees that may be achievable, to provide a means for projecting what future values of the thing may arise. Explanation, then, involves the statement of the place the thing explained occupies in total existent reality. While it might give grounds for prediction of future outcomes of actions or events, it follows that explanation and prediction (i.e., the actual projection of future values) are very different intellectual activities. Moreover, by reason of the insurmountable entanglements of the reality under investigation, both description and explanation at any moment of time must necessarily be partial and incomplete. And, in addition, explanation, in the form of scientific hypotheses, for example, is tentative to varying degrees, often awaiting confirmation or disproof depending on what is held as the logical or methodological significance of the explanatory procedure.

Against such realizations, the preceding chapters have been motivated by two awarenesses. First is the importance of understanding that there are significant distinctions between explanatory enterprise in the physical sciences and in economics. In sharp contrast with the former, the objects of explanation in the latter are the actions of sentient, often rational and responsible decision-making agents, and it is therefore imperative to take account of the nature of, and the reasons for, the decisions they make, along with the outcomes that follow as a result. For this reason and for the numerous additional reasons stated in Chapter 1, it was concluded there that an epistemological parity between physical and economic sciences does not exist. Second, due to the complexity of real-world environments and affairs, the disparity between description and explanation in economics is particularly acute. As a result, economic explanation, as it differs from economic description, often takes the form of model building, with all of the abstractions from, and simplifications of, reality that models inevitably imply and which have been referred to in the foregoing.

The relevant point can be stated differently. The twists and knots of economic affairs defy exhaustive description of past or currently existing states; the impossibility of knowing the future rules out description of things to come. In our world, therefore, to understand frequently means to explain. And model building is not only a possible, but for many purposes an unavoidable approach to explanation.

This claim, along with the matters addressed in this volume, viz., those of model building, the logical and frequently mathematical problems associated with it, and the detailed procedures of model construction abut, in the end, a significant philosophical issue. Why, again, is model building in the service of economic explanation so necessary? In effect, that question has been answered in the previous recognition of the uncertainties and ignorance thrown up by the fact that economic activity takes place in real (or historical), as opposed to what has earlier been referred to as logical time. The world is not ergodic or fully repetitive. Uniformity of outcomes or determining causes, in the sense that outcomes and causes are durable across all time and space, does not, in any comprehensive manner, obtain. The determining forces and the structures they bequeath are in no way stable in their description and existential impact. As yesterday gives birth to today, and as time moves on its unpredictable trajectory to tomorrow, there is no reason to believe, and every reason to disbelieve, that the same thing as before will occur and the same complex of affairs will eventuate. On a definitive level, then, and lying beyond any exercise in explaining reality, is the fact that history, while it might move in essential respects on a linear path to appointed ends, is observable in disturbed realities. It does not exhibit at any point of its journey a naive uniformity of outcomes and causations. Determining forces modify their structures and impacts, people change, inventiveness and technology alters as historical time challenges with its jagged edges.

As to the instincts of uniformity, there is every justification, of course, for what might be called methodological uniformity, or the theoretical assumption of uniformity for the purposes of imaginative constructions of explanatory analytical structures and hypotheses. That is simply saying in that regard that explanation, or science in general, proceeds by building bridges to quantitative and unquantified empirical reality, by hypothesis testing, and by their implied attempts at falsification and disproof. In previous chapters, some aspects of what is to be affirmed at those levels have been observed. But what is at issue here is something different. That can be put in the single question harking back to that raised above: Why in its final challenge and analysis is economic model building, the activity that has engaged this volume, necessary? It is because, in short, and quite apart from methodological uniformity, actual uniformity in the real world of human activity does not exist. And the building of models is an important way of dealing with explanation in its absence. Without model building, our ability to explain would be that much poorer.

However, the question in economic explanation frequently is not that of whether to build an explanatory model, but how building that model is to be done. The preceding chapters have attempted to bring to prominence the principal elements or logical stages of model construction and to provide some preliminary examples of effective modeling procedures. The model-building process itself has been viewed as a five-stage linear progression from initial inspiration through rough formulation, operationalization, empirical testing where appropriate, and lastly a judgment as to the cogency and explanatory competence of the result. It involves simplification of, and abstraction from, what may be referred to as the real, dialectical economic complex to be explained. As a practical matter this means, in particular, the selection from that complex of the specific elements thought to be the most relevant for the purpose at hand, the extraction from those elements of arithmomorphic variables with which to proceed, and then the fabrication of arithmomorphic relations or functions among the latter. Along the way, and especially at the operational stage, appropriate assumptions not a part of, but perhaps suggested by, the dialectical base are introduced. It follows that models are, at best, only approximations of what is to be modeled, and necessarily contain components that sit some distance from reality. And the stage-five judgments of cogency and explanatory competence are heavily influenced by the investigator's cultural background and that of the professional milieu in which he works.

Of course, the nature of the model that is built, and that which determines the particularities of the model components incorporated in the five-stage procedure described in Chapter 3, also depends on the explanatory objective the investigator has in mind. On the one hand, the aim could be to describe the configuration of the relations, that is, the structure of an economic entity, how it, as a whole, might work, and how its various parts might fit together. On the other, the purpose could be to explain how certain observed outcomes might have come about. In either case, as has been seen, the outputs produced by the model could be either a collection of variable values or a collection of behavioral functions. The identification of the appropriate outputs with what has been observed is what permits it to be said that the constructed model explains the observations. Models built to explain a structure are not, as a totality, generally testable; and models that fail empirical tests may not be rejected as explanations of that which was observed. The model of organizational forms in Chapter 7 exemplifies the former (although expansions of that model were described there that would allow for empirical testing of parts of the enlarged model). As an illustration of the latter, the possibility of model acceptance while failing empirical tests was discussed in relation to the utility-maximization model of the consumer as a general explanation of consumer demand behavior. While it is not appropriate to repeat here the details of the arguments that have already been explored, it will be useful to take note of some of the issues raised in earlier chapters that bear on the nature of models themselves.

First, economic affairs and outcomes exist and occur in real historical time as opposed to what has been referred to as logical time. That being so, economic models have been constructed in varying ways that have attempted to capture the uncertainties of time and its unforeseen deliverances. Some models, as has been seen, have incorporated the notion that the future can be reduced to the present by invoking the apparatus of probability and mathematical expectations in such a way as to reduce future possible magnitudes to present-day certainty equivalents. Other models have abstracted completely from time itself and have concentrated on a fully static construction. That has generally occurred in the context of the assumption that perfect knowledge is possessed by all economic agents in whatever model is under consideration. Still other models have taken time in its historical form and uncertainty in its non-probabilistic state, and accounted for some of the peculiarities that that approach requires.

Second, it is noteworthy, again by reason of the complexity of economic affairs, that explanatory models have been very various as to what it is about the real world that has been impounded in a ceteris paribus (other things being equal) clause or assumption. The content of the ceteris paribus depends on the stage (i) vision of the model builder and the manner in which he infuses that vision into the structure and properties of his model as he constructs it through stage (iii). At this point it is sufficient to say that the extent of the ceteris paribus will bear on the possibility and reach of empirical testing of the model and on the possibility of observing meaningful bridges between either model relations or other model components and actual real-world instances. Indeed, the degree to which confidence can be placed in the model's purported explanation may well depend on the faith one has in the stability over time of what is corralled in the ceteris paribus postulate.

Third, it is a troublesome feature of economic explanation, unlike that of the physical sciences, that the very definition of the thing being explained may itself not be stable over time. How is meaning to be imported to the explanation of changes in the demand for automobiles, for example, when the notion of automobile, as to questions of design and technical capabilities, is not invariant over time? Or again, what degree of credence can be placed in a model that assumes the constancy of individual preferences and tastes from one moment to the next?

Fourth, a tangled and perplexing set of issues has to do with the penchant of economists for quantification and the measurement of not necessarily measurable explanatory variables, for ignoring the subtleties and traps that are present in confusion between cardinally stated and ordinally stated measures and the frequently illegitimate employment of the latter, and for the possibly injudicious use of surrogate explanatory variables. Within that assemblage, and referring to the strong predilection for measurement, an insufficiently clear understanding still exists regarding the meaning of, and the possible effective development of, explanatory models containing variables such as culture, freedom, and feelings of security that are both non-quantifiable and frequently relevant for understanding economic phenomena. It was for that reason that emphasis was placed in the preceding chapters on the use and manipulation of unmeasured arithmomorphic variables. In fact, the example of model building to which Chapter 7 was devoted focused, partly for illustrative purposes, on the use of such unscaled variables and the interpretation of results obtained in their presence.

Lastly, and in a significant way overriding all that has been said as to the unavoidability and use of explanatory economic models, it has been stated that, in addition to the role culture plays in the stage-five judgment of cogency and explanatory significance, important influences on the appropriate form and content of models emanate from the cultural context in which economic activity takes place. Complete sense and meaning does not inhere, for example, in the use of model elements that set out to explain "Western" economic actions of individual agents (as in, say, the United States) to explain affairs and developments in a country whose cultural complex and therefore economic determinants are vastly different from those of the West (as they are in, say, Japan).

But the principal conclusion remains. Existential realities insist that model building in economic explanation is in many instances an inevitable necessity. The real question confronting economists is that of how, most efficiently and effectively, that inevitable necessity of model building is to be accommodated.

When that has been said, a final matter of some importance for economics as an intellectual discipline still needs to be faced. Model building in economics is addressed, in the ways that have now been exhibited, to the task of explaining concrete real-world phenomena and states of affairs. Examples of models of several kinds, useful for different purposes, can be contemplated or have been adduced in preceding chapters – models of individual demand for a designated commodity; of observed price and quantity outcomes in a commodity market or the entire economy; of static or dynamically changing market conditions; of macroeconomic cycles or growth; of agent decision making under assumed conditions of probabilistic uncertainty or of true (non-probabilistic) uncertainty in historical time situations. But a question of implied import remains beyond the actual explanatory power and success of any or each of such model constructions. What, it is to be asked finally, is the contribution that any or all such models, whatever the degree of analytical sophistication they contain, make to wider economic understanding and larger objectives?

It can be said that at a minimum, as Lionel Robbins [1, p. 16] observed almost a century ago, economics is the study of the issues and problems involved in the system-wide allocation to competing ends of scarce resources that have alternative uses. If, then, as previously suggested, a model can be constructed to explain, for example, the determination of economy-wide market outcomes, the question follows as to what, in fact, and at a stage further removed, those properly explained market outcomes, that is the model outputs, are themselves describing or explaining. The answer at its most immediate level is that the price and quantity solution values observed in the various markets and explained by the model are determinants of the system-wide allocation of economic resource endowments that is being achieved. In another example, the solution outputs in models of financial markets are indicative of the ways in which available money capital is being allocated to alternative investment uses. Models of intertemporal growth aim to explain the respects in which given resource endowments and constraints permit the achievement of desired or sustainable rates of economic advance. Conceivably, the system-wide allocation of resources at a given time, or their allocation to expansive investment over time, are aimed to satisfy some criteria of social optima or, in other words, to make the most efficient contribution to economy-wide benefit or social welfare.

Now specific models that are designed to explain specific situations and conditions such as have been referred to by way of illustration in this volume are not themselves, even in the case of the Walrasian general equilibrium model, fully addressed to those wider tasks and objectives, nor, in the conceptual scheme of things, are they designed to do so. Model building requires abstractions and simplifications that necessarily leave out elements relating in important ways to individual benefit and social welfare. But it is of no small importance to see, at the same time, that the real justification for the economist's investment of intellectual resources in specific, or in a sense isolated, model building is that he is thereby contributing to the explanation of the economy's wider tasks and larger objectives.

The importance of that realization is not only that it provides in that manner a justification for the economic model-builder's activity. Beyond that, and of larger moment, it raises the possibility that, and the possible ways in which, the understanding provided by the explanation the model precipitates can provide the basis for recommendations of changes in economic behavior or policy. In its conscious awareness of, and its contribution to, such larger ends and objectives, economics as a discipline vindicates its description as a *social* science. Its significance as potentially contributing to the realization of what might in some sense be defined as optimal society-wide economic objectives thereby comes into view.

Reference

[1] Robbins, L., *An Essay on the Nature and Significance of Economic Science*, 2nd ed. (London: Macmillan, 1952).

Index